Mistake-Stitch Ribbing:

Multiple of 4 sts plus 3.

* K2, P2; rep from *, end K2, P1

Repeat this row.

(Copied from Sister's pattern book)

One-Piece Knits That Fit

How to Knit and Crochet One-Piece Garments

Margaret Hubert

Photography by Christopher Hubert

VNR VAN NOSTRAND REINHOLD COMPANY
New York   Cincinnati   Toronto   London   Melbourne

To R.M.H.

*Most buttons shown are La Mode Buttons by
B. Blumenthal.*

*The two photographs on pages 108 and 109 were taken
by John Bisesi.*

Copyright © 1978 by Litton Educational Publishing, Inc.
Library of Congress Catalog Card Number 78-17516
ISBN 0-442-23567-4

Printed in United States of America

Published in 1978 by Van Nostrand Reinhold Company
A division of Litton Educational Publishing, Inc.
135 West 50th Street, New York, NY, 10020, U.S.A.

Van Nostrand Reinhold Limited
1410 Birchmount Road
Scarborough, Ontario M1P 2E7, Canada

Van Nostrand Reinhold Australia Pty. Ltd.
17 Queen Street
Mitcham, Victoria 3132, Australia

Van Nostrand Reinhold Company Limited
Molly Millars Lane
Wokingham, Berkshire, England

16 15 14 13 12 11 10 9 8 7 6 5 4 3 2

Library of Congress Cataloging in Publication Data

Hubert, Margaret.
  One-piece knits that fit.

  Includes index.
  1. Knitting. 2. Crocheting. I. Title.
TT825.H8   746.4'32   78-17516
ISBN 0-442-23567-4

God gave me my hands;
they are my life

Acknowledgments

How do you thank people who have given so freely of their time and energy to help you put a book together? My list is so long that I truly do not know where to begin. My son Chris gave so many hours of his time doing the photography. My mother, Carmela Mancuso, not only taught me how to knit, but her nimble fingers are responsible for turning more than half of my "paper designs" into the beautiful creations shown in the photographs. My friend Katherine Ghirardi, who also knit some of the garments for me; Marianne Lesko, who did sketches for me; Nancy Green, without whom I could not have progressed past the outline stage; Susan Rosenthal, who shaped and edited my work; the many yarn companies that donated yarn; the models, who patiently posed; my customers, who encouraged me by their loyalty; they all deserve many thanks. Last, but by no means least, thank you to my husband, Robert, whose confidence propelled me, my son Robert Jr., whose knowledge of New York City and unique chauffering ability managed to get me to appointments on time, and my son Mark and daughter, Sharon, who often ended up doing the household chores and errands. This book was really a "family affair."

Thanks again to all of the models: Connie Bock, Joseph Campanaro, Lynn Campanaro, Rachel Companaro, Christopher DiMarco, Stephanie DiMarco, Kathleen Federico, Philip J. Federico, Stacy Federico, Sandra Fishman, Lisa Marie Gaccino, John Giacco, Victoria Gonda, Peter Gradoni, Sue Gradoni, Dorothy Gusick, Robert Hubert, Sharon E. Hubert, Joseph Isidori, Caroline Keindl, Bernadette Lawler, Brain Lawler, Celeste Lawler, Clare Lawler, Marianne Lesko, Kelly Ann McManus, Susan Manucuso, Marguerite Mendes, Dana Mills, Darby Mills, Wayne Nadorf, Cathy Olmsted, Rosanne Raneri, Virginia Richardson, Pamela Roberts, Melissa Savino, Anne Marie Stephens, Diane Tarasco, and Joseph Tarasco.

Contents

1. Why One-Piece Knitting?

In these days of increased leisure time and revived interest in do-it-yourself activities, both knitting and crocheting are enjoying great popularity. It's a wonderful feeling to complete a homemade knit (in this book, the term *knit* will refer to knitted or crocheted garments); and, for a multitude of reasons, it is even more satisfying to create one-piece knits than regular knitted garments. Before you read about the merits of one-piece knitting and crocheting, however, it might be interesting to learn something about the history of these crafts.

Knitting can be traced all the way back to the Phonenician and Egyptian cultures. In fact, the oldest known knitted garment was discovered in an Egyptian tomb that dates back to the fourth century B.C. (The oldest known knitting needle, by the way, is on display in the Corinium Museum in Gloucestershire, England.) The word *knitting* comes from an Anglo-Saxon word, *cynntan*, which means "to tie" or "to knot." This ancient knotting craft was passed on from generation to generation. Interestingly enough, while knitting is considered to be "women's work," until rather recent times knitting was an occupation held by men. During the Middle Ages, in fact, men trained for six years to become master knitters. After completing their apprenticeships, each had to pass an extremely difficult examination before he could go into business for himself. It was not until the Industrial Revolution that knitting became "women's work." Women went on to design their own garments and then passed on their techniques to others, who improved or changed them to suit their particular needs. This method of learning continued right up to the nineteenth century, before ladies' magazines came into being. Women then began to depend on the patterns supplied by these magazines, and the tradition of passing on patterns slowly and unfortunately came to a halt.

Crochet is a relatively new craft. The earliest evidence of *crochet* (from the French word, *croche*, meaning "hook") traces it back to the sixteenth century. During this period, crochet trimmings were used to adorn church vestments. In fact, crocheting was done almost exclusively in convents. The earliest known written instruction books for crochet were printed in the early nineteenth century, and crocheting became popular by the end of that century when well-born ladies began to take up the hobby. Crochet designs can be very simple or very complex. The simple designs continue to be popular, as they are fun to do and go quickly. But the very fine crochet, such as Irish and lace designs and intricate bedspread and tablecloth patterns are done by relatively fewer women. In general, the simpler knitting and crochet patterns do tend to be the most popular ones.

But, why *one-piece* knitting and crocheting? Over the years, I have found that the one thing that most knitters or crocheters cannot do well is sew their garments together. Even if they can do it properly, most people do not enjoy this part of the job; the biggest problem seems to be setting in the sleeves. One-piece knitting and crocheting eliminates this boring task entirely. This simple technique is really just a matter of sectioning off parts of the sweater—front, back, sleeves—and placing some sections on holders while others are being worked. In addition to eliminating the sewing tasks, the one-piece garment fits better and can be more easily altered to keep up with growing children and fickle fashion. Also, working in one piece enables the knitter or crocheter to quickly become a designer just by learning some basic techniques and principles and by learning how to add your own special touches. You'll learn how to make the same sweater in an infinite variety of patterns and sizes, adding your own special touches and truly making each garment your very own creation.

Doesn't one-piece knitting get very heavy on the needles? Do you need circular needles and are they difficult to work with? Could I master the method even though I'm not all that experienced? Why haven't I seen more patterns like these in other instruction books? These are just a few of the questions I'm asked by nonbelievers; that is, until they have completed their first garment. Almost without exception, they are so pleased with the professional-looking garment they've created that they cannot wait to get started on a second project. This book was inspired by these former nonbelievers, the literally hundreds of people who have remarked, "Why don't you write a book?"

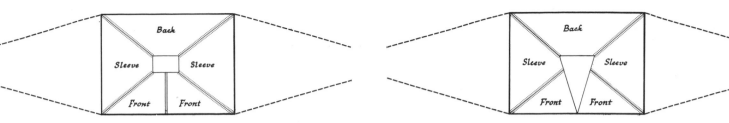

Figure 1. The parts of a raglan crew neck cardigan.

Figure 2. The parts of a raglan V neck cardigan.

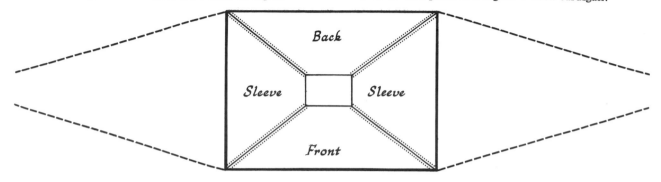

Figure 3. The parts of a raglan crew neck pullover.

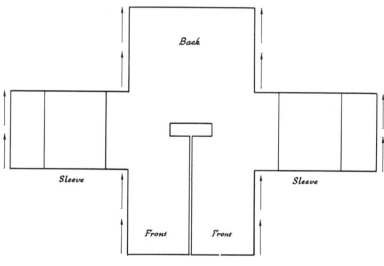

Figure 4. The parts of a T top crew neck cardigan worked from bottom to top.

Figure 5. The parts of a T top V neck cardigan worked from bottom to top.

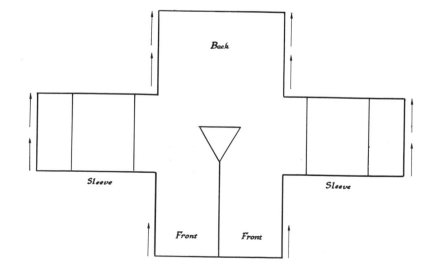

8

In an attempt to explain the facts about working a garment in one piece I've written the answers to some of these commonly asked questions. First of all, one-piece knitting does not get very heavy on the needles. Infants', children's, teenagers', and women's small sizes are no problem at all. Any size larger than these—women's larger sizes and men's—can become a bit of a problem; at one point, just when you are about to divide for sections, there does seem to be an unending line of stitches on the needle. Fortunately, this situation lasts only for a short time, and I feel that the finished results are worth this little bit of temporary discomfort.

While most knitters seem to think that all one-piece knitting requires circular needles, this simply is not so. All cardigans knitted from the top down and most cardigans and pull-overs knitted from the bottom up or side over do not require circular needles. The larger cardigans do require circular needles, simply because of the extra stitches on the needles; all pullovers knitted from the top down or side over also require circular needles because they are worked round and round. The point must be made, however, that working on circular needles is not difficult. On the contrary, many knitters welcome the change of pace.

Knitting or crocheting in one piece requires no more patience or concentration than regular work. Markers are used, which, in fact, make counting unneccesary once the marking row is done. Some of the fancier, expanded styles, which, you'll find in Part III, will require more concentration, but this is true for any craft. And, if you're well grounded in the basics, you'll have no trouble with the variations.

Could I master this method even though I don't have much experience? I have been asked this question by brand-new knitters and crocheters and by those who have been knitting and crocheting since childhood. Anybody who can knit and purl and anyone who can single crochet or double crochet can master these skills. They can not only master the skills, but become expert in a very short time. I have yet to meet the person who does not love the technique once they've tried it.

As to why more of these patterns are not given in instruction books, I can only say that this remains a mystery to me too. Some pattern books do include one or two of these styles and most knitting books devote a small chapter to one-piece knitting. There are one or two good leaflets with knitted one-piece garments, but crocheted one-piece instructions are few and far between. I personally feel that the virtues of one-piece garments have been ignored far too long; thus, this book.

Since I believe that the best way to become an expert at something is to start off with the basic steps, I've divided this book into three parts. This first part will explain some of the terms I've used frequently throughout the book and will refresh your memory with regard to the knitter's or crocheter's terminology and conventions. Part II is devoted to the classic styles. Here you will learn four techniques—the knitted raglan (from the top down), the crocheted raglan (from the top down), the knitted T top (from the bottom up or side over), and the crocheted T top (from the bottom up or side over). For each of these techniques you will learn three types of sweaters—the crew neck cardigan, the V neck cardigan, and the crew neck pullover. (Instructions are given on page 16 for adapting crew neck pullovers to turtlenecks or V necks, so actually there are five types of sweaters taught in each technique.) See Figures 1 through 9 for schematic diagrams. For each of these categories instructions are given in infants', children's, women's, and men's sizes in sport weight, knitting worsted, and bulky yarns. (The only exception to this are the infants' sweaters which are not given in bulky yarns. I doubt whether anyone will miss these patterns, since sweaters for infants are traditionally, and, for good reason, done in lighter weight wools.) You'll notice that most of these sweaters are very similar. The instructions for the Men's Classic Sport Weight Crew Neck Cardigan, for example, will be pretty much the same as the instructions for the Infant's Classic Sport Weight Crew Neck Cardigan. The main difference will be the numbers. The directions for each sweater type and size are detailed almost completely so that there will be a minimum of cross-referencing for you to do. I know how annoying it can be to have to stop everything and turn to another section of the book.

Once you've mastered the classic sweaters, you're ready to move on to the expanded styles in Part III. Here you'll find dresses, tunics, sweaters, ponchos, jackets, and coats that look fancy and difficult to make, but that are really just variations of the classics you've already done. Some are simple variations, such as a stripe pattern or a shorter sleeve; others incorporate cable patterns, decorative cuffs and collars, and all sorts of fashionable embellishments. The point is that you will no longer be a beginner at one-piece knitting or crocheting and you will be ready to take on any of these expanded styles—difficult or easy.

Hopefully, these expanded styles will show you how easy it is to vary instructions, thus creating an entirely different piece. Perhaps they will stir your imagination and give you the confidence you need to try your own improvisations. Change a collar, add a stripe, crochet an edging; anything you do is fine as long as you adhere to the basic skills and techniques of one-piece knitting or crocheting. Many women find it easier to copy patterns from an instruction book solely. This is unfortunate, because the joys of creating from scratch are truly fantastic. It is my hope that this book will inspire readers to create their own designs; have fun, and let your imaginations go.

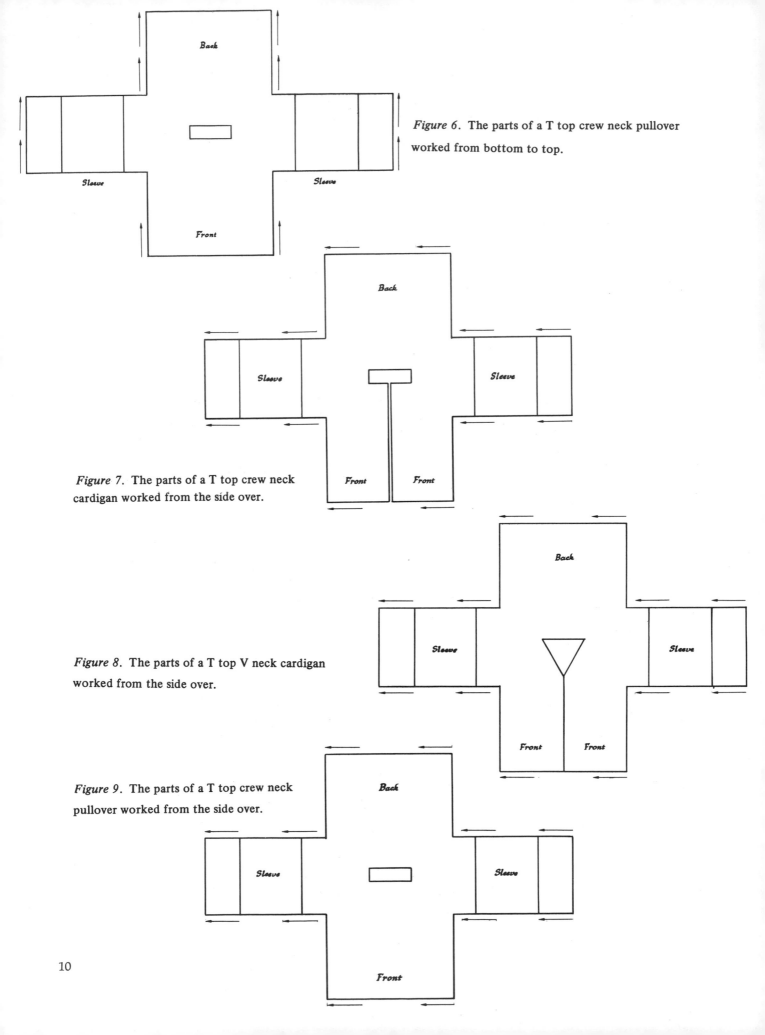

Figure 6. The parts of a T top crew neck pullover worked from bottom to top.

Figure 7. The parts of a T top crew neck cardigan worked from the side over.

Figure 8. The parts of a T top V neck cardigan worked from the side over.

Figure 9. The parts of a T top crew neck pullover worked from the side over.

10

2. Knitting and Crocheting Basics

If you've never knitted or crocheted before, you should certainly start out by reading this chapter. But, even if you are an experienced knitter or crocheter, it's a good idea to skim over the next few pages. I've included definitions of terms and abbreviations, knitting and crocheting tips, instructions on sizing, and other useful facts that I consider essential for good professional-looking results.

STYLES

Part II contains classic raglans and T tops and Part III contains variations of these classic styles, so perhaps you should start out by learning what these stylistic terms actually mean.

Classic: If you are talking about music or literature, "classic" refers to works of the highest rank; works that serve as models of their kind and that have survived the test of time and are still in accordance with established principles and methods. When you speak of fashion, these definitions should still describe the classic garment. The classic knit should be of good proportion and fit, with emphasis placed on simplicity and form. It should look as suitable today as it would ten years from today. The classic should be comfortable to wear and should always look attractive, whether it is being worn casually or for a more formal occasion. Every person should have several classics in their wardrobe.

Expanded Styles: This is a term I've adopted for the purpose of this book. I've used it to mean styles that are based on the classics, but that have been varied in some way. The change might be a different sleeve or neckline, a longer length, a cabled pattern, or perhaps just the addition of a stripe design.

Raglan Sleeve: This is a loose-fitting sleeve that slants away from the shoulder. It is not a new concept, by the way. During the Crimean War, the British Commander in Chief, Lord Raglan, felt that his men were hampered in their activities by the design of their uniforms. Their overcoats were bulky and tight-fitting and the men could hardly move in them. Lord Raglan designed a loose overcoat, with sleeves that continued into the collar, so that there were no shoulder seams. The coats kept the men warm, but gave them the freedom they needed to handle guns and equipment. The design proved to be a good one, as is proven by its immense popularity today.

T Tops: This is the name given to garments that are made in one piece that look exactly like a letter *T*. That is, the sleeve is extended out from the body of the garment, back and front, like a kimono. T tops are made by one of two methods. They can be worked from the bottom up or worked from the side over, starting with the sleeve. The finished garment has the same look whether it is made from bottom up or side over. The reason I teach both methods is that you can create different effects with stripes and patterns by changing the approach. For example, if you wanted a stripe effect to be horizontal you would make the garment from the bottom up; if you wanted the stripe effect to be vertical, you would work from the sleeve over. This same principle applies to patterns such as cables or ribbing, or any other pattern that is lined. There are several examples of this in Part III.

Cardigan: This is the term used to describe a sweater that opens completely down the center front. Buttons or a zipper are usually used as fasteners.

Pullover: This term is used quite simply to describe sweaters pulled over the head.

Crew Neck: The crew neck sweater is a favorite of everyone's. A crew neck is a slightly rounded, 1-inch band around the neckline. It is compatible with blouse collars, turtlenecks, or with scarves. The crew neck is comfortable and flattering to all.

V Neck: This is a lower neckline than the crew neck, dipping into a deep V shape on the chest. Although quite suitable for many occasions, this style is especially flattering in evening wear. Men in particular like V neck sweaters because the lower neckline allows a shirt and tie to show through.

Turtleneck: This seems to be particularly popular among sports enthusiasts. The neckline is usually 6 inches high, worn folded in half, and the extra fabric at the neckline makes for a very warm sweater. It's great for skiing, ice skating, and all outdoor activities for that reason.

Cowl Neckline: This is just a turtleneck made to be worn very loose. It drapes, as opposed to the turtleneck which stays very close to the neck. This style has become quite popular in recent years.

Kimono Sleeve: This is a loose-fitting sleeve that is not shaped. It is worked the same width from bottom to armhole.

Cap Sleeve: This is a tiny, short sleeve that just covers the top of the shoulder. It usually only extends 1 or 2 inches away from the shoulder seam.

ABBREVIATIONS

Anyone who has ever looked at knitting or crocheting instructions is familiar with the fact that knitters and crocheters have their own "language." All those numbers, terms, and abbreviations may be intimidating to the novice at the very beginning, but once their meanings are learned, their use becomes second nature. By way of review, and, because some instructors use different terms and abbreviations, it's a good idea to go over the following list. If British usage differs from American usage, I've added the correct term in parentheses.

Abbreviations or Symbols	Meanings	British Meanings That Differ
beg	begin or beginning	
cc	contrasting color	
ch(s)	chain(s)	
cir	circular	
col	color	
dc	double crochet(s)	(treble)
dec(s)	decrease	
dp	double pointed	
hdc	half double crochet	(half treble)
inc(s)	increase(s)	
k	knit	
mc	main color	
p	purl	
pat(s)	pattern(s)	
psso	pass slipped stitch over	
rem	remaining	
rib	ribbing	
sc	single crochet(s)	
sk	skip	
sl	slip	
slst	slipstitch	
sp	space	
st(s)	stitch(es)	
tog	together	
tr	triple crochet(s)	(double treble)
yo	yarn over	
*	Used to indicate that a group of stitches will be repeated for a certain number of times.	
( )	Used to enclose directions for larger sizes or to indicate that the directions contained within are to be repeated for a specified number of times.	

SIZES

Before starting a garment, be sure that you are making the correct size and using the proper weight yarn and the proper hook or needles to conform to the gauge. Although each garment was made with a specific yarn, substitutes may be used. Always make sure, however, that the yarn you are using falls into the same weight class as that specified in the instructions. Most Mohairs, for example, are equal to knitting worsted yarn in weight. Some of the imported tweeds are equal to knitting worsted and some are equal to sport yarn. The best way to check is to take a gauge. In any case, try the yarn you wish to use on the same size needle that is called for in the instructions. If the gauge is the same, that yarn may be substituted for the yarn in the instructions.

To determine correct size for a knitted or crocheted garment, take body measurements at fullest part of chest, hips, and natural waistline. Allowances have been made for ease and proper fit. Use the size that is nearest to the chest measurement. Other adjustments may be made in the blocking or while you are working the pattern.

INFANTS' AND TODDLERS' SIZES

	6 mos	1	2	3	4
Chest:	19	20	21	22	23
Waist:	20	19½	20	20½	21
Hips:	20	21	22	23	24
Height:	22	25	29	31	33

CHILDREN'S SIZES

	4	6	8	10	12	14
Chest:	23	24	26	28	30	32
Waist:	21	22	23½	24½	25½	26½
Hips:	24	26	28	30	32	34

PRETEENS' SIZES

	8	10	12	14	16
Chest:	28	29	31	33	34
Waist:	23	24	25	26	29
Hips:	31	32	34	36	38

WOMEN'S SIZES

	8	10	12	14	16	18
Bust:	31½	32½	34	36	38	40
Waist:	23	24	25½	27	29	31
Hips:	33½	34½	36	38	40	42

MEN'S SIZES

	34	36	38	40	42	44	46
Chest:	34	36	38	40	42	44	46
Waist:	30	32	34	36	38	40	42

13

ALPHABET STITCHING CHARTS

Use these stitching charts for the filet crochet sweater
on page 138 or for any sweater you'd like to personalize.

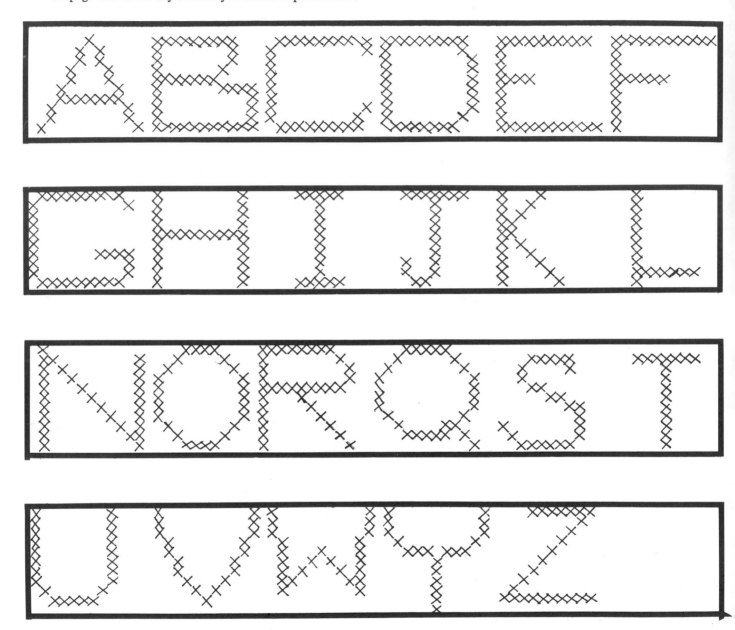

POINTERS

The following list will serve as a refresher course for some and a how-to section for others. Read it over carefully before starting your first project.

● To make the stockinette stitch on regular needles, knit 1 row and purl the next row. On circular or double-pointed needles, knit every row.

● To make the garter stitch on regular needles, knit every row. When working on circular or double-pointed needles, knit 1 row and purl the next.

● To make the seed stitch (sometimes called the "moss" stitch) with an odd number of stitches, knit 1, purl 1 across the row, ending with a knit-1. Repeat this row, making a knit-1 over a purl-1 and a purl-1 over a knit-1. Seed stitch is usually worked on an odd number of stitches because it is easier that way, but it may be done on an even number by reversing stitches.

● Ribbing is a combination of knitting and purling, as in knit 2, purl 2, or knit 1, purl 1. Ribbing is most often used for waistbands, cuffs, and neckbands because of its elastic quality.

● Beading refers to a row of holes made by knitting 2 stitches together, yarning over and then repeating this across row. Usually this is used for decorative purposes or for a place to draw a ribbon or chain through.

● Reverse stockinette stitch means to use the purl side as the right side.

● Picots are made by folding in a hemline right at the row of yarnovers, as in beading, and stitching in place. The yarnovers make little points along an edge.

● To decrease in knitting, unless otherwise specified, knit 2 stitches together as one.

● Double-pointed needles have a point at each end. They are used for working in rounds (no seams) and are sold in sets of four.

● Double-pointed needles and circular needles are both used for working in rounds. Circular needles may be used to work back and forth also, but double-pointed needles are only used for working in rounds. Sometimes you must use both double-pointed needles and circular needles because when you are working on a small number of stitches the circular needle does not reach around. The double points are used until enough increases are made and then the circular needle is used.

● Cable needles have a dip in the middle and points at either end. They are used specifically for twisting cables and come in two sizes—regular and bulky. Double-pointed needles may be used instead of cable needles.

● Placing a marker on a needle means that a marker, which may be a commercially sold marker, a paper clip, or a piece of yarn tied into a little ring, is to indicate a certain spot in your work. This marker is slipped from the left to the right needle as you work each row.

● The recommended gauge refers to the number of stitches and rows that should make up 1 inch of knitted or crocheted fabric in order to achieve the correct results. The gauge is what the designer bases the instructions on.

● The number of stitches that are worked to form one pattern is referred to as the multiple. If you increase or decrease the number of stitches in a pattern, you must do so in the multiple.

● Slipstitch means to slip a stitch from the left to the right needle without working the stitch. Insert the right needle as if to purl, unless otherwise specified.

● To increase in knitting, unless otherwise specified, knit in the front of the stitch and leave it on the needle. Then knit in back of the same stitch and slip both stitches off the needle.

● To yarn over when knitting, bring yarn under the right needle to the front as if to purl. Then knit the next stitch with yarn in the purling position. To yarn over when purling, wind the yarn around the right needle once and purl the next stitch. Sometimes you are told to yarn over when you need to increase in delicate open-work patterns.

● Yarn over is used in crocheting also. To do so, wrap yarn around the crochet hook as many times as the pattern calls for.

● To pick up stitches, always have the right side of the garment facing you. Using a crochet hook and a separate strand of yarn, evenly space and pick up stitches along the edge. As you work, slip the stitches off the hook from the back and onto your knitting needle. This takes a little practice. If you pick up enough stitches so that there will be no holes in your work and then increase or decrease to the amount of stitches needed, you will have a neat line of picked-up stitches.

● It is best to join yarn at the outside edges of work, except when making a one-piece raglan. In that case, adding under the arm is best.

• To change colors, pick up the color to be worked from underneath the dropped color. This is done to prevent holes.

• Binding off should always be done in the pattern you are working and should be done loosely. To bind off, work 2 stitches in the pattern. *With the left needle, lift the first stitch worked over the second and drop off the needle. This makes 1 bound-off stitch. Work another stitch and repeat from * as often as required. If you are binding off completely, cut yarn after the last stitch, leaving a 5-inch end. Bring the cut end through the last stitch.

• Backstitching is the best method for sewing most seams. Always pin right sides together and take a running stitch with a backstitch about every ¼ inch.

• Blocking and steaming is not recommended for heavily patterned work. The best procedure is to wet the garment thoroughly, remove as much moisture as possible by rolling in towels, and then lay it flat to dry after "pressing" into shape with your fingertips. Steaming is fine for flat knits. Always use a damp cloth. Pass the iron slowly over the garment, not allowing the weight of the iron to press the garment. The trick is to bring the iron as close as possible without really pressing. Never block ribbing or 100 percent acrylic yarns with steaming or they will stretch permanently.

• Lengthening or shortening a garment that has been worked from the top down is a fairly simple job. If the sleeves are too short, open up the bound-off row, rip back the border, and continue the pattern for the desired length. Then reknit the border. If the same color yarn is not available, work two or three contrasting color stripes and then reknit the border. The same thing can be done at the bottom of sweaters, dresses, coats, and ponchos. If the garment is too long, rip back the border, count the stitches on the last row, and then rip back till 2 inches less than the desired length. If necessary, decrease to the same amount of stitches that were on the last row. Then reknit the border.

• Lengthening sweaters worked from bottom up or side over is easy too. With separate yarn and crochet hook, pick up stitches along bottom, one in each stitch, and place on circular needle. Work garter stitch desired length.

• To make V neck pullovers in any raglan or T Top size, start as for a classic V neck cardigan and complete as for pullover at the underarm.

• To make turtlenecks in any raglan sleeve size, cast on the same number of stitches as for a classic crew neck cardigan, using the larger needles. Work 3 inches for children, 4 inches for teenagers, and 5 inches for adults. Change to smaller needles, work in ribbing for 1 inch, and continue as for a classic pullover.

• To make turtlenecks in any T top pick up stitches around neck picking up the first stitch in each stitch and row around the neck opening. Then knit 1, purl 1 in ribbing for 4 inches for children, 5 inches for teenagers, 6 inches for men and women. Bind off in ribbing.

• For teen sizes 16, 18, and 20, start the same as for women's sizes 10, 12, or 14. Work till there are 78 (82, 86) stitches on the back section. Follow the remaining instructions, making the sleeves 1 inch shorter and the body 2 inches shorter.

• For women's large sizes 20, 22, and 24 follow women's size 18 directions. Work till there are 104 (108, 112) stitches on the back section. Divide as for size 18 and follow the remaining instructions for sleeve decreases and length. The body length is the same.

Color Plate 2. A striped honeycomb pattern is the major feature of this knitted coat and hat. Coat, hat, and dress make a perfect ensemble. Yarn: coat and hat—Aspen Bulky Yarn by Brunswick, dress—Germanntown Knitting Worsted by Brunswick.

Color Plate 1. The ribbed collar, deep cuffs, and tweed yarn set this knitted raglan cardigan apart. Yarn: Donegal Tweed by Tahki. The slacks are Ultra-Suede by Skinner.

Color Plate 3. This nubby tweed coat can also be knitted as a jacket. Yarn: Vail by Brunswick.

Color Plate 4: This knitted ensemble features an interesting cable pattern on the coat sleeves. Yarn: Vail by Brunswick.

Color Plate 5. An interesting ribbing pattern that extends from bodice to border at the waist is the main feature of this cowl-neck tunic. Yarn: Indiecita Alpaca by Plymouth Yarns.

Color Plate 6. Opposite: Two textured sweaters are featured here. Both were knitted in a pattern of knit one row, rib the next. Yarn: Nantuck by Columbia Minerva.

Color Plate 7. Right: This tunic, which was knitted from the side over, features vertical stripes. The tunic can be worn front side out or back side out. Yarn: Indiecita Alpaca by Plymouth Yarns.

Color Plate 8. Below: The cardigan shown features wishbone cables, which can be done as easily as any other cable pattern. The mohair tunic shown here has a subtle diamond motif on the front. Yarn: cabled cardigan—Germanntown Knitting Worsted by Brunswick, tunic—Dji Dji by Stanley Woolen Company.

Color Plate 9. This little sweater set consists of a cardigan, pullover, and tam. The delicate cable pattern on the pullover is repeated on the borders of the tam and cardigan. Yarn: Unger's Nanette.

Color Plate 10. The sweater set of zippered cardigan and crew neck pullover was knitted with two strands of yarn held together for the tweed effect. Yarn: Nantuck by Columbia-Minerva.

Color Plate 11. This casual shawl-collared wraparound can also be knitted for a man. It is knitted with two strands of yarn held together. Yarn: Columbia-Minerva Sport Weight.

Color Plate 12. The simple tweed dress in this ensemble complements the textured coat perfectly. Yarn: coat—Alaska Tweed by Galler, dress—Eskimo Spezial by Galler.

Color Plate 13. A fitted, striped bodice is the main feature of this beautiful blouson. The cuffs repeat the bodice pattern.

3. Raglans Knitted from Top to Bottom

Figure 10. Classic raglan sweaters are attractive and easy to wear. The sweater on the left is a zippered version of the crew neck cardigan; the one on the right is a V neck pullover. The sweater in the middle is, of course, just a smaller version of the one on the left. Yarns: left—Brunswick Aspen, right and center—Germanntown Knitting Worsted by Brunswick.

When making a knitted raglan for the first time, it is wise to start with one of the classic styles. After you are familiar with the method of working, completing an expanded style will be much easier for you. It is very helpful to have three holders and a box of markers at your disposal before you start. These items are not absolutely essential, since pieces of yarn can be used for marking and holding stitches, but the proper tools do make the job easier.

Instructions are given here for crew neck cardigans, V neck cardigans, and crew neck pullovers but remember that it's quite easy to adapt these directions to V neck pullovers and turtleneck pullovers (see page 16). Directions are given in infants', children's, women's, and men's sizes, but remember that you can easily adapt them for teenagers and large women's sizes (see page 16). Also, refer back to Figures 1, 2, and 3 on page 7 for schematic diagrams of the classic styles taught in this chapter.

The knitted raglans in this chapter are staples of our you'll probably find a few of the classic sweaters shown in Figures 10, 11, and 12. They're basic, attractive, comfortable, and extremely versatile, so it's no wonder they're such favorites; and, as you'll see once you've started your first project, knitting one-piece raglans is easy.

INFANTS' CLASSIC SPORT WEIGHT SWEATERS

Crew Neck Cardigan

Infants' Sizes: Directions are for 6 months. Changes for 1, 2, and 3 are in parentheses.
Materials: 4 (6, 8, 10) oz sport weight yarn
Needles: #3 and #5; crochet hook #3
Gauge: 6 sts = 1 inch; 6 rows = 1 inch

Yoke:
With #3 needles cast on 68 sts. K 1, p 1 in rib for 1 inch. Change to #5 needles and work as follows: P 12 sts, place marker (front), p 10 sts, place marker (sleeve), p 24 sts, place marker (back), p 10 sts, place marker (sleeve), p 12 sts, (front). *Next row, k all across, inc 1 st before and after each marker (8 incs). Next row p. Repeat from * till there are 60 (64, 66, 68) sts on back section. End with a right side row.

Front, Back, and Sleeves:
P across to first marker, place sts just worked on holder, p to 3rd marker, place sts between 2nd and 3rd marker on holder, p to 4th marker, place rem sts not worked on holder. Mark this front and remove all other markers. You now have 2 sleeve sections left on needles. Working both at once and joining 2nd ball of yarn for 2nd sleeve, work as follows: Dec 1 st each side of each sleeve, every 1 inch, 4 (5, 5, 6) times. Work even till 5½ (6, 6½, 7) inches or desired length. Change to #3 needles, k 1, p 1 in rib for 1 (1, 1½, 1½) inch. Bind off loosely in rib. Join yarn at underarm of marked front. P across this front section, turn, k same front, k back section, k other front section. Continue body in 1 piece, working till 5 (5½, 6, 6½) inches from underarm or 1½ inches less than desired length. Change to #3 needles, k 1, p 1 in rib for 1½ inches. Bind off loosely in rib.

Finishing:
Sew underarm seams. *For Zipper:* With right side facing you, work 2 rows sc on each front edge and sew in zipper. *For Buttonholes:* With right side facing you, work 5 rows sc on each front edge, placing buttonholes evenly spaced on the 3rd row. Make buttonholes on the right for girls, on the left for boys. To make buttonholes, ch 2, sk 2 sts. On the 4th row, make 2 sc in the ch-2 sp.

V Neck Cardigan

Infants' Sizes: Directions are for 6 months. Changes for 1, 2, and 3 are in parentheses.
Materials: 4 (6, 8, 10) oz sport weight yarn
Needles: #3 and #5; crochet hook #3
Gauge: 6 sts = 1 inch; 6 rows = 1 inch

Yoke:

With #5 needles cast on 48 sts and work as follows: P 2 sts, place marker (front), p 10 sts, place marker (sleeve), p 24 sts, place marker (back), p 10 sts, place marker (sleeve), p 2 sts (front). *Next row, k all across, inc 1 st in the first st, 1 st before and after each marker (10 incs). Next row p. Next row, k all across, inc 1 st before and after each marker (8 incs). Next row p. Repeat from * till there are 60 (64, 66, 68) sts on back section. End with a right side row.

Continue as for front, back, and sleeves of Infants' Classic Sport Weight Sweaters—Crew Neck Cardigan.

Finishing:

Sew underarm seams. *For Zipper:* With right side facing you, work 2 rows sc around entire front and neck edges. Sew in zipper up to where V shaping starts. *For Buttonholes:* With right side facing you, work 5 rows sc around entire front and neck edge, placing buttonholes evenly spaced on the 3rd row, between bottom and start of V shaping. Make buttonholes on the right for girls, on the left for boys. To make buttonholes, ch 2, sk 2 sts. On the 4th row, make 2 sc in the ch-2 sp.

Crew Neck Pullover

Infants' Sizes: Directions are for 6 months. Changes for 1, 2, and 3 are in parentheses.
Materials: 4 (6, 8, 10) oz sport weight yarn
Needles: dp #3 and #5; 24-inch cir #3 and #5
Gauge: 6 sts = 1 inch; 6 rows = 1 inch

Yoke:

With dp #3 needles cast on 74 sts. Join, being careful not to twist, working round and round, k 1, p 1 in rib for 1 inch. Change to dp #5 needles and work as follows: k 26 sts, place marker (front), k 11 sts, place marker (sleeve), k 26 sts, place marker (back), k 11 sts, (sleeve). Next row, k all around, inc 1 st before and after each marker (8 incs). Next row, k. Continue to k every row, inc 1 st before and after each marker, every other row, and changing to cir #5 needle after 2 inches. Work till there are 60 (64, 66, 68) sts on back section.

Front, Back, and Sleeves:

Place front, back, and 1 sleeve section on holders. Work rem sleeve as follows: *With dp #5 needles, place marker at underarm and dec 1 st each side of the marker every 1 inch 4 (5, 5, 6) times. Work even till 5½ (6, 6½, 7) inches or desired length. Change to dp #3 needles, k 1, p 1 in rib for 1 (1, 1½, 1½) inches. Bind off loosely in rib. Repeat from * for other sleeve. Join yarn at underarm. With cir #5 needle, work in rnds till 5 (5½, 6, 6½) inches from underarm. Change to cir #3 needle and k 1, p 1 in rib for 1½ inches. Bind off loosely in rib.

Finishing:

Sew small hole at underarm. Block lightly.

INFANTS' CLASSIC KNITTING WORSTED SWEATERS

CREW NECK CARDIGAN

Infants' Sizes: Directions are for 6 months. Changes for 1, 2, and 3 are in parentheses.
Materials: 4 (6, 8, 8) oz knitting worsted
Needles: #5 and #8; crochet hook #5
Gauge: 5 sts = 1 inch; 5 rows = 1 inch

Yoke:

With #5 needles cast on 48 (48, 50, 50) sts. K 1, p 1 in rib for 1 inch. Change to #8 needles and work as follows: p 9 sts, place marker (front), p 6 (6, 7, 7) sts, place marker (sleeve), p 18 sts, place marker (back), p 6 (6, 7, 7) sts, place marker (sleeve), p 9 sts, (front). *Next row, k all across, inc 1 st before and after each marker (8 incs). Next row p. Repeat from * till there are 48 (50, 52, 54) sts on back section. End with a right side row.

Front, Back, and Sleeves:

P across to first marker, place sts just worked on holder, p to 3rd marker, place sts between 2nd and 3rd marker on holder, p to 4th marker, place rem sts not worked on holder. Mark this front and remove all other markers. You now have 2 sleeve sections left on needles. Working both at once and joining 2nd ball of yarn for 2nd sleeve, work as follows: Dec 1 st each side of each sleeve, every 1 inch, 4 (5, 5, 6) times. Work even till 5½ (6, 6½, 7) inches or desired length. Change to #5 needles, k 1, p 1 in rib for 1 (1, 1½, 1½) inch. Bind off loosely in rib. Join yarn at underarm of marked front. P across this front section, turn, k same front, k back section, k other front section. Continue body in 1 piece, working till 5 (5½, 6, 6½) inches from underarm or 1½ inches less than desired length. Change to #5 needles, k 1, p 1 in rib for 1½ inches. Bind off loosely in rib.

Finishing:

Sew underarm seams. *For Zipper:* With right side facing you, work 2 rows sc on each front edge and sew in zipper. *For Buttonholes:* With right side facing you, work 3 rows sc on each front edge, placing buttonholes evenly spaced on the 2nd row. Make buttonholes on the right for girls, on the left for boys. To make buttonholes, ch 1, sk 1. On the 3rd row, make 1 sc in the ch-1 sp.

V NECK CARDIGAN

Infants' Sizes: Directions are for 6 months. Changes for 1, 2, and 3 are in parentheses.
Materials: 4 (6, 8, 8) oz knitting worsted
Needles: #5 and #8; crochet hook #5
Gauge: 5 sts = 1 inch

Yoke:

With #8 needles cast on 34 (34, 36, 36) sts and work as follows: P 2 sts, place marker (front), p 6 (6, 7, 7) sts, place marker (sleeve), p 18 sts, place marker (back), p 6 (6, 7, 7) sts, place marker (sleeve), p 2 sts, (front). *Next row, k all across, inc 1 st in the first st, 1 st before and after each marker, and 1 st in the last st (10 incs). Next row p. Next row, k all across, inc 1 st before and after each marker (8 incs). Next row p. Repeat from * till there are 48 (50, 52, 54) sts on back section. End with a right side row.

Continue as for front, back, and sleeves of Infants' Classic Knitting Worsted Sweaters—Crew Neck Cardigan.

Finishing:

Sew underarm seams. *For Zipper:* With right side facing you, work 2 rows sc around entire front and neck edges. Sew in zipper up to where V shaping starts. *For Buttonholes:* With right side facing you, work 3 rows sc around entire front and neck edge, placing buttonholes evenly spaced on the 2nd row, between bottom and start of V shaping. Make buttonholes on the right for girls, on the left for boys. To make buttonholes, ch 1, sk 1. On the 3rd row, make 1 sc in the ch-1 sp.

CREW NECK PULLOVER

Infants' Sizes: Directions are for 6 months. Changes for 1, 2, and 3 are in parentheses.
Materials: 4 (6, 8, 8) oz knitting worsted
Needles: dp #5 and #8; 24-inch cir #5 and #8
Gauge: 5 sts = 1 inch; 5 rows = 1 inch

Yoke:

With dp #5 needles cast on 54 (54, 56, 56) sts. Join, being careful not to twist, working round and round, k 1, p 1 in rib for 1 inch. Change to dp #8 needles and work as follows: K 20 sts, place marker (front), k 7 (7, 8, 8) sts, place marker (sleeve), k 20 sts, place marker (back), k 7 (7, 8, 8) sts, (sleeve). Next row, k all around, inc 1 st before and after each marker (8 incs). Next row k. Continue to k every row, inc 1 st before and after each marker, every other row, and changing to cir #8 needle after 2 inches. Work till there are 48 (50, 52, 54) sts on back section.

Front, Back, and Sleeves:

Place front, back, and 1 sleeve section on holders. Work rem sleeve as follows: *With dp #8 needles, place marker at underarm and dec 1 st each side of marker, every 1 inch, 4 (5, 5, 6) times. Work even till 5½ (6, 6½, 7) inches. Change to dp #5 needles, k 1, p 1 in rib for 1 (1, 1½, 1½) inches. Bind off loosely in rib. Repeat from * for other sleeve. Join yarn at underarm. With cir #8 needle, work in rnds till 5 (5½, 6, 6½) inches from underarm. Change to cir #5 needle and k 1, p 1 in rib for 1½ inches. Bind off loosely in rib.

Finishing:

Sew small hole at underarm. Block lightly.

Figure 11. A buttoned version of the classic crew neck cardigan. Notice the ribbing at the neck, waistband, and cuffs. This is typical of knitted raglan sweaters. Yarn: Nantuck by Columbia-Minerva.

CHILDREN'S CLASSIC SPORT WEIGHT SWEATERS

CREW NECK CARDIGAN

Children's Sizes: Directions are for size 4. Changes for 6, 8, 10, 12, and 14 are in parentheses.
Materials: 10 (10, 12, 12, 14, 14) oz sport weight yarn
Needles: #3 and #5; crochet hook #3
Gauge: 6 sts = 1 inch

Yoke:

With #3 needles cast on 68 (68, 68, 76, 76, 76) sts. K 1, p 1 in rib for 1 inch. Change to #5 needles and work as follows: P 12 (12, 12, 14, 14, 14) sts, place marker (front), p 10 sts, place marker (sleeve), p 24 (24, 24, 28, 28, 28) sts, place marker (back), p 10 sts, place marker (sleeve), p 12 (12, 12, 14, 14, 14) sts, (front). *Next row, k all across, inc 1 st before and after each marker (8 incs). Next row p. Repeat from * till there are 70 (76, 82, 88, 94, 100) sts on back section. End with a right side row.

Front, Back, and Sleeves:

P across to first marker, place sts just worked on holder, p to 3rd marker, place sts between 2nd and 3rd marker on holder, p to 4th marker, place rem sts not worked on holder. Mark this front and remove all other markers. You now have 2 sleeve sections left on needles. Working both at once and joining 2nd ball of yarn for 2nd sleeve, work as follows: Dec 1 st each side of each sleeve every 1 inch, 7 (8, 9, 10, 11, 11) times. Work even till 9½ (10½, 11½, 12½, 13½, 14) inches or desired length. Change to #3 needles, k 1, p 1 in rib for 2 inches. Bind off loosely in rib. Join yarn at underarm of marked front. P across this front section, turn, k same front, k back section, k other front section. Continue body in 1 piece, working till 8 (9, 10, 11, 12, 13) inches from underarm or 2 inches less than desired length. Change to #3 needles, k 1, p 1 in rib for 2 inches. Bind off loosely in rib.

Finishing:

Sew underarm seams. *For Zipper:* With right side facing you, work 2 rows sc on each front edge and sew in zipper. *For Buttonholes:* With right side facing you, work 5 rows sc on each front edge, placing buttonholes evenly spaced on the 3rd row. Make buttonholes on the right for girls, on the left for boys. To make buttonholes, ch 2, sk 2 sts. On the 4th row, make 2 sc in the ch-2 sp.

V NECK CARDIGAN

Children's Sizes: Directions are for size 4. Changes for 6, 8, 10, 12, and 14 are in parentheses.
Materials: 10 (10, 12, 12, 14, 14) oz sport weight yarn
Needles: #3 and #5; crochet hook #3
Gauge: 6 sts = 1 inch; 6 rows = 1 inch

Yoke:

With #5 needles cast on 48 (48, 48, 52, 52, 52) sts and work as follows: P 2 sts, place marker (front), p 10 sts, place marker (sleeve), p 24 (24, 24, 28, 28, 28) sts, place marker (back), p 10 sts, place marker (sleeve), p 2 sts, (front). *Next row, k all across, inc 1 st in first st, 1 st before and after each marker, and 1 st in last st (10 incs). Next row p. Next row, k all across, inc 1 st before and after each marker (8 incs). Next row p. Repeat from * till there are 70 (76, 82, 88, 94, 100) sts on back section. End with a right side row.

Continue as for front, back, and sleeves of Children's Classic Sport Weight Sweaters—Crew Neck Cardigan.

Finishing:

Sew underarm seams. *For Zipper:* With right side facing you, work 2 rows sc around entire front and neck edges. Sew in zipper up to where V shaping starts. *For Buttonholes:* With right side facing you, work 5 rows sc around entire front and neck edge, placing buttonholes evenly spaced on the 3rd row, between bottom and start of V shaping. Make buttonholes on the right for girls, on the left for boys. To make buttonholes, ch 2, sk 2 sts. On the 4th row, make 2 sc in the ch-2 sp.

CREW NECK PULLOVER

Children's Sizes: Directions are for size 4. Changes for 6, 8, 10, 12, and 14 are in parentheses.
Materials: 10 (10, 12, 12, 14, 14) oz sport weight yarn
Needles: dp #3 and #5, 24-inch cir #3 and #5
Gauge: 6 sts = 1 inch; 6 rows = 1 inch

Yoke:

With dp #3 cast on 74 (74, 74, 82, 82, 82) sts. Join, being careful not to twist, working round and round, k 1, p 1 in rib for 1 inch. Change to dp #5 needles and work as follows: K 26 (26, 26, 30, 30, 30) sts, place marker (front), k 11 sts, place marker (sleeve), k 26 (26, 26, 30, 30, 30) sts, place marker (back), k 11 sts, (sleeve). Next row, k all around, inc 1 st before and after each marker (8 incs). Next row k. Continue to k every row, inc 1 st before and after each marker, every other row, and changing to cir #5 needle after 2 inches. Work till there are 70 (76, 82, 88, 94, 100) sts on back section.

Front, Back, and Sleeves

Place front, back, and 1 sleeve section on holders. Work rem sleeve as follows: *With dp #5 needles, place marker at underarm and dec 1 st each side of marker every 1 inch, 7 (8, 9, 10, 11, 11) times. Work even till 9½ (10½, 11½, 12½, 13½, 14) inches. Change to dp #3 needles, k 1, p 1 in rib for 2 inches. Bind off loosely in rib. Repeat from * for other sleeve. Join yarn at underarm. With cir #5 needle, work in rnds till 8 (9, 10, 11, 12, 13) inches from underarm. Change to cir #3 needle and k 1, p 1 in rib for 2 inches. Bind off loosely in rib.

Finishing:

Sew small hole at underarm. Block lightly.

CHILDREN'S CLASSIC KNITTING WORSTED SWEATERS

CREW NECK CARDIGAN

Children's Sizes: Directions are for size 4. Changes for 6, 8, 10, 12, and 14 are in parentheses.
Materials: 12 (12, 14, 16, 16, 20) oz knitting worsted
Needles: #5 and #8; crochet hook #5
Gauge: 5 sts = 1 inch; 5 rows = 1 inch

Yoke:

With #5 needles cast on 56 (56, 56, 60, 60, 60) sts. K 1, p 1 in rib for 1 inch. Change to #8 needles and work as follows: P 10 (10, 10, 11, 11, 11) sts, place marker (front), p 8 sts, place marker (sleeve), p 20 (20, 20, 22, 22, 22) sts, place marker (back), p 8 sts, place marker (sleeve), p 10, (10, 10 11, 11, 11) sts, (front). *Next row, k all across, inc 1 st before and after each marker (8 incs). Next row p. Repeat from * till there are 56 (60, 64, 66, 70, 74) sts on back section. End with a right side row.

Front, Back, and Sleeves:

P across to first marker, place sts just worked on holder, p to 3rd marker, place sts between 2nd and 3rd marker on holder, p to 4th marker, place rem sts not worked on holder. Mark this front and remove all other markers. You now have 2 sleeve sections left on needles. Working both at once and joining 2nd ball of yarn for 2nd sleeve, work as follows: Dec 1 st each side of each sleeve, every 1 inch, 7 (8, 9, 10, 11, 11) times. Work even till 9½ (10½, 11½, 12½, 13½, 14) inches or desired length. Change to #5 needles, k 1, p 1 in rib for 2 inches. Bind off loosely in rib. Join yarn at underarm of marked front. P across this front section, turn, k same front, k back section, k other front section. Continue body in 1 piece, work till 8 (9, 10, 11, 12, 13) inches from underarm or 2 inches less than desired length. Change to #5 needles, k 1, p 1 in rib for 2 inches. Bind off loosely in rib.

Finishing:

Sew underarm seams. *For Zipper:* With right side facing you, work 2 rows sc on each front edge and sew in zipper. *For Buttonholes:* With right side facing you, work 5 rows sc on each front edge, placing buttonholes evenly spaced on the 3rd row. Make buttonholes on the right for girls, on the left for boys. To make buttonholes, ch 2, sk 2 sts. On the 4th row, make 2 sc in the ch-2 sp.

V Neck Cardigan

Children's Sizes: Directions are for size 4. Changes for 6, 8, 10, 12, and 14 are in parentheses.
Materials: 12 (12, 14, 14, 16, 16, 20) oz knitting worsted
Needles: #5 and #8; crochet hook #5
Gauge: 5 sts = inch

Yoke:

With #8 needles cast on 40 (40, 40, 42, 42, 42) sts and work as follows: P 2 sts, place marker (front), p 8 sts, place marker (sleeve), p 20 (20, 20, 22, 22, 22) sts, place marker (back), p 8 sts, place marker, (sleeve), p 2 sts, (front). *Next row, k all across, inc 1 st in the first st, 1 st before and after each marker, and 1 st in the last st (10 incs). Next row p. Next row, k all across, inc 1 st before and after each marker (8 incs). Next row p. Repeat from * till there are 56 (60, 64, 66, 70, 74) sts on back section. End with a right side row.

Continue as for front, back, and sleeves of Children's Classic Knitting Worsted Sweaters—Crew Neck Cardigan.

Finishing:

Sew Underarm seams. *For Zipper:* With right side facing you, work 2 rows sc around entire front and neck edges. Sew in zipper up to where V shaping starts. *For Buttonholes:* With right side facing you, work 5 rows sc around entire front and neck edge, placing buttonholes evenly spaced on the 3rd row, between bottom and start of V shaping. Make buttonholes on the right for girls, on the left for boys. To make buttonholes, ch 2, sk 2 sts. On the 4th row, make 2 sc in the ch-2 sp.

Crew Neck Pullover

Children's Sizes: Directions are for size 4. Changes for 6, 8, 10, 12, and 14 are in parentheses.
Materials: 12 (12, 14, 16, 16, 20) oz knitting worsted
Needles: dp #5 and #8; 24-inch cir #5 and #8
Gauge: 5 sts = 1 inch; 5 rows = 1 inch

Yoke:

With dp #5 needles cast on 62 (62, 62, 66, 66, 66,) sts. Join, being careful not to twist, working round and round, k 1, p 1 in rib for 1 inch. Change to dp #8 needles and work as follows: K 22 (22, 22, 24, 24, 24) sts, place marker (front), k 9 sts, place marker (sleeve), k 22 (22, 22, 24, 24, 24) sts, place marker (back), k 9 sts, (sleeve). Next row, k all around, inc 1 st before and after each marker (8 incs). Next row k. Continue to k every row, inc 1 st before and after each marker, every other row, and changing to cir #8 needle after 2 inches. Work till there are 56 (60, 64, 66, 70, 74) sts on back section.

Front, Back, and Sleeves:

Place front, back, and 1 sleeve section on holders. Work rem sleeve as follows: *With dp #8 needles, place marker at underarm and dec 1 st each side of marker, every 1 inch, 7 (8, 9, 10, 11, 11) times. Work even till 9½ (10½, 11½, 12½, 13½, 14) inches. Change to dp #5 needles, k 1, p 1 in rib for 2 inches. Bind off loosely in rib. Repeat from * for other sleeve. Join yarn at underarm. With cir #8 needle, work in rnds till 8 (9, 10, 11, 12, 13) inches from underarm. Change to cir #5 needle and k 1, p 1 in rib for 2 inches. Bind off loosely in rib.

Finishing:

Sew small hole at underarm. Block lightly.

CHILDREN'S CLASSIC BULKY YARN SWEATERS

CREW NECK CARDIGAN

Children's Sizes: Directions are for size 4. Changes for 6, 8, 10, 12, and 14 are in parentheses.
Materials: 20 (22, 24, 26, 28, 30) oz bulky yarn
Needles: #9 and #10½; crochet hook #9
Gauge: 3½ sts = 1 inch; 4 rows = 1 inch

Yoke:
With #9 needles cast on 34 (34, 38, 38, 42, 42) sts. K 1, p 1 in rib for 1 inch. Change to #10½ needles and work as follows: P 6 (6, 7, 7, 8, 8) sts, place marker (front), p 5 (5, 5, 5, 6, 6) sts, place marker (sleeve), p 12 (12, 14, 14, 14, 14) sts, place marker (back), p 5 (5, 5, 5, 6, 6) sts, place marker (sleeve), p 6 (6, 7, 7, 8, 8) sts, (front). *Next row, k all across, inc 1 st before and after each marker (8 incs). Next row p. Repeat from * till there are 40 (44, 48, 52, 56, 60) sts on back section. End with a right side row.

Front, Back, and Sleeves:
P across to first marker, place sts just worked on holder, p to 3rd marker, place sts between 2nd and 3rd marker on holder, p to 4th marker, place rem sts not worked on holder. Mark this front and remove all other markers. You now have 2 sleeve sections left on needles. Working both at once and joining 2nd ball of yarn for 2nd sleeve, work as follows: Dec 1 st each side of each sleeve, every 2 inches, 3 (4, 4, 5, 5, 5) times. Work even till 9½ (10½, 11½, 12½, 13½, 14) inches or desired length. Change to #9 needles, k 1, p 1 in rib for 2 inches. Bind off loosely in rib. Join yarn at underarm of marked front. P across this front section, turn, k same front, k back section, k other front section. Continue body in 1 piece, working till 8 (9, 10, 11, 12, 13) inches from underarm or 2 inches less than desired length. Change to #9 needles, k 1, p 1 in rib for 2 inches. Bind off loosely in rib.

Finishing:
Sew underarm seams. *For Zipper:* With right side facing you, work 2 rows sc on each front edge and sew in zipper. *For Buttonholes:* With right side facing you, work 3 rows sc on each front edge, placing buttonholes evenly spaced on the 2nd row. Make buttonholes on the right for girls, on the left for boys. To make buttonholes, ch 1, sk 1. On the 3rd row, make 1 sc in the ch-1 sp.

V NECK CARDIGAN

Children's Sizes: Directions are for size 4. Changes for 6, 8, 10, 12 and 14 are in parentheses.
Materials: 20 (22, 24, 26, 28, 30) oz bulky yarn
Needles: #9 and #10½; crochet hook #9
Gauge: 3½ sts = 1 inch; 4 rows = 1 inch

Yoke:
With #10½ needles cast on 26 (26, 28, 28, 30, 30) sts and work as follows: P 2 sts, place marker (front), p 5 (5, 5, 5, 6, 6) sts, place marker (sleeve), p 12 (12, 14, 14, 14, 14) sts, place marker (back), p 5 (5, 5, 5, 6, 6) sts, place marker (sleeve), p 2 sts, (front). *Next row, k all across, inc 1 st in the first st, 1 st before and after each marker, and 1 st in the last st (10 incs). Next row p. Next row, k all across, inc 1 st before and after each marker (8 incs). Next row p. Repeat from * till there are 40 (44, 48, 52, 56, 60) sts on back section. End with a right side row.

Continue as for front, back, and sleeves of Children's Classic Bulky Yarn Sweaters–Crew Neck Cardigan.

Finishing:
Sew underarm seams. *For Zipper:* With right side facing you, work 2 rows sc around entire front and neck edges. Sew in zipper up to where V shaping starts. *For Buttonholes:* With right side facing you, work 3 rows sc around entire front and neck edge, placing buttonholes evenly spaced on the 2nd row, between bottom and start of V shaping. Make buttonholes on the right for girls, on the left for boys. To make buttonholes, ch 1, sk 1. On the 3rd row, make 1 sc in the ch-1 sp.

CREW NECK PULLOVER

Children's Sizes: Directions are for size 4. Changes for 6, 8, 10, 12, and 14 are in parentheses.
Materials: 20 (22, 24, 26, 28, 30) oz bulky yarn
Needles: dp #9 and #10½; 24-inch cir #9 and #10½
Gauge: 3½ sts = 1 inch; 4 rows = 1 inch

Yoke:
With dp #9 needles cast on 38 (38, 42, 42, 44, 44) sts. Join, being careful not to twist, working round and round, k 1, p 1 in rib for 1 inch. Change to dp #10½ needles and work as follows: K 13 (13, 15, 15, 15, 15) sts, place marker (front), k 6 (6, 6, 6, 7, 7) sts, place marker (sleeve), k 13 (13, 15, 15, 15, 15) sts, place marker (back), k 6 (6, 6, 6, 7, 7) sts, (sleeve). Next row, k all around, inc 1 st before and after each marker (8 incs). Next row k. Continue to k every row, inc 1 st before and after each marker, every other row, and changing to cir #10½ needle after 2 inches. Work till there are 40 (44, 48, 52, 56, 60) sts on back section.

Front, Back, and Sleeves:

Place front, back, and 1 sleeve section on holders. Work rem sleeve as follows: *With dp #10½ needles, place marker at underarm and dec 1 st each side of marker, every 2 inches, 3 (4, 4, 5, 5, 5) times. Work even till 9½ (10½, 11½, 12½, 13½, 14) inches. Change to dp #9 needles, k 1, p 1 in rib for 2 inches. Bind off loosely in rib. Repeat from * for other sleeve. Join yarn at underarm. With cir #10½ needle, work in rnds till 8 (9, 10, 11, 12, 13) inches from underarm. Change to cir #9 needle and k 1, p 1 in rib for 2 inches. Bind off loosely in rib.

Finishing:

Sew small hole at underarm. Block lightly.

Figure 12. The V neck, buttoned cardigan on the right is a particularly versatile style. It provides warmth, but allows some of the blouse, shirt, or sweater underneath to show through. Turtleneck pullovers like the one shown on the left are immensely popular among sports enthusiasts. Any crew neck pullover can be converted to a turtleneck just by adding rows at the neck. Yarn: Germanntown Knitting Worsted by Brunswick.

WOMEN'S CLASSIC SPORT WEIGHT SWEATERS

CREW NECK CARDIGAN

Women's Sizes: Directions are for size 8. Changes for 10, 12, 14, 16, and 18 are in parentheses.
Materials: 14 (14, 16, 16, 18, 18) oz sport weight yarn
Needles: #3 and #5; crochet hook #3
Gauge: 6 sts = 1 inch; 6 rows = 1 inch

Yoke:

With #3 needles cast on 76 (76, 76, 82, 82, 82) sts. K 1, p 1 in rib for 1 inch. Change to #5 needles and work as follows: P 14 (14, 14, 15, 15, 15) sts, place marker (front), p 10 (10, 10, 11, 11, 11) sts, place marker (sleeve), p 28 (28, 28, 30, 30, 30) sts, place marker (back), p 10 (10, 10, 11, 11, 11) sts, place marker (sleeve), p 14 (14, 14, 15, 15, 15) sts, (front). *Next row, k all across, inc 1 st before and after each marker (8 incs). Next row p. Repeat from * till there are 96 (102, 108, 112, 118, 124) sts on back section. End with a right side row.

Front, Back, and Sleeves:

P to first marker, place sts just worked on holder, p to 3rd marker, place sts between 2nd and 3rd marker on holder, p to 4th marker, place rem sts not worked on holder. Mark this front and remove all other markers. You now have 2 sleeve sections left on needles. Working both at once and joining a 2nd ball of yarn for 2nd sleeve, work as follows: Dec 1 st each side of each sleeve, every 1 inch, 12 (12, 12, 12, 13, 13) times. Work even till 14 (14, 14½, 14½, 15½, 15½) inches or desired length. Change to #3 needles, k 1, p 1 in rib for 2 inches. Bind off loosely in rib. Join yarn at underarm of marked front. P across this front section, turn, k same front, k back section, k other front section. Continue body in 1 piece, work till 13 (13, 14, 14, 15, 15) inches from underarm or 2 inches less than desired length. Change to #3 needles, k 1, p 1 in rib for 2 inches. Bind off loosely in rib.

Finishing:

Sew underarm seams. *For Zipper:* With right side facing you, work 2 rows sc on each front edge and sew in zipper. *For Buttonholes:* With right side facing you, work 5 rows sc on each front edge, placing buttonholes evenly spaced on the 3rd row. Make buttonholes on the right for girls, on the left for boys. To make buttonholes, ch 2, sk 2 sts. On the 4th row, make 2 sc in the ch-2 sp.

V NECK CARDIGAN

Women's Sizes: Directions are for size 8. Changes for 10, 12, 14, 16, and 18 are in parentheses.
Materials: 14 (14, 16, 16, 18, 18) oz sport weight yarn
Needles: #3 and #5; crochet hook #3
Gauge: 6 sts = 1 inch; 6 rows = 1 inch

Yoke:

With #5 needles cast on 54 (54, 54, 58, 58, 58) sts and work as follows: P 3 sts, place marker (front), p 10 (10, 10, 11, 11, 11) sts, place marker (sleeve), p 28 (28, 28, 30, 30, 30) sts, place marker (back), p 10 (10, 10, 11, 11, 11) sts, place marker (sleeve), p 3 sts, (front). *Next row, k all across, inc 1 st in the first st, 1 st before and after each marker, and 1 st in the last st (10 incs). Next row p. Next row, k all across, inc 1 st before and after each marker (8 incs). Next row p. Repeat from * till there are 96 (102, 108, 112, 118, 124) sts on back section. End with a right side row.

Continue as for front, back, and sleeves of Women's Classic Sport Weight Sweaters—Crew Neck Cardigan.

Finishing:

Sew underarm seams. *For Zipper:* With right side facing you, work 2 rows sc around entire front and neck edges. Sew in zipper up to where V shaping starts. *For Buttonholes:* With right side facing you, work 5 rows sc around entire front and neck edge, placing buttonholes evenly spaced on the 3rd row, between bottom and start of V shaping. Make buttonholes on the right for girls, on the left for boys. To make buttonholes, ch 2, sk 2 sts. On the 4th row, make 2 sc in the ch-2 sp.

CREW NECK PULLOVER

Women's Sizes: Directions are for size 8. Changes for 10, 12, 14, 16, and 18 are in parentheses.
Materials: 14 (14, 16, 16, 18, 18) oz sport weight yarn
Needles: dp #3 and #5; 24-inch cir #3 and #5
Gauge: 6 sts = 1 inch; 6 rows = 1 inch

Yoke:

With dp #3 needles cast on 82 (82, 82, 88, 88, 88) sts. Join, being careful not to twist, working round and round, k 1, p 1 in rib for 1 inch. Change to dp #5 needles and work as follows: K 30 (30, 30, 32, 32, 32) sts, place marker (front), k 11 (11, 11, 12, 12, 12) sts, place marker (sleeve), k 30 (30, 30, 32, 32, 32) sts, place marker (back), k 11 (11, 11, 12, 12, 12) sts, (sleeve). Next row, k all around, inc 1 st before and after each marker (8 incs). Next row k. Continue to k every row, inc 1 st before and after each marker every other row and changing to cir #5 needle after 2 inches. Work till there are 96 (102, 108, 112, 118, 124) sts on back section.

Front, Back, and Sleeves:
Place front, back, and 1 sleeve section on holders. Work rem sleeve as follows: *With dp #5 needles, place marker at underarm and dec 1 st each side of markers, every 1 inch, 12 (12, 12, 12, 13, 13) times. Work even till 14 (14, 14½, 14½, 15½, 15½) inches. Change to dp #3 needles, k 1, p 1 in rib for 2 inches. Bind off loosely in rib. Repeat from * for other sleeve. Join yarn at underarm. With cir #5 needle, work in rnds till there are 13 (13, 14, 14, 15, 15) inches from underarm. Change to cir #3 needle and k 1, p 1 in rib for 2 inches. Bind off loosely in rib.

Finishing:
Sew small hole at underarm. Block lightly.

WOMEN'S CLASSIC KNITTING WORSTED SWEATERS

CREW NECK CARDIGAN

Women's Sizes: Directions are for size 8. Changes for 10, 12, 14, 16, and 18 are in parentheses.
Materials: 16 (20, 20, 20, 24, 24) oz knitting worsted
Needles: #5 and #8; crochet hook #5
Gauge: 5 sts = 1 inch; 5 rows = 1 inch

Yoke:
With #5 needles cast on 60 (60, 60, 64, 64, 64) sts. K 1, p 1 in rib for 1 inch. Change to #8 needles and work as follows: P 11 (11, 11, 12, 12, 12) sts, place marker on needle (front), p 8 sts, place marker (sleeve), p 22 (22, 22, 24, 24, 24) sts, place marker (back), p 8 sts, place marker (sleeve), p 11 (11, 11, 12, 12, 12) sts, (front). *Next row, k all across, inc 1 st before and after each marker (8 incs). Next row p. Repeat from * till there are 78 (82, 86, 90, 94, 98) sts on back section. End with a right side row.

Front, Back, and Sleeves:
P across to first marker, place sts just worked on holder, p to 3rd marker, place sts between 2nd and 3rd marker on holder, work to 4th marker, place rem sts not worked on holder. Mark this front and remove all other markers. You now have 2 sleeve sections left on needles. Working both at once and joining 2nd ball of yarn for 2nd sleeve, work as follows: Dec 1 st each side of each sleeve, every 1 inch, 12 (12, 12, 12, 13, 13) times. Work even till 14 (14, 14½, 14½, 15½, 15½) inches or desired length. Change to #5 needles, k 1, p 1 in rib for 2 inches. Bind off loosely in rib. Join yarn at underarm of marked front. P across this front section, turn, k same front, k back section, k other front section. Continue body in 1 piece, working till 13 (13, 14, 14, 15, 15) inches from underarm or 2 inches less than desired length. Change to #5 needles, k 1, p 1 in rib for 2 inches. Bind off loosely in rib.

Finishing:
Sew underarm seams. *For Zipper:* With right side facing you, work 2 rows sc on each front edge and sew in zipper. *For Buttonholes:* With right side facing you, work 5 rows sc on each front edge, placing buttonholes evenly spaced on the 3rd row. Make buttonholes on the right for girls, on the left for boys. To make buttonholes, ch 2, sk 2 sts. On the 4th row, make 2 sc in the ch-2 sp.

V Neck Cardigan

Women's Sizes: Directions are for size 8. Changes for 10, 12, 14, 16, and 18 are in parentheses.
Materials: 16 (20, 20, 20, 24, 24) oz knitting worsted
Needles: #5 and #8; crochet hook #5
Gauge: 5 sts = 1 inch; 5 rows = 1 inch

Yoke:

With #8 needles cast on 42 (42, 42, 44, 44, 44) sts and work as follows: P 2 sts, place marker (front), p 8 sts, place marker (sleeve), p 22 (22, 22, 24, 24, 24) sts, place marker (back), p 8 sts, place marker (sleeve), p 2 sts (front). *Next row, k all across, inc 1 st in the first st, 1 st before and after each marker, and 1 st in the last st (10 incs). Next row p. Next row, k all across, inc 1 st before and after each marker (8 incs). Next row p. Repeat from * till there are 78 (82, 86, 90, 94, 98) sts on back section. End with a right side row.

Continue as for front, back, and sleeves of Women's Classic Knitting Worsted Sweaters—Crew Neck Cardigan.

Finishing

Sew underarm seams. *For Zipper:* With right side facing you, work 2 rows sc around entire front and neck edges. Sew in zipper up to where V shaping starts. *For Buttonholes:* With right side facing you, work 5 rows sc around entire front and neck edge, placing buttonholes evenly spaced on the 3rd row, between bottom and start of V shaping. Make buttonholes on the right for girls, on the left for boys. To make buttonholes, ch 2, sk 2 sts. On the 4th row, make 2 sc in the ch-2 sp.

Crew Neck Pullover

Women's Sizes: Directions are for size 8. Changes for 10, 12, 14, 16, and 18 are in parentheses.
Materials: 16 (20, 20, 20, 24, 24) oz knitting worsted
Needles: dp #5 and #8; 24-inch cir #5 and #8
Gauge: 5 sts = 1 inch; 5 rows = 1 inch

Yoke:

With dp #5 needles cast on 66 (66, 66, 70, 70, 70) sts. Join, being careful not to twist, working round and round, k 1, p 1 in rib for 1 inch. Change to dp #8 needles and work as follows: K 24 (24, 24, 26, 26, 26) sts, place marker (front), k 9 sts, place marker (sleeve), k 24 (24, 24, 26, 26, 26) sts, place marker (back), k 9 sts, (sleeve). Next row, k all around, inc 1 st before and after each marker (8 incs). Next row k. Continue to k every row, inc 1 st before and after each marker every other row and changing to cir #8 needle after 2 inches. Work till there are 78 (82, 86, 90, 94, 98) sts on back section.

Front, Back, and Sleeves:

Place front, back, and 1 sleeve section on holders. Work rem sleeve as follows: *With dp #8 needles place marker at underarm and dec 1 st each side of marker, every 1 inch, 12 (12, 12, 12, 13, 13) times. Work even till 14 (14, 14½, 14½, 15½, 15½) inches. Change to dp #5 needles, k 1, p 1 in rib for 2 inches. Bind off loosely in rib. Repeat from * for other sleeve. Join yarn at underarm. With cir #8 needle work in rnds till 13 (13, 14, 14, 15, 15) inches from underarm. Change to cir #5 needle and k 1, p 1 in rib for 2 inches. Bind off loosely in rib.

Finishing:

Sew small hole at underarm. Block lightly.

WOMEN'S CLASSIC BULKY YARN SWEATERS

CREW NECK CARDIGAN

Women's Sizes: Directions are for size 8. Changes for 10, 12, 14, 16, and 18 are in parentheses.
Materials: 40 (42, 44, 46, 48, 50) oz bulky yarn
Needles: #9 and #10½; crochet hook #9
Gauge: 3½ sts = 1 inch; 4 rows = 1 inch

Yoke:
With #9 needles cast on 42 (42, 42, 48, 48, 48) sts. K 1, p 1 in rib for 1 inch. Change to #10½ needles and work as follows: P 8 (8, 8, 9, 9, 9) sts, place marker (front), p 6 (6, 6, 7, 7, 7) sts, place marker (sleeve), p 14 (14, 14, 16, 16, 16) sts, place marker (back), p 6 (6, 6, 7, 7, 7) sts, place marker (sleeve), p 8 (8, 8, 9, 9, 9) sts, (front). *Next row, k all across, inc 1 st before and after each marker (8 incs). Next row p. Repeat from * till there are 56 (60, 62, 66, 70, 74) sts on back section. End with a right side row.

Front, Back, and Sleeves:
P to first marker, place sts just worked on holder, p to 3rd marker, place sts between 2nd and 3rd marker on holder, p to 4th marker, place rem sts not worked on holder. Mark this front and remove all other markers. You now have 2 sleeve sections left on needles. Working both at once and joining a 2nd ball of yarn for 2nd sleeve, work as follows: Dec 1 st each side of each sleeve, every 2 inches, 5 (5, 5, 6, 6, 6) times. Work even till 14 (14, 14½, 14½, 15½, 15½) inches or desired length. Change to #9 needles, k 1, p 1 in rib for 2 inches. Bind off loosely in rib. Join yarn at underarm of marked front. P across this front section, turn k same front, k back section, k other front section. Continue body in 1 piece, working till 13 (13, 14, 14, 15, 15) inches from underarm or 2 inches less than desired length. Change to #9 needles, k 1, p 1 in rib for 2 inches. Bind off loosely in rib.

Finishing:
Sew underarm seams. *For Zipper*: With right side facing you, work 2 rows sc on each front edge and sew in zipper. *For Buttonholes*: With right side facing you, work 3 rows sc on each front edge, placing buttonholes evenly spaced on the 2nd row. Make buttonholes on the right for girls, on the left for boys. To make buttonholes, ch 1, sk 1. On the 3rd row, make 1 sc in the ch-1 sp.

V NECK CARDIGAN

Women's Sizes: Directions are for size 8. Changes for 10, 12, 14, 16, and 18 are in parentheses.
Materials: 40 (42, 44, 46, 48, 50) oz bulky yarn
Needles: #9 and #10½; crochet hook #9
Gauge: 3½ sts = 1 inch; 4 rows = 1 inch

Yoke:
With #10½ needles cast on 30 (30, 30, 34, 34, 34) sts and work as follows: P 2 sts, place marker (front), p 6 (6, 6, 7, 7, 7) sts, place marker (sleeve), p 14 (14, 14, 16, 16, 16) sts, place marker (back), p 6 (6, 6, 7, 7, 7) sts, place marker (sleeve), p 2 sts, (front). *Next row, k all across, inc 1 st in the first st, 1 st before and after each marker, and 1 st in the last st (10 incs). Next row p. Next row, k all across, inc 1 st before and after each marker (8 incs). Next row p. Repeat from * till there are 56 (60, 62, 66, 70, 70) sts on back section. End with a right side row.

Continue as for front, back, and sleeves of Women's Classic Bulky Yarn Sweater—Crew Neck Cardigan.

Finishing:
Sew underarm seams. *For Zipper*: With right side facing you, work 2 rows sc around entire front and neck edges. Sew in zipper up to where V shaping starts. *For Buttonholes*: With right side facing you, work 3 rows sc around entire front and neck edge, placing buttonholes evenly spaced on the 2nd row, between bottom and start of V shaping. Make buttonholes on the right for girls, on the left for boys. To make buttonholes, ch. 1 sk 1. On the 3rd row, make 1 sc in the ch-1 sp.

CREW NECK PULLOVER

Women's Sizes: Directions are for size 8. Changes for 10, 12, 14, 16, and 18 are in parentheses.
Materials: 40 (42, 44, 46, 48, 50) oz bulky yarn
Needles: dp #9 and #10½; 36-inch cir #9 and #10½
Gauge: 3½ sts = 1 inch; 4 rows = 1 inch

Yoke:

With dp #9 needles cast on 46 (46, 46, 52, 52, 52) sts. Join, being careful not to twist, working round and round, k 1, p 1 in rib for 1 inch. Change to dp #10½ needles and work as follows: K 16 (16, 16, 18, 18, 18) sts, place marker (front), k 7 (7, 7, 8, 8, 8) sts, place marker (sleeve), k 16 (16, 16, 18, 18, 18) sts, place marker (back), k 7 (7, 7, 8, 8, 8) sts, (sleeve). Next row, k all around, inc 1 st before and after each marker (8 incs). Next row k. Continue to k every row, inc 1 st before and after each marker, every other row, and changing to cir #10½ needle after 2 inches. Work till there are 56 (60, 62, 66, 70, 74) sts on back section.

Front, Back, and Sleeves:

Place front, back, and 1 sleeve section on holders. Work rem sleeve as follows: *With dp #10½ needles, place marker at underarm and dec 1 st each side of marker, every 2 inches, 5 (5, 5, 6, 6, 6) times. Work even till 14 (14, 14½, 14½, 15½, 15½) inches. Change to dp #9 needles, k 1, p 1 in rib for 2 inches. Bind off loosely in rib. Repeat from * for other sleeve. Join yarn at underarm. With cir #10½ needle work in rnds till 13 (13, 14, 14, 15, 15) inches from underarm. Change to cir #9 needle and k 1, p 1 in rib for 2 inches. Bind off loosely in rib.

Finishing:

Sew small hole at underarm. Block lightly.

MEN'S CLASSIC SPORT WEIGHT SWEATERS

CREW NECK CARDIGAN

Men's Sizes: Directions are for size 36. Changes for 38, 40, 42, 44, and 46 are in parentheses.
Materials: 16 (18, 18, 20, 22, 22) oz sport weight yarn
Needles: #3 and #5; crochet hook #3
Gauge: 6 sts = 1 inch; 6 rows = 1 inch

Yoke:

With #3 needles cast on 82 (82, 82, 88, 88, 88) sts. K 1, p 1 in rib for 1 inch. Change to #5 needles and work as follows: P 15 (15, 15, 16, 16, 16) sts, place marker (front), p 11 (11, 11, 12, 12, 12) sts, place marker (sleeve), p 30 (30, 30, 32, 32, 32) sts, place marker (back), p 11 (11, 11, 12, 12, 12) sts, place marker (sleeve), p 15 (15, 15, 16, 16, 16) sts, (front). *Next row, k all across, inc 1 st before and after each marker (8 incs). Next row p. Repeat from * till there are 110 (116, 122, 128, 134, 140) sts on back section. End with a right side row.

Front, Back, and Sleeves:

P across to first marker, place sts just worked on holder, p to 3rd marker, place sts between 2nd and 3rd marker on holder, p to 4th marker, place rem sts not worked on holder. Mark this front. Remove all other markers. You now have 2 sleeve sections left on needles. Working both at once and joining 2nd ball of yarn for 2nd sleeve, work as follows: Dec 1 st each side of each sleeve, every 1 inch, 14 (14, 14, 15, 15, 15) times. Work even till 16½ (16½, 17, 17, 17½, 17½) inches or desired length. Change to #3 needles, k 1, p 1 in rib for 2 inches. Bind off loosely in rib. Join yarn at underarm of marked front. P across this front section, turn, k same front, k back section, k other front section. Continue body in 1 piece, working till 14 (14, 15, 15, 16, 16) inches from underarm or 2 inches less than desired length. Change to #3 needles, k 1, p 1 in rib for 2 inches. Bind off loosely in rib.

Finishing:

Sew underarm seams. *For Zipper*: With right side facing you, work 2 rows sc on each front edge and sew in zipper. *For Buttonholes*: With right side facing you, work 5 rows sc on each front edge, placing buttonholes evenly spaced on the 3rd row. Make buttonholes on the right for girls, on the left for boys. To make buttonholes, ch 2, sk 2 sts. On the 4th row, make 2 sc in the ch-2 sp.

V Neck Cardigan

Men's Sizes: Directions are for size 36. Changes for 38, 40, 42, 44, and 46 are in parentheses.
Materials: 16 (18, 18, 20, 22, 22) oz sport weight yarn
Needles: #3 and #5; crochet hook #3
Gauge: 6 sts = 1 inch; 6 rows = 1 inch

Yoke:

With #5 needles cast on 58 (58, 58, 62, 62, 62) sts and work as follows: P 3 sts, place marker (front), p 11 (11, 11, 12, 12, 12) sts, place marker (sleeve), p 30 (30, 30, 32, 32, 32) sts, place marker (back), p 11 (11, 11, 12, 12, 12) sts, place marker (sleeve), p 3 sts, (front). *Next row, k all across, inc 1 st in first st, 1 st before and after each marker, and 1 st in the last st (10 incs). Next row p. Next row, k all across inc 1 st before and after each marker (8 incs). Next row p. Repeat from * till there are 110 (116, 122, 128, 134, 140) sts on back section. End with a right side row.

Continue as for front, back, sleeves of Men's Classic Sport Weight Sweaters—Crew Neck Cardigan.

Finishing:

Sew underarm seams. *For Zipper*: With right side facing you, work 2 rows sc around entire front and neck edges. Sew in zipper up to where V shaping starts. *For Buttonholes*: With right side facing you, work 5 rows sc around entire front and neck edge, placing buttonholes evenly spaced on the 3rd row, between bottom and start of V shaping. Make buttonholes on the right for girls, on the left for boys. To make buttonholes, ch 2, sk 2 sts. On the 4th row, make 2 sc in the ch-2 sp.

Crew Neck Pullover

Men's Sizes: Directions are for size 36. Changes for 38, 40, 42, 44, and 46 are in parentheses.
Materials: 16 (18, 18, 20, 22, 22) oz sport weight yarn
Needles: dp #3 and #5; 36-inch cir #3 and #5
Gauge: 6 sts = 1 inch; 6 rows = 1 inch

Yoke:

With dp #3 needles cast on 92 (92, 92, 98, 98, 98) sts. Join, being careful not to twist, working round and round, k 1, p 1 in rib for 1 inch. Change to dp #5 needles and work as follows: K 33 (33, 33, 35, 35, 35) sts, place marker (front), k 13 (13, 13, 14, 14, 14) sts, place marker (sleeve), k 33 (33, 33, 35, 35, 35) sts, place marker (back), k 13 (13, 13, 14, 14, 14) sts, (sleeve). Next row, k all around, inc 1 st before and after each marker (8 incs). Next row k. Continue to k every row, inc 1 st before and after each marker, every other row, and changing to cir #5 needle after 2 inches. Work till there are 110 (116, 122, 128, 134, 140) sts on back section.

Front, Back, and Sleeves:

Place front, back, and 1 sleeve section on holders. Work rem sleeve as follows: *With dp #5 needles, place marker at underarm and dec 1 st each side of marker, every 1 inch, 14 (14, 14, 15, 15, 15) times. Work even till 16½ (16½, 17, 17, 17½, 17½) inches. Change to dp #3 needles, k 1, p 1 in rib for 2 inches. Bind off loosely in rib. Repeat from * for other sleeve. Join yarn at underarm. With cir #5 needle work in rnds till there are 14 (14, 15, 15, 16, 16) inches from underarm. Change to cir #3 needle and k 1, p 1 in rib for 2 inches. Bind off loosely in rib.

Finishing:

Sew small hole at underarm. Block lightly.

MEN'S CLASSIC KNITTING WORSTED SWEATERS

CREW NECK CARDIGAN

Men's Sizes: Directions are for size 36. Changes for 38, 40, 42, 44, and 46 are in parentheses.
Materials: 24 (24, 28, 28, 32, 32) oz knitting worsted
Needles: #5 and #8; crochet hook #5
Gauge: 5 sts = 1 inch; 5 rows = 1 inch

Yoke:

With #5 needles cast on 70 (70, 70, 74, 74, 74) sts. K 1, p 1 in rib for 1 inch. Change to #8 needles and work as follows: P 12 (12, 12, 13, 13, 13) sts, place marker (front), p 11 sts, place marker (sleeve), p 24 (24, 24, 26, 26, 26) sts, place marker (back), p 11 sts, place marker (sleeve), p 12 (12, 12, 13, 13, 13) sts, (front). *Next row, k all across, inc 1 st before and after each marker (8 incs). Next row p. Repeat from * till there are 86 (90, 94, 98, 104, 108) sts on back section. End with a right side row.

Front, Back and Sleeves:

P across to first marker, place sts just worked on holder, p to 3rd marker, place sts between 2nd and 3rd marker on holder, p to 4th marker, place rem sts not worked on holder. Mark this front and remove all other markers. You now have 2 sleeve sections left on needles. Working both at once and joining 2nd ball of yarn for 2nd sleeve, work as follows: Dec 1 st each side of each sleeve, every 1 inch, 14 (14, 14, 15, 15, 15) times. Work even till 16½ (16½, 17, 17, 17½, 17½) inches or desired length. Change to #5 needles, k 1, p 1 in rib for 2 inches. Bind off loosely in rib. Join yarn at underarm of marked front. P across this front section, turn, k same front, k back section, k other front section. Continue body in 1 piece, working till 14 (14, 15, 15, 16, 16) inches from underarm or 2 inches less than desired length. Change to #5 needles, k 1, p 1 in rib for 2 inches. Bind off loosely in rib.

Finishing:

Sew underarm seams. *For Zipper*: With right side facing you, work 2 rows sc on each front edge and sew in zipper. *For Buttonholes*: With right side facing you, work 5 rows sc on each front edge, placing buttonholes evenly spaced on the 3rd row. Make buttonholes on the right for girls, on the left for boys. To make buttonholes, ch 2, sk 2 sts. On the 4th row, make 2 sc in the ch-2 sp.

V NECK CARDIGAN

Men's Sizes: Directions are for size 36. Changes for 38, 40, 42, 44, and 46 are in parentheses.
Materials: 24 (24, 28, 28, 32, 32) oz knitting worsted
Needles: #5 and #8; crochet hook #5
Gauge: 5 sts = 1 inch; 5 rows = 1 inch

Yoke:

With #8 needles cast on 48 (48, 48, 50, 50, 50) sts and work as follows: P 2 sts, place marker (front), p 10 sts, place marker (sleeve), p 24 (24, 24, 26, 26, 26) sts, place marker (back), p 10 sts, place marker (sleeve), p 2 sts, (front). *Next row, k all across, inc 1 st in the first st, 1 st before and after each marker, and 1 st in the last st (10 incs). Next row p. Next row k, inc 1 st before and after each marker (8 incs). Next row p. Repeat from * till there are 86 (90, 94, 98, 104, 108) sts on back section. End with a right side row.

Continue as for front, back, and sleeves of Men's Classic Knitting Worsted Sweaters—Crew Neck Cardigan.

Finishing:

Sew underarm seams. *For Zipper*: With right side facing you, work 2 rows sc around entire front and neck edges. Sew in zipper up to where V shaping starts. *For Buttonholes*: With right side facing you, work 5 rows sc around entire front and neck edge, placing buttonholes evenly spaced on the 3rd row, between bottom and start of V shaping. Make buttonholes on the right for girls, on the left for boys. To make buttonholes, ch 2, sk 2 sts. On the 4th row, make 2 sc in the ch-2 sp.

CREW NECK PULLOVER

Men's Sizes: Directions are for size 36. Changes for 38, 40, 42, 44, and 46 are in parentheses.
Materials: 24 (24, 28, 28, 32, 32) oz knitting worsted
Needles: dp #5 and #8; 24-inch cir #5 and #8
Gauge: 5 sts = 1 inch; 5 rows = 1 inch

Yoke:

With dp #5 needles cast on 76 (76, 76, 80, 80, 80) sts. Join, being careful not to twist, working round and round, k 1, p 1 in rib for 1 inch. Change to dp #8 needles and work as follows: K 26 (26, 26, 28, 28, 28) sts, place marker (front), k 12 sts, place marker (sleeve), k 26 (26, 26, 28, 28, 28) sts, place marker (back), k 12 sts, (sleeve). Next row, k all around, inc 1 st before and after each marker (8 incs). Next row k. Continue to k every row, inc 1 st before and after each marker, every other row, and changing to cir #8 needle after 2 inches. Work till there are 86 (90, 94, 98, 104, 108) sts on back section.

Front, Back, and Sleeves:

Place front, back, and 1 sleeve section on holders. Work rem sleeve as follows: *With dp #8 needles, place marker at underarm, dec 1 st each side of marker, every 1 inch, 14 (14, 14, 15, 15, 15) times. Work even till 16½ (16½, 17, 17, 17½, 17½) inches. Change to dp #5 needles, k 1, p 1 in rib for 2 inches. Bind off loosely in rib. Repeat from * for other sleeve. Join yarn at underarm. With cir #8 needle work in rnds till there are 14 (14, 15, 15, 16, 16) inches from underarm. Change to cir #5 needle and k 1, p 1 in rib for 2 inches. Bind off loosely in rib.

Finishing:

Sew small hole at underarm. Block lightly.

MEN'S CLASSIC BULKY YARN SWEATERS

CREW NECK CARDIGAN

Men's Sizes: Directions are for size 36. Changes for 38, 40, 42, 44, and 46 are in parentheses.
Materials: 44 (46, 48, 50, 52, 52) oz bulky yarn
Needles: #9 and #10½; crochet hook #9
Gauge: 3½ sts = 1 inch; 4 rows = 1 inch

Yoke:

With #9 needles cast on 48 (48, 48, 54, 54, 54) sts. K 1, p 1 in rib for 1 inch. Change to #10½ needles and work as follows: P 9 (9, 9, 10, 10, 10) sts, place marker (front), p 7 (7, 7, 8, 8, 8) sts, place marker (sleeve), p 16 (16, 16, 18, 18, 18) sts, place marker (back), p 7 (7, 7, 8, 8, 8) sts, place marker (sleeve), p 9 (9, 9, 10, 10, 10) sts, (front). *Next row, k all across, inc 1 st before and after each marker (8 incs). Next row p. Repeat from * till there are 66 (70, 74, 78, 82, 86) sts on back section. End with a right side row.

Front, Back, and Sleeves:

P across to first marker, place sts just worked on holder, p to 3rd marker, place sts between 2nd and 3rd marker on holder, p to 4th marker, place rem sts not worked on holder. Mark this front and remove all other markers. You now have 2 sleeve sections left on needles. Working both at once and joining 2nd ball of yarn for 2nd sleeve, work as follows: Dec 1 st each side of each sleeve, every 2 inches, 5 (5, 5, 6, 6, 6) times. Work even till 16½ (16½, 17, 17, 17½, 17½) inches or desired length. Change to #9 needles, k 1, p 1 in rib for 2 inches. Bind off loosely in rib. Join yarn at underarm of marked front. P across this front section, turn, k same front, k back section, k other front section. Continue body in 1 piece, working till 14 (14, 15, 15, 16, 16) inches from underarm or 2 inches less than desired length. Change to #9 needles, k 1, p 1 in rib for 2 inches. Bind off loosely in rib.

Finishing:

Sew underarm seams. *For Zipper*: With right side facing you, work 2 rows sc on each front edge and sew in zipper. *For Buttonholes*: With right side facing you, work 3 rows sc on each front edge, placing buttonholes evenly spaced on the 2nd row. Make buttonholes on the right for girls, on the left for boys. To make buttonholes, ch 1, sk 1. On the 3rd row, make 1 sc in the ch-1 sp.

V NECK CARDIGAN

Men's Sizes: Directions are for size 36. Changes for 38, 40, 42, 44, and 46 are in parentheses.
Materials: 44 (46, 48, 50, 52, 52) oz bulky yarn
Needles: #9 and #10½; crochet hook #9
Gauge: 3½ sts = 1 inch; 4 rows = 1 inch

Yoke:

With #10½ needles cast on 34 (34, 34, 38, 38, 38) sts and work as follows: P 2 sts, place marker (front), p 7 (7, 7, 8, 8, 8) sts, place marker (sleeve), p 16 (16, 16, 18, 18, 18) sts, place marker (back), p 7 (7, 7, 8, 8, 8) sts, place marker (sleeve), p 2 sts, (front). *Next row, k all across, inc 1 st in the first st, 1 st before and after each marker, and 1 st in the last st (10 incs). Next row p. Next row, k all across, inc 1 st before and after each marker (8 incs). Next row p. Repeat from * till there are 66 (70, 74, 78, 82, 86) sts on back section. End with a right side row.

Continue as for front, back, and sleeves of Men's Bulky Yarn Sweaters—Crew Neck Cardigan.

Finishing:

Sew underarm seams. *For Zipper*: With right side facing you, work 2 rows sc around entire front and neck edges. Sew in zipper up to where V shaping starts. *For Buttonholes*: With right side facing you, work 3 rows sc around entire front and neck edge, placing buttonholes evenly spaced on the 2nd row, between bottom and start of V shaping. Make buttonholes on the right for girls, on the left for boys. To make buttonholes, ch 1, sk 1. On the 3rd row, make 1 sc in the ch-1 sp.

CREW NECK PULLOVER

Men's Sizes: Directions are for size 36. Changes for 38, 40, 42, 44, and 46 are in parentheses.
Materials: 44 (46, 48, 50, 52, 52) oz bulky yarn
Needles: dp #9 and #10½; 24-inch cir #9 and #10½
Gauge: 3½ sts = 1 inch; 4 rows = 1 inch

Yoke:

With dp #9 needles cast on 52 (52, 52, 58, 58, 58) sts. Join, being careful not to twist, working round and round, k 1, p 1 in rib for 1 inch. Change to dp #10½ needles and work as follows: K 18 (18, 18, 20, 20, 20) sts, place marker (front), k 8 (8, 8, 9, 9, 9) sts, place marker (sleeve), k 18 (18, 18, 20, 20, 20) sts, place marker (back), k 8 (8, 8, 9, 9, 9) sts (sleeve). Next row, k all around, inc 1 st before and after each marker (8 incs). Next row k. Continue to k every row, inc 1 st before and after each marker, every other row, and changing to cir #10½ needle after 2 inches. Work till there are 66 (70, 74, 78, 82, 86) sts on back section.

Front, Back, and Sleeves:

Place front, back, and 1 sleeve section on holders. Work rem sleeve as follows: *With dp #10½ needles, place marker at underarm and dec 1 st each side of marker, every 2 inches, 5 (5, 5, 6, 6, 6) times. Work even till 16½ (16½, 17, 17, 17½, 17½) inches. Change to dp #9 needles, k 1, p 1 in rib for 2 inches. Bind off loosely in rib. Repeat from * for other sleeve. Join yarn at underarm. With cir #10½ needle, work till there are 14 (14, 15, 15, 16, 16) inches from underarm. Change to cir #9 needle and k 1, p 1 in rib for 2 inches. Bind off loosely in rib.

Finishing:

Sew small hole at underarm. Block lightly.

4. Raglans Crocheted from Top to Bottom

Several years after I had discovered the joys of knitting from the top down, I began to experiment with crocheting from the top down. I had seen several baby sweaters done in a yoke method from the top down, but virtually no other patterns were available in this method. The results of my experimentation were indeed gratifying. In this chapter I have included instructions for all the classic sweaters. You'll be happy to know that crocheting one-piece garments is even easier than knitting one-piece garments.

There are a few things to look out for, however. For one thing, obtaining the proper gauge with a crochet hook is much more difficult than it is to do with knitting needles, and you must be sure that your gauge is correct. Use a smaller or larger hook than what is called for to obtain the proper gauge, if necessary. Another problem that sometimes occurs is foundation chains are too tight. In that case, use a larger hook for the chain and then change to the proper hook when starting the foundation row.

As far as materials are concerned, you will not need the marker or the holders that are used for the knitted raglans. The points of increase are quite visible on crocheted pieces. Some people, however, do like to place colored strands of yarn to mark these spots.

Crocheted raglans are not quite so common as knitted raglans, but as crochet becomes more and more popular so will the demand for classic sweaters. Figures 13, 14, 15, and 16 show each of the classic crocheted raglans. See page 16 for directions on how to make a turtleneck or a V neck pullover. Also on that page are instructions for teen sizes and ladies' larger sizes. Figures 1, 2, and 3 on page 7 will help you visualize the sweaters as you go along.

Figure 13. The crocheted version of the classic crew neck raglan cardigan. The diagonal raglan sleeve line is hardly visible on the crocheted sweaters. Yarn: Nantuck by Columbia-Minerva.

INFANTS' CLASSIC SPORT WEIGHT SWEATERS

CREW NECK CARDIGAN

Infants' Sizes: Directions are for 6 months. Changes for 1, 2, and 3 are in parentheses.
Materials: 4 (6, 8, 10) oz sport weight yarn
Aluminum Hook: #4 or E
Gauge: 5 sts = 1 inch

Yoke:
Ch 57 loosely.
Foundation Row: 1 dc in 3rd ch from hook, 1 dc in each of next 8 chs, (1 dc, ch 1, 1 dc) all in next ch (front), 1 dc in each of next 7 chs, (1 dc, ch 1, 1 dc) all in next ch (sleeve), 1 dc in each of next 18 chs, (1 dc, ch 1, 1 dc) all in next ch (back), 1 dc in each of next 7 chs, (1 dc, ch 1, 1 dc) all in next ch (sleeve), 1 dc in each of last 9 chs (front).
Row 1: Ch 3, turn (ch-3 always counts as first dc), sk first st, 1 dc in each of next 9 sts, (1 dc, ch 1, 1 dc) all in ch-1 sp (inc), 1 dc in each of next 9 sts, (1 dc ch 1, 1 dc) all in ch-1 sp (inc), 1 dc in each of next 20 sts, (1 dc, ch 1, 1 dc) all in ch-1 sp (inc), 1 dc in each of next 9 sts, (1 dc, ch 1, 1 dc) all in ch-1 sp (inc), 1 dc in each of last 10 sts (last st is top of turning ch).
Row 2: Ch 3, turn, 1 dc in each st to first ch-1 sp, (1 dc, ch 1, 1 dc) all in ch-1 sp, *1 dc in each st to next ch-1 sp, (1 dc, ch 1, 1 dc) all in ch-1 sp. Repeat from * twice more, ending with 1 dc in each st, 1 dc in top of turning ch.
Repeat Row 2 till there are 50 (54, 56, 58) dc in back section.

Front and Back:
Work across front to first ch-1 sp, ch 2, sk sleeve section, work across back section, ch 2, sk other sleeve section, work across front section. Continue in pat as established, omitting incs and working 2 dc on the added ch at underarm. Work entire body section till 6½ (7, 7½, 8) inches from underarm, end off.

Sleeves:
Join yarn at underarm, ch 3, work 1 dc in each st around sleeve section, work 1 dc on ch at underarm. Ch 3, turn. Working back and forth in pat as established, dec 1 st each side, every other row, 3 times. Work even till 6½ (7, 7½, 8) inches or desired length, end off.

Finishing:
Sew underarm seams. *For Zipper:* With right side facing you, starting at bottom right corner, work 2 rows sc around entire front and neck edges, making 3 sc in each corner st at neck. Sew in zipper. *For Buttonholes:* With right side facing you, work 5 rows sc around entire front and neck edges, making 3 sc in each corner st at neck and placing buttonholes evenly spaced on the 3rd row. Make buttonholes on the right for girls, on the left for boys. To make buttonholes, ch 2, sk 2 sts. On the 4th row, make 2 sc in the ch-2 sp.

V NECK CARDIGAN

Infants' Sizes: Directions are for 6 months. Changes for 1, 2, and 3 are in parentheses.
Materials: 4 (6, 8, 10) oz sport weight yarn
Aluminum Hook: #4 or E
Gauge: 5 sts = 1 inch

Yoke:
Ch 41 loosely.
Foundation Row: 1 dc in 3rd ch from hook, (1 dc, ch 1, 1 dc) all in next ch (front), 1 dc in each of next 7 chs, (1 dc, ch 1, 1 dc) all in next ch (sleeve), 1 dc in each of next 18 chs, (1 dc, ch 1, 1 dc) all in next ch (back), 1 dc in each of next 7 chs, (1 dc, ch 1, 1 dc) all in next ch (sleeve), 1 dc in last ch (front).
Row 1: Ch 3, turn (ch-3 always counts as first dc), 1 dc in first st (inc), (1 dc, ch 1, 1 dc) all in ch-1 sp (inc), 1 dc in each of next 9 sts, (1 dc, ch 1, 1 dc) in ch-1 sp (inc), 1 dc in each of next 20 sts, (1 dc, ch 1, 1 dc) all in ch-1 sp (inc), 1 dc in each of next 9 sts, (1 dc, ch 1, 1 dc) all in ch-1 sp (inc), 2 dc in last st.
Row 2: Ch 3, turn, 1 dc in first st, 1 dc in each st to first ch-1 sp (1 dc, ch 1, 1 dc) all in ch-1 sp, *1 dc in each st to next ch-1 sp, (1 dc, ch 1, 1 dc) all in ch-1 sp. Repeat from * twice more, ending with 1 dc in each st, 2 dc in top of turning ch.
Repeat Row 2 till there are 50 (54, 56, 58) dc in back section.
Continue as for front, back, and sleeves of Infants' Classic Sport Weight Sweaters—Crew Neck Cardigan.

Finishing:
Sew underarm seams. *For Zipper:* With right side facing you, starting at bottom right corner, work 2 rows sc around entire front and neck edges. Sew in zipper up to where V shaping starts. *For Buttonholes:* With right side facing you, work 5 rows sc around entire front and neck edges, place buttonholes evenly spaced on the 3rd row, between bottom of garment and start of V shaping. Make buttonholes on the right for girls, on the left for boys. To make buttonholes, ch 2, sk 2. On the 4th row, make 2 sc in the ch-2 sp.

CREW NECK PULLOVER

Infants' Sizes: Directions are for 6 months. Changes for 1, 2 and 3 are in parentheses.
Materials: 4 (6, 8, 10) oz sport weight yarn
Aluminum Hook: #4 or E
Gauge: 5 sts = 1 inch

Yoke:
Ch 48 (48, 52, 52) loosely, join to form a ring.
Foundation Row: Ch 3 (ch-3 always counts as first dc), 1 dc in each of next 5 chs, (1 dc, ch 1, 1 dc) all in next ch (sleeve), 1 dc in each of next 16 (16, 18, 18) chs, (1 dc, ch 1, 1 dc) all in next ch (front), 1 dc in each of next 6 chs, (1 dc, ch 1, 1 dc) all in next ch (sleeve), 1 dc in each of next 16 (16, 18, 18) chs, (1 dc, ch 1, 1 dc) all in next ch (back), join with a slst to starting ch-3.

Row 1: Ch 3, *1 dc in each st to ch-1 sp, (1 dc, ch 1, 1 dc) all in ch-1 sp, repeat from * 3 times more, join with a slst to top of starting ch.
Repeat Row 1 till there are 48 (50, 52, 54) sts on back section.

Front and Back:
On next row, ch 3 sk sleeve section, work across front section, ch 2, sk other sleeve section, work back section, ch 2, join to top of starting ch-3. Working round and round, starting each round with ch-3, and ending with a slst to join, work till body is 6 (7, 8, 9) inches from underarm, end off.

Sleeves:
Join yarn at underarm, ch 3, work 1 dc in each st around sleeve, work 1 dc on the underarm ch, join with a slst. Working round and round, dec 1 st at the underarm every 3rd row, 2 (2, 3, 3) times. Work even till 6 (7, 8, 9) inches from underarm, end off.

Finishing:
Sew underarm seams. Work 4 rows sc around neck opening.

INFANTS' CLASSIC KNITTING WORSTED SWEATERS

CREW NECK CARDIGAN

Infants' Sizes: Directions are for 6 months. Changes for 1, 2, and 3 are in parentheses.
Materials: 4 (6, 8, 8) oz knitting worsted
Aluminum Hook: #6 or G
Gauge: 4 st = 1 inch

Yoke:
Ch 39 loosely.
Foundation Row: 1 dc in 3rd ch from hook, 1 dc in each of next 5 chs, (1 dc, ch 1, 1 dc) all in next ch (front), 1 dc in each of next 4 chs, (1 dc, ch 1, 1 dc) all in next ch (sleeve), 1 dc in each of next 12 chs, (1 dc, ch 1, 1 dc) all in next ch (back), 1 dc in each of next 4 chs, (1 dc, ch 1, 1 dc) all in next ch (sleeve), 1 dc in each of last 6 chs (front).
Row 1: Ch 3, turn (ch-3 always counts as first dc), sk first st, 1 dc in each of next 6 sts, (1 dc, ch 1, 1 dc) all in ch-1 sp (inc), 1 dc in each of next 6 sts, (1 dc, ch 1, 1 dc) all in ch-1 sp (inc), 1 dc in each of next 14 sts, (1 dc, ch 1, 1 dc) all in ch-1 sp (inc), 1 dc in each of next 6 sts, (1 dc, ch 1, 1 dc) all in ch-1 sp (inc), 1 dc in each of last 7 sts (last st is top of turning ch).
Row 2: Ch 3, turn, 1 dc in each st to first ch-1 sp, (1 dc, ch 1, 1 dc) all in ch-1 sp, *1 dc in each st to next ch-1 sp, (1 dc, ch 1, 1 dc) all in ch-1 sp. Repeat from * twice more, ending with 1 dc in each st, 1 dc in top of turning ch.

Repeat Row 2 till there are 34 (36, 38, 40) dc in back section.

Front and Back:
Work across front to first ch-1 sp, ch 2, sk sleeve section, work across back section, ch 2, sk other sleeve section, work across front section. Continue in pat as established, omitting incs and working 2 dc on the added ch at underarm. Work entire body section till 6½ (7, 7½, 8) inches from underarm, end off.

Sleeves:
Join yarn at underarm, ch 3, work 1 dc in each st around sleeve section, work 1 dc on ch at underarm. Ch 3, turn. Working back and forth in pat as established, dec 1 st each side, every other row, 3 times. Work even till 6½ (7, 7½, 8) inches from underarm, end off.

Finishing:
Sew underarm seams. *For Zipper:* With right side facing you, starting at bottom right corner, work 2 rows sc around entire front and neck edges, making 3 sc in each corner st at neck. Sew in zipper. *For Buttonholes:* With right side facing you, work 3 rows sc around entire front and neck edges, making 3 sc in each corner st at neck and placing buttonholes evenly spaced on the 2nd row. Make buttonholes on the right for girls, on the left for boys. To make buttonholes, ch 2, sk 2. On the 3rd row, make 2 sc in the ch-2 sp.

V NECK CARDIGAN

Infants' Sizes: Directions are for 6 months. Changes for 1, 2, and 3 are in parentheses.
Materials: 4 (6, 8, 8) oz knitting worsted
Aluminum Hook: #6 or G
Gauge: 4 sts = 1 inch

Yoke:
Ch 29 loosely.
Foundation Row: 1 dc in 3rd ch from hook, (1 dc, ch 1, 1 dc) all in next ch (front), 1 dc in each of next 4 chs, (1 dc, ch 1, 1 dc) all in next ch (sleeve), 1 dc in each of next 12 chs, (1 dc, ch 1, 1 dc) all in next ch (back), 1 dc in each of next 4 chs, (1 dc, ch 1, 1 dc) all in next ch (sleeve), 1 dc in each of last 2 chs (front).
Row 1: Ch 3, turn (ch-3 always counts as first dc), 1 dc in first st (inc), 1 dc in each st to the ch-1 sp, (1 dc, ch 1, 1 dc) all in ch-1 sp, 1 dc in each of next 6 sts, (1 dc, ch 1, 1 dc) all in ch-1 sp, 1 dc in each of next 14 sts, (1 dc, ch 1, 1 dc) all in ch-1 sp, 1 dc in each of next 6 sts, (1 dc, ch 1, 1 dc) all in ch-1 sp, 1 dc in each st to end, 2 dc in top of turning ch (inc).
Row 2: Ch 3, turn, 1 dc in first st, 1 dc in each st to first ch-1 sp, (1 dc, ch 1, 1 dc) in ch-1 sp, *1 dc in each st to next ch-1 sp, (1 dc, ch 1, 1 dc) all in ch-1 sp. Repeat from * twice more, ending with 1 dc in each st, 2 dc in top of turning ch.

Repeat Row 2 till there are 34 (36, 38, 40) sts in back section.

Continue as for front, back, and sleeves of Infants' Classic Knitting Worsted Sweaters—Crew Neck Cardigan.

Finishing:
Sew underarm seams. *For Zipper:* With right side facing you, starting at bottom right corner, work 2 rows sc around entire front and neck edges. Sew in zipper up to where V shaping starts. *For Buttonholes:* With right side facing you, work 3 rows sc around entire front and neck edges, place buttonholes evenly spaced on the 2nd row, between bottom of garment and start of V shaping. Make buttonholes on the right for girls, on the left for boys. To make buttonholes, ch 2, sk 2. On the 3rd row, make 2 sc in the ch-2 sp.

CREW NECK PULLOVER

Infants' Sizes: Directions are for 6 months. Changes for 1, 2, and 3 are in parentheses.
Materials: 4 (6, 8, 8) oz knitting worsted
Aluminum Hook: #6 or G
Gauge: 4 sts = 1 inch

Yoke:
Ch 36 loosely, join to form a ring.
Foundation Row: Ch 3 (ch-3 always counts as first dc), 1 dc in each of next 3 chs, (1 dc, ch 1, 1 dc) all in next ch (sleeve), 1 dc in each of next 12 chs, (1 dc, ch 1, 1 dc) all in the next ch (front), 1 dc in each of next 4 chs, (1 dc, ch 1, 1 dc) all in next ch (sleeve), 1 dc in each of next 12 chs, (1 dc, ch 1, 1 dc) all in next ch (back), join with a slst to starting ch-3.
Row 1: Ch 3, *1 dc in each st to ch-1 sp, (1 dc, ch 1, 1 dc) all in ch-1 sp, repeat from * 3 times more, join with a slst to top of starting ch.
  Repeat Row 1 till there are 34 (36, 38, 40) sts on back section.

Front and Back:
On next row, ch 3, sk sleeve section, work across front section, ch 2, sk other sleeve section, work back section, ch 2, join to top of starting ch-3. Working round and round, starting each round with a ch-3, and ending with a slst to join, work till body is 6½ (7, 7½, 8) inches from underarm, end off.

Sleeves:
Join yarn at underarm, ch 3, work 1 dc in each st around sleeve, work 1 dc on the underarm ch, join with a slst. Working round and round, dec 1 st at the underarm every row, 4 times. Work even till 6½ (7, 7½, 8) inches from underarm, end off.

Finishing:
Sew underarm seams. Work 4 rows sc around neck opening.

CHILDREN'S CLASSIC SPORT WEIGHT SWEATERS

CREW NECK CARDIGAN

Children's Sizes: Directions are for size 4. Changes for 6, 8, 10, 12, and 14 are in parentheses.
Materials: 10 (10, 12, 12, 14, 14) oz sport weight yarn
Aluminum Hook: #4 or E
Gauge: 5 sts = 1 inch

Yoke:
Ch 59 (59, 59, 63, 63, 63) loosely.
Foundation Row: 1 dc in 3rd ch from hook, 1 dc in each of next 9 (9, 9, 10, 10, 10) chs, (1 dc, ch 1, 1 dc) all in next ch (front), 1 dc in each of next 6 chs, (1 dc, ch 1, 1 dc) all in next ch (sleeve), 1 dc in each of next 20 (20, 20, 22, 22, 22) chs, (1 dc, ch 1, 1 dc) all in next ch (back), 1 dc in each of next 6 chs, (1 dc, ch 1, 1 dc) all in next ch (sleeve), 1 dc in each of last 10 (10, 10, 11, 11, 11) chs (front).
Row 1: Ch 3, turn (ch-3 always counts as first dc), sk first st, 1 dc in each of next 10 (10, 10, 11, 11, 11) sts, (1 dc, ch 1, 1 dc) all in ch-1 sp (inc), 1 dc in each of next 8 sts, (1 dc, ch 1, 1 dc) all in ch-1 sp (inc), 1 dc in each of next 22, (22, 22, 24, 24, 24) sts, (1 dc, ch 1, 1 dc) all in ch-1 sp (inc), 1 dc in each of next 8 sts, (1 dc, ch 1, 1 dc) all in ch-1 sp (inc), 1 dc in each of last 11 (11, 11, 12, 12, 12) sts (last st is in top of turning ch).
Row 2: Ch 3, turn, 1 dc in each st to first ch-1 sp, (1 dc, ch 1, 1 dc) all in ch-1 sp, *1 dc in each st to next ch-1 sp, (1 dc, ch 1, 1 dc) all in ch-1 sp. Repeat from * twice more, ending with 1 dc in each st, 1 dc in top of turning ch.
  Repeat Row 2 till there are 56 (60, 64, 66, 70, 74) dc in back section.

Front and Back:
Work across front to first ch-1 sp, ch 2, sk sleeve section, work across back section, ch 2, sk other sleeve section, work across front section. Continue in pat as established, omitting incs and working 2 dc on the added ch at underarm. Work entire body section till 10 (11, 12, 13, 14, 15) inches from underarm or desired length, end off.

Sleeves:
Join yarn at underarm, ch 3, work 1 dc in each st around sleeve section, work 1 dc on ch at underarm. Ch 3, turn. Working back and forth in pat as established, dec 1 st each side, every 3rd row, 3 (3, 4, 4, 5, 5) times. Work even till 11½ (12½, 13½, 14½, 15½, 16) inches, end off.

Finishing:

Sew underarm seams. *For Zipper:* With right side facing you, starting at bottom right corner, work 2 rows sc around entire front and neck edges, making 3 sc in each corner st at neck. Sew in zipper. *For Buttonholes:* With right side facing you, work 5 rows sc around entire front and neck edges, making 3 sc in each corner st at neck and placing buttonholes evenly spaced on the 3rd row. Make buttonholes on the right for girls, on the left for boys. To make buttonholes, ch 2, sk 2 sts. On the 4th row, make 2 sc in the ch-2 sp.

V NECK CARDIGAN

Children's Sizes: Directions are for size 4. Changes for 6, 8, 10, 12, and 14 are in parentheses.
Materials: 10 (10, 12, 12, 14, 14) oz sport weight yarn
Aluminum Hook: #4 or E
Gauge: 5 sts = 1 inch

Yoke:

Ch 41 (41, 41, 43, 43, 43) loosely.
Foundation Row: 1 dc in 3rd ch from hook, (1 dc, ch 1, 1 dc) all in next ch (front), 1 dc in each of next 6 chs (1 dc, ch 1, 1 dc) all in next ch (sleeve), 1 dc in each of next 20 (20, 20, 22, 22, 22) chs, (1 dc, ch 1, 1 dc) all in next ch (back), 1 dc in each of next 6 chs, (1 dc, ch 1, 1 dc) all in next ch (sleeve), 1 dc in each of 2 chs (front).

Row 1: Ch 3, turn (ch-3 always counts as first dc), 1 dc in first st (inc), 1 dc in each st to first ch-1 sp, (1 dc, ch 1, 1 dc) all in ch-1 sp (inc), 1 dc in each of next 8 sts, (1 dc, ch 1, 1 dc) all in ch-1 sp (inc), 1 dc in each of next 22 (22, 22, 24, 24, 24) sts, (1 dc, ch 1, 1 dc) all in ch-1 sp (inc), 1 dc in each of next 8 sts, (1 dc, ch 1, 1 dc) all in ch-1 sp (inc), 1 dc in each of last 2 sts, 2 dc in top of turning ch (inc.).
Row 2: Ch 3, turn, 1 dc in first st, 1 dc in each st to first ch-1 sp, (1 dc, ch 1, 1 dc) all in ch-1 sp, *1 dc in each st to next ch-1 sp, (1 dc, ch 1, 1 dc) all in ch-1 sp. Repeat from * twice more, ending with 1 dc in each st, 2 dc in top of turning ch.
Repeat Row 2 till there are 56 (60, 64, 66, 70, 74) dc in back section.
Continue as for front, back, and sleeves of Children's Classic Sport Weight Sweaters—Crew Neck Cardigan.

Finishing:

Sew underarm seams. *For Zipper:* With right side facing you, starting at bottom right corner, work 2 rows sc around entire front and neck edges. Sew in zipper up to where V shaping starts. *For Buttonholes:* With right side facing you, work 5 rows sc around entire front and neck edges, place buttonholes evenly spaced on the 3rd row, between bottom of garment and start of V shaping. Make buttonholes on the right for girls, on the left for boys. To make buttonholes, ch 2, sk 2. On the 4th row, make 2 sc in the ch-2 sp.

CREW NECK PULLOVER

Children's Sizes: Directions are for size 4. Changes for 6, 8, 10, 12, and 14 are in parentheses.
Materials: 10 (10, 12, 12, 14, 14) oz sport weight yarn
Aluminum Hook: #4 or E
Gauge: 5 sts = 1 inch

Yoke:

Ch 56, (56, 56, 60, 60, 60) loosely, join to form a ring.
Foundation Row: Ch 3 (ch-3 always counts as first dc), 1 dc in each of next 5 chs, (1 dc, ch 1, 1 dc) all in next ch (sleeve), 1 dc in each of next 20 (20, 20, 22, 22, 22) sts, (1 dc, ch 1, 1 dc) all in next ch (front), 1 dc in each of next 6 chs, (1 dc, ch 1, 1 dc) all in next ch (sleeve), 1 dc in each of next 20 (20, 20, 22, 22, 22) chs, (1 dc, ch 1, 1 dc) all in next ch (back), join with a slst to starting ch.
Row 1: Ch 3, *1 dc in each st to ch-1 sp, (1 dc, ch 1, 1 dc) all in ch-1 sp. Repeat from * 3 times more, join with a slst to top of starting ch.
Repeat Row 1 till there are 56 (60, 64, 66, 70, 74) sts on back section.

Front and Back:

On next row, ch 3, sk sleeve section, work across front section, ch 2, sk other sleeve section, work back section, ch 2, join to top of starting ch-3. Working round and round, starting each round with ch-3, and ending with a slst to join, work till body is 10 (11, 12, 13, 14, 15) inches from underarm, end off.

Sleeves:

Join yarn at underarm, ch 3, work 1 dc in each st around sleeve, work 1 dc on the underarm ch, join with a slst. Working round and round, dec 1 st at the underarm, every 3rd row, 3 (3, 4, 4, 5, 5) times. Work even till 11½ (12½, 13½, 14½, 15½, 16) inches from underarm, end off.

Finishing:

Sew underarm seams. Work 4 rows, sc around neck opening.

CHILDREN'S CLASSIC KNITTING WORSTED SWEATERS

CREW NECK CARDIGAN

Children's Sizes: Directions are for size 4. Changes for 6, 8, 10, 12, and 14 are in parentheses.
Materials: 12 (12, 14, 16, 16, 20) oz knitting worsted
Aluminum Hook: #6 or G
Gauge: 4 sts = 1 inch

Yoke:
Ch 40 (40, 44, 44, 48, 48) loosely.
Foundation Row: 1 dc in 3rd ch from hook, 1 dc in each of next 5 (5, 6, 6, 7, 7) chs, (1 dc, ch 1, 1 dc) all in next ch (front), 1 dc in each of next 5 (5, 5, 5, 6, 6) chs, (1 dc, ch 1, 1 dc) all in next ch (sleeve), 1 dc in each of next 12 (12, 14, 14, 14, 14) chs, (1 dc, ch 1, 1 dc) all in next ch (back), 1 dc in each of next 5 (5, 5, 5, 6, 6) chs (sleeve), 1 dc in each of last 6 (6, 7, 7, 8, 8) chs (front).
Row 1: Ch 3, turn (ch-3 always counts as first dc), sk first st, 1 dc in each of next 6 (6, 7, 7, 8, 8) sts, (1 dc, ch 1, 1 dc) all in ch-1 sp (inc), 1 dc in each of next 7 (7, 7, 7, 8, 8) sts, (1 dc, ch 1, 1 dc) all in ch-1 sp (inc), 1 dc in each of next 14 (14, 16, 16, 16, 16) sts, (1 dc, ch 1, 1 dc) all in ch-1 sp (inc), 1 dc in each of next 7 (7, 7, 7, 8, 8) sts, (1 dc, ch 1, 1 dc) all in ch-1 sp (inc), 1 dc in each of last 7 (7, 8, 8, 9, 9) sts (last st is in top of turning ch).
Row 2: Ch 3, turn, 1 dc in each st to first ch-1 sp (1 dc, ch 1, 1 dc) all in ch-1 sp, *1 dc in each st to next ch-1 sp, (1 dc, ch 1, 1 dc) all in ch-1 sp. Repeat from * twice more, ending with 1 dc in each st, 1 dc in top of turning ch.

Repeat Row 2 till there are 46 (48, 50, 52, 54, 56) dc in back section.

Front and Back:
Work across front to first ch-1 sp, ch 2, sk sleeve section, work across back section, ch 2, sk other sleeve section, work across front section. Continue in pat as established, omitting incs and working 2 dc on the added ch at underarm. Work entire body section till 10 (11, 12, 13, 14, 15) inches from underarm, end off.

Sleeves:
Join yarn at underarm, ch 3, work 1 dc in each st around sleeve section, work 1 dc on ch at underarm. Ch 3, turn. Working back and forth in pat as established, dec 1 st each side, every 3rd row, 3 (3, 4, 4, 5, 5) times. Work even till 11½ (12½, 13½, 14½, 15½, 16) inches, end off.

Finishing:
Sew underarm seams. *For Zipper:* With right side facing you, starting at bottom right corner, work 2 rows sc around entire front and neck edges, making 3 sc in each corner st at neck. Sew in zipper. *For Buttonholes:* With right side facing you, work 3 rows sc around entire front and neck edges, making 3 sc in each corner st at neck and placing buttonholes evenly spaced on the 2nd row. Make buttonholes on the right for girls, on the left for boys. To make buttonholes, ch 2, sk 2. On the 3rd row, make 2 sc in the ch-2 sp.

V NECK CARDIGAN

Children's Sizes: Directions are for size 4. Changes for 6, 8, 10, 12, and 14 are in parentheses.
Materials: 12 (12, 14, 16, 16, 20) oz knitting worsted
Aluminum Hook: #6 or G
Gauge: 4 sts = 1 inch

Yoke:
Ch 32 (32, 34, 34, 36, 36) loosely.
Foundation Row: 1 dc in 3rd ch from hook, 1 dc in next ch, (1 dc, ch 1, 1 dc) all in next ch (front), 1 dc in each of next 5 (5, 5, 5, 6, 6) chs, (1 dc, ch 1, 1 dc) all in next ch (sleeve), 1 dc in each of next 12 (12, 14, 14, 14, 14) chs, (1 dc, ch 1, 1 dc) all in next ch (back), 1 dc in each of next 5 (5, 5, 5, 6, 6) chs, (1 dc, ch 1, 1 dc) all in next ch (sleeve), 1 dc in each of last 2 chs (front).
Row 1: Ch 3, turn (ch-3 always counts as first dc), 1 dc in first st (inc), 1 dc in each st to first ch-1 sp, (1 dc, ch 1, 1 dc) all in ch-1 sp, 1 dc in each of next 7 (7, 7, 7, 8, 8) sts, (1 dc, ch 1, 1 dc) all in ch-1 sp, 1 dc in each of next 14 (14, 16, 16, 16, 16) sts, (1 dc, ch 1, 1 dc) all in ch-1 sp, 1 dc in each of next 7 (7, 7, 7, 8, 8) sts, (1 dc, ch 1, 1 dc) all in ch-1 sp, 1 dc in each st to end, 2 dc in top of turning ch (inc).
Row 2: Ch 3, turn, 1 dc in first st, 1 dc in each st to first ch-1 sp, (1 dc, ch 1, 1 dc) all in ch-1 sp, *1 dc in each st to next ch-1 sp, (1 dc, ch 1, 1 dc) all in ch-1 sp. Repeat from * twice more, ending with 1 dc in each st, 2 dc in top of turning ch.

Repeat Row 2 till there are 46 (48, 50, 52, 54, 56) sts in back section.

Continue as for front, back, and sleeves Children's Classic Knitting Worsted Sweaters—Crew Neck Cardigan.

Finishing:
Sew underarm seams. *For Zipper:* With right side facing you, starting at bottom right corner, work 2 rows sc around entire front and neck edges. Sew in zipper up to where V shaping starts. *For Buttonholes:* With right side facing you, work 3 rows sc around entire front and neck edges, place buttonholes evenly spaced on the 2nd row, between bottom of garment and start of V shaping. Make buttonholes on the right for girls, on the left for boys. To make buttonholes, ch 2, sk 2. On the 3rd row, make 2 sc in the ch-2 sp.

Figure 14. The classic V neck crocheted raglan cardigan. Note how the soft quality of this yarn gives the sweater a delicate quality. Picture this same sweater with another yarn weight for a completely different result. Yarn: Frostlon Petite by Spinnerin.

Figure 15. This classic crew neck pullover has a more rugged look partly because of the yarn used. Yarn: Nan-tuck by Columbia-Minerva.

CREW NECK PULLOVER

Children's Sizes: Directions are for size 4. Changes for 6, 8, 10, 12, and 14 are in parentheses.
Materials: 12 (12, 14, 16, 16, 20) oz knitting worsted
Aluminum Hook: #6 or G
Gauge: 4 sts = 1 inch

Yoke:

Ch 38 (38, 42, 42, 46, 46) loosely, join to form a ring.
Foundation Row: Ch 3 (ch-3 always counts as first dc), 1 dc in each of next 4 (4, 4, 4, 5, 5) chs, (1 dc, ch 1, 1 dc) all in next ch (sleeve), 1 dc in each of next 12 (12, 14, 14, 15, 15) chs, (1 dc, ch 1, 1 dc) all in next ch (front), 1 dc in each of next 5 (5, 5, 5, 6, 6) chs, (1 dc, ch 1, 1 dc) all in next ch (sleeve), 1 dc in each of next 12 (12, 14, 14, 15, 15) chs, (1 dc, ch 1, 1 dc) all in next ch (back), join with a slst to starting ch-3.
Row 1: Ch 3, *1 dc in each st to ch-1 sp, (1 dc, ch 1, 1 dc) all in ch-1 sp. Repeat from * 3 times more, join with a slst to top of starting ch.
  Repeat Row 1 till there are 46 (48, 50, 52, 54, 56) sts on back section.

Front and Back:

On next row, ch 3, sk sleeve section, work across front section, ch 2, sk other sleeve section, work back section, ch 2, join to top of starting ch-3. Working round and round, starting each round with a ch-3, and ending with a slst to join, work till body is 10 (11, 12, 13, 14, 15) inches from underarm, end off.

Sleeves:

Join yarn at underarm, ch 3, work 1 dc in each st around sleeve, work 1 dc on the underarm ch, join with a slst. Working round and round, dec 1 st at the underarm, every 3rd row, 3 (3, 4, 4, 5, 5) times. Work even till 11½ (12½, 13½, 14½, 15½, 16) inches from underarm, end off.

Finishing:

Sew underarm seams. Work 4 rows sc around neck opening.

CHILDREN'S CLASSIC BULKY YARN SWEATERS

CREW NECK CARDIGAN

Children's Sizes: Direction are for size 4. Changes for 6, 8, 10, 12, and 14 are in parentheses.
Materials: 20 (22, 24, 26, 28, 30) oz bulky yarn
Aluminum Hook: #10½ or K
Gauge: 5 sts = 2 inches

Yoke:

Ch 33 (33, 37, 37, 41, 41) loosely.
Foundation Row: 1 dc in 3rd ch from hook, 1 dc in each of next 3 (3, 4, 4, 5, 5) chs, (1 dc, ch 1, 1 dc) all in next ch (front), 1 dc in each of next 5 chs, (1 dc, ch 1, 1 dc) all in next ch (sleeve), 1 dc in each of next 8 (8, 10, 10, 12, 12) chs, (1 dc, ch 1, 1 dc) all in next ch (back), 1 dc in each of next 5 chs, (1 dc, ch 1, 1 dc) all in next ch (sleeve), 1 dc in each of last 4 (4, 5, 5, 6, 6) chs (front).
Row 1: Ch 3, turn (ch-3 always counts as first dc), sk first st, 1 dc in each of next 4 (4, 5, 5, 6, 6) sts, (1 dc, ch 1, 1 dc) all in ch-1 sp (inc), 1 dc in each of next 7 sts, (1 dc, ch 1, 1 dc) all in ch-1 sp (inc), 1 dc in each of next 10 (10, 12, 12, 14, 14) sts, (1 dc, ch 1, 1 dc) all in ch-1 sp (inc), 1 dc in each of next 7 sts, (1 dc, ch 1, 1 dc) all in ch-1 sp (inc), 1 dc in each of last 5 (5, 6, 6, 7, 7) sts (last st is in top of turning ch).
Row 2: Ch 3, turn, 1 dc in each st to first ch-1 sp, (1 dc, ch 1, 1 dc) all in ch-1 sp, *1 dc in each st to next ch-1 sp, (1 dc, ch 1, 1 dc) all in ch-1 sp. Repeat from * twice more, ending with 1 dc in each st, 1 dc in top of turning ch.
  Repeat Row 2 till there are 30 (32, 34, 36, 38, 40) sts in back section.

Front and Back:

Work across front to first ch-1 sp, ch 2, sk sleeve section, work across back section, ch 2, sk other sleeve section, work across front section. Continue in pat as established, omitting incs and working 2 dc on the added ch at underarm. Work entire body section till 10 (11, 12, 13, 14, 15) inches from underarm, end off.

Sleeves:

Join yarn at underarm, ch 3, work 1 dc in each st around sleeve section, work 1 dc on ch at underarm. Ch 3, turn. Working back and forth in pat as established, dec 1 st each side, every 5th row, 2 (2, 3, 3, 4, 4) times. Work even till 11½ (12½, 13½, 14½, 15½ 16) inches, end off.

Finishing:

Sew underarm seams. *For Zipper:* With right side facing you, starting at bottom right corner, work 2 rows sc around entire front and neck edges, making 3 sc in each corner st at neck. Sew in zipper. *For Buttonholes:* With right side facing you, work 3 rows sc around entire front and neck edges, making 3 sc in each corner at neck and placing buttonholes evenly spaced on the 2nd row. Make buttonholes on the right for girls, on the left for boys. To make buttonholes, ch 2, sk 2. On the 3rd row, make 2 sc in the ch-2 sp.

V NECK CARDIGAN

Children's Sizes: Direction are for size 4. Changes for 6, 8, 10, 12, and 14 are in parentheses.
Materials: 20 (22, 24, 26, 28, 30) oz bulky yarn
Aluminum Hook: #10½ or K
Gauge: 5 sts = 2 inches

Yoke:

Ch 25 (25, 27, 27, 29, 29) loosely.
Foundation Row: (1 dc, ch 1, 1 dc) all in 3rd ch from hook (front), 1 dc in each of next 5 chs, (1 dc, ch 1, 1 dc) all in next ch (sleeve), 1 dc in each of next 8 (8, 10, 10, 12, 12) chs, (1 dc, ch 1, 1 dc) all in next ch (back), 1 dc in each of next 5 chs, (1 dc, ch 1, 1 dc) all in next ch (sleeve), 2 dc in last ch (front).
Row 1: Ch 3, turn (ch-3 always counts as first dc), 1 dc in first st (inc), 1 dc in each st to first ch-1 sp, (1 dc, ch 1, 1 dc) all in ch-1 sp (inc), 1 dc in each of next 7 sts, (1 dc, ch 1, 1 dc) all in ch-1 sp (inc), 1 dc in each of next 10 (10, 12, 12, 14, 14) sts, (1 dc, ch 1, 1 dc) all in ch-1 sp (inc), 1 dc in each of next 7 sts, (1 dc, ch 1, 1 dc) all in ch-1 sp (inc), 1 dc in each st to end, 2 dc in top of turning ch (inc).
Row 2: Ch 3, turn, 1 dc in first st, 1 dc in each st to first ch-1 sp, (1 dc, ch 1, 1 dc) all in ch-1 sp, *1 dc in each st to next ch-1 sp, (1 dc, ch 1, 1 dc) all in ch-1 sp. Repeat from * twice more, ending with 1 dc in each st, 2 dc in top of turning ch.

Repeat Row 2 till there are 30 (32, 34, 36, 38, 40) sts in back section.

Continue as for front, back, and sleeves of Children's Classic Bulky Weight Sweaters—Crew Neck Cardigan.

Finishing:

Sew underarm seams. *For Zipper:* With right side facing you, starting at bottom right corner, work 2 rows sc around entire front and neck edges. Sew in zipper up to where V shaping starts. *For Buttonholes:* With right side facing you, work 3 rows sc around entire front and neck edges, place buttonholes evenly spaced on the 2nd row, between bottom of garment and start of V shaping. Make buttonholes on the right for girls, on the left for boys. To make buttonholes, ch 2, sk 2. On the 3rd row, make 2 sc in the ch-2 sp.

CREW NECK PULLOVER

Children's Sizes: Directions are for size 4. Changes for 6, 8, 10, 12, and 14 are in parentheses.
Materials: 20 (22, 24, 26, 28, 30) oz bulky yarn
Aluminum Hook: #10½ or K
Gauge: 5 sts = 2 inches

Yoke:

Ch 30 (30, 34, 34, 38, 38) loosely, join to form a ring.
Foundation Row: Ch 3 (ch-3 always counts as first dc), 1 dc in each of next 4 chs, (1 dc, ch 1, 1 dc) all in next ch (sleeve), 1 dc in each of next 8 (8, 10, 10, 12, 12) chs, (1 dc, ch 1, 1 dc) all in next ch (front), 1 dc in each of next 5 chs, (1 dc, ch 1, 1 dc) all in next ch (sleeve), 1 dc in each of next 8 (8, 10, 10, 12, 12) chs, (1 dc, ch 1, 1 dc) all in next ch (back), join with a slst to starting ch-3.
Row 1: Ch 3, *1 dc in each st to ch-1 sp, (1 dc, ch 1, 1 dc) all in ch-1 sp. Repeat from * 3 times more, join with a slst to top of starting ch.

Repeat Row 1 till there are 30 (32, 34, 36, 38, 40) sts on back section.

Front and Back:

On next row, ch 3, sk sleeve section, work across front section, ch 2, sk other sleeve section, work back section, ch 2, join to top of starting ch-3. Working round and round, starting each round with a ch-3, and ending with a slst to join, work till body is 10 (11, 12, 13, 14, 15) inches from underarm.

Sleeves:

Join yarn at underarm, ch 3, work 1 dc in each st around sleeve, work 1 dc on the underarm ch, join with a slst. Working round and round, dec 1 st at the underarm, every 5th row, 2 (2, 3, 3, 4, 4) times. Work even till 11½, (12½, 13½, 14½, 15½, 16) inches from underarm, end off.

Finishing:

Sew underarm seams. Work 4 rows sc around neck opening.

Figure 16. The crocheted raglan V neck pullover. Yarn: Nantuck by Columbia-Minerva.

WOMEN'S CLASSIC SPORT WEIGHT SWEATERS

CREW NECK CARDIGAN

Women's Sizes: Directions are for size 8. Changes for 10, 12, 14, 16, and 18 are in parentheses.
Materials: 14 (14, 16, 16, 18, 18) oz sport weight yarn
Aluminum Hook: #4 or E
Gauge: 5 sts = 1 inch

Yoke:
Ch 63 (63, 63, 67, 67, 67) loosely.
Foundation Row: 1 dc in 3rd ch from hook, 1 dc in each of next 9 (9, 9, 10, 10, 10) chs, (1 dc, ch 1, 1 dc) all in next ch (front), 1 dc in each of next 8 chs, (1 dc, ch 1, 1 dc) all in next ch (sleeve), 1 dc in each of next 20 (20, 20, 22, 22, 22) chs, (1 dc, ch 1, 1 dc) all in next ch (back), 1 dc in each of next 8 chs, (1 dc, ch 1, 1 dc) all in next ch (sleeve), 1 dc in each of last 10 (10, 10, 11, 11, 11) chs (front).
Row 1: Ch 3, turn (ch-3 always counts as first dc), sk first st, 1 dc in each of next 10 (10, 10, 11, 11, 11) sts, (1 dc, ch 1, 1 dc) all in ch-1 sp (inc), 1 dc in each of next 10 sts, (1 dc, ch 1, 1 dc) all in ch-1 sp (inc), 1 dc in each of next 22 (22, 22, 24, 24, 24) sts, (1 dc, ch 1, 1 dc) all in ch-1 sp (inc), 1 dc in each of next 10 sts, (1 dc, ch 1, 1 dc) all in ch-1 sp (inc), 1 dc in each of last 11 (11, 11, 12, 12, 12) sts (last st is in top of turning ch).
Row 2: Ch 3, turn, 1 dc in each st to first ch-1 sp, (1 dc, ch 1, 1 dc) all in ch-1 sp, *1 dc in each st to next ch-1 sp, (1 dc, ch 1, 1 dc) all in ch-1 sp. Repeat from * twice more, ending with 1 dc in each st, 1 dc in top of turning ch.
   Repeat Row 2 till there are 78 (82, 86, 90, 94, 98) dc in back section.

Front and Back:
Work across front to first ch-1 sp, ch 3, sk sleeve section, work across back section, ch 3, sk other sleeve section, work across front section. Continue in pat as established, omitting incs and working 3 dc on the added ch at underarm. Work entire body section till 15 (15, 16, 16, 17, 17) inches from underarm, end off.

Sleeves:
Join yarn at underarm, ch 3, work 1 dc in each st around sleeve section, work 1 dc on ch at underarm. Ch 3, turn. Working back and forth in pat as established, dec 1 st each side, every 4th row, 4 (4, 5, 5, 6, 6) times. Work even till 16 (16, 16, 16, 17, 17) inches, end off.

Finishing:
Sew underarm seams. *For Zipper:* With right side facing you, starting at bottom right corner, work 2 rows sc around entire front and neck edges, making 3 sc in each corner st at neck. Sew in zipper. *For Buttonholes:* With right side facing you, work 5 rows sc around entire front and neck edges, making 3 sc in each corner st at neck and placing buttonholes evenly spaced on the 3rd row. Make buttonholes on the right for girls, on the left for boys. To make buttonholes, ch 2, sk 2 sts. On the 4th row, make 2 sc in the ch-2 sp.

V NECK CARDIGAN

Women's Sizes: Directions are for size 8. Changes for 10, 12, 14, 16, and 18 are in parentheses.
Materials: 14 (14, 16, 16, 18, 18) oz sport weight yarn
Aluminum Hook: #4 or E
Gauge: 5 sts = 1 inch

Yoke:
Ch 45 (45, 45, 47, 47, 47) loosely.
Foundation Row: 1 dc in 3rd ch from hook, (1 dc, ch 1, 1 dc) all in next ch (front), 1 dc in each of next 8 chs, (1 dc, ch 1, 1 dc) all in next ch (sleeve), 1 dc in each of next 20 (20, 20, 22, 22, 22) chs, (1 dc, ch 1, 1 dc) all in next ch (back), 1 dc in each of next 8 chs, (1 dc, ch 1, 1 dc) all in next ch (sleeve), 1 dc in next ch, 1 dc in last ch (front).
Row 1: Ch 3, turn (ch-3 always counts as first dc), 1 dc in first st (inc), 1 dc in each st to first ch-1 sp, (1 dc, ch 1, 1 dc) all in ch-1 sp (inc), 1 dc in each of next 10 sts, (1 dc, ch 1, 1 dc) all in ch-1 sp (inc), 1 dc in each of next 22 (22, 22, 24, 24, 24) sts, (1 dc, ch 1, 1 dc) all in ch-1 sp (inc), 1 dc in each of next 10 sts, (1 dc, ch 1, 1 dc) all in ch-1 sp (inc), 1 dc in each of last 2 sts, 2 dc in top of turning ch (inc).
Row 2: Ch 3, turn, 1 dc in first st, 1 dc in each st to first ch-1 sp, (1 dc, ch 1, 1 dc) all in ch-1 sp, *1 dc in each st to next ch-1 sp, (1 dc, ch 1, 1 dc) all in ch-1 sp. Repeat from * twice more, ending with 1 dc in each st, 2 dc in top of turning ch.
   Repeat Row 2 till there are 78 (82, 86, 90, 96, 98) dc in back section.
   Continue as for front, back, and sleeves of Women's Classic Sport Weight Sweaters—Crew Neck Cardigan.

Finishing:
Sew underarm seams. *For Zipper:* With right side facing you, starting at bottom right corner, work 2 rows sc around entire front and neck edges. Sew in zipper up to where V shaping starts. *For Buttonholes:* With right side facing you, work 5 rows sc around entire front and neck edges, place buttonholes evenly spaced on the 3rd row, between bottom of garment and start of V shaping. Make buttonholes on the right for girls, on the left for boys. To make buttonholes, ch 2, sk 2. On the 4th row, make 2 sc in the ch-2 sp.

CREW NECK PULLOVER

Women's Sizes: Directions are for size 8. Changes for
10, 12, 14, 16, and 18 are in parentheses.
Materials: 14 (14, 16, 16, 18, 18) oz sport weight yarn
Aluminum Hook: #4 or E
Gauge: 5 sts = 1 inch

Yoke:

Ch 60 (60, 60, 64, 64, 64) loosely, join to form a ring.
Foundation Row: Ch 3 (ch-3 always counts as first dc),
1 dc in each of next 7 chs, (1 dc, ch 1, 1 dc) all in next
ch (sleeve), 1 dc in each of next 20 (20, 20, 22, 22, 22)
chs, (1 dc, ch 1, 1 dc) all in next ch (front), 1 dc in each
of next 8 chs, (1 dc, ch 1, 1 dc) all in next ch (sleeve),
1 dc in each of next 20 (20, 20, 22, 22, 22) chs, (1 dc,
ch 1, 1 dc) all in next ch (back), join with a slst to
starting ch-3.
Row 1: Ch 3, *1 dc in each st to ch-1 sp, (1 dc, ch 1,
1 dc) all in ch-1 sp. Repeat from * 3 times more, join
with a slst to top of starting ch.
   Repeat Row 1 till there are 78 (82, 86, 90, 94, 98) sts
on back section.

Front and Back:

On next row, ch 3, sk sleeve section, work across front
section, ch 3, sk other sleeve section, work back section,
ch 3, join to top of starting ch-3. Working round and
round, starting each rnd with a ch-3, and ending with a
slst to join, work till body is 15 (15, 16, 16, 17, 17)
inches from underarm, end off.

Sleeves:

Join yarn at underarm, ch 3, work 1 dc in each st around
sleeve, work 1 dc on the underarm ch, join with a slst.
Working round and round, dec 1 st at underarm, every
4th row, 4 (4, 5, 5, 6, 6) times. Work even till 16 (16,
16, 16, 17, 17) inches from underarm, end off.

Finishing:

Sew underarm seams. Work 4 rows sc around neck
opening.

WOMEN'S CLASSIC KNITTING WORSTED SWEATERS

CREW NECK CARDIGAN

Women's Sizes: Directions are for size 8. Changes for
10, 12, 14, 16, and 18 are in parentheses.
Materials: 16 (20, 20, 20, 24, 24) oz knitting worsted
Aluminum Hook: #6 or G
Gauge: 4 sts = 1 inch

Yoke:

Ch 49 (49, 51, 51, 53, 53) loosely.
Foundation Row: 1 dc in 3rd ch from hook, 1 dc in
each of next 7 (7, 7, 7, 8, 8) chs, (1 dc, ch 1, 1 dc) all in
next ch (front), 1 dc in each of next 6 chs, (1 dc, ch 1,
1 dc) all in next ch (sleeve), 1 dc in each of next 14 (14,
16, 16, 16, 16) chs, (1 dc, ch 1, 1 dc) all in next ch
(back), 1 dc in each of next 6 chs, (1 dc, ch 1, 1 dc) all
in next ch (sleeve), 1 dc in each of last 8 (8, 8, 8, 9, 9)
chs (front).
Row 1: Ch 3, turn (ch-3 always counts as first dc), sk
first st, 1 dc in each of next 8 (8, 8, 8, 9, 9) sts, (1 dc,
ch 1, 1 dc) all in ch-1 sp (inc), 1 dc in each of next 8 sts,
(1 dc, ch 1, 1 dc) all in ch-1 sp (inc), 1 dc in each of next
16 (16, 18, 18, 18, 18) sts, (1 dc, ch 1, 1 dc) all in ch-1
sp (inc), 1 dc in each of next 8 sts, (1 dc, ch 1, 1 dc) all
in ch-1 sp (inc), 1 dc in each of last 9 (9, 9, 9, 10, 10)
sts (last st is in top of turning ch).
Row 2: Ch 3, turn, 1 dc in each st to first ch-1 sp, (1 dc,
ch 1, 1 dc) all in ch-1 sp, *1 dc in each st to next ch-1
sp, (1 dc, ch 1, 1 dc) all in ch-1 sp. Repeat from * twice
more, ending with 1 dc in each st, 1 dc in top of turning
ch.
   Repeat Row 2 till there are 64 (66, 68, 72, 76, 80) sts
in back section.

Front and Back:

Work across front to first ch-1 sp, ch 3, sk sleeve section,
work across back section, ch 3, sk other sleeve section,
work across front section. Continue in pat as established,
omitting incs and working 3 dc on the added ch at
underarm. Work entire body section till 15 (15, 16, 16,
17, 17) inches from underarm, end off.

Sleeves:

Join yarn at underarm, ch 3, work 1 dc in each st around
sleeve section, work 1 dc on ch at underarm. Ch 3, turn.
Working back and forth in pat as established, dec 1 st
each side, every 4th row, 4 (4, 5, 5, 6, 6) times. Work
even till 16 (16, 16, 16, 17, 17) inches, end off.

Finishing:
Sew underarm seams. *For Zipper:* With right side facing you, starting at bottom right corner, work 2 rows sc around entire front and neck edges, making 3 sc in each corner st at neck. Sew in zipper. *For Buttonholes:* With right side facing you, work 3 rows sc around entire front and neck edges, making 3 sc in each corner st at neck and placing buttonholes evenly spaced on the 2nd row. Make buttonholes on the right for girls, on the left for boys. To make buttonholes, ch 2, sk 2. On the 3rd row, make 2 sc in the ch-2 sp.

V Neck Cardigan

Women's Sizes: Directions are for size 8. Changes for 10, 12, 14, 16, and 18 are in parentheses.
Materials: 16 (20, 20, 20, 24, 24) oz knitting worsted
Aluminum Hook: #6 or G
Gauge: 4 sts = 1 inch

Yoke:
Ch 37 (37, 39, 39, 39, 39) loosely.
Foundation Row: 1 dc in 3rd ch from hook, 1 dc in next ch, (1 dc, ch 1, 1 dc) all in next ch (front), 1 dc in each of next 6 chs, (1 dc, ch 1, 1 dc) all in next ch (sleeve), 1 dc in each of next 14 (14, 16, 16, 16, 16) chs, (1 dc, ch 1, 1 dc) all in next ch (back), 1 dc in each of next 6 chs, (1 dc, ch 1, 1 dc) all in next ch (sleeve), 1 dc in each of last 2 chs (front).
Row 1: Ch 3, turn (ch-3 always counts as first dc), 1 dc in first st (inc), 1 dc in each st to first ch-1 sp, (1 dc, ch 1, 1 dc) all in ch-1 sp, 1 dc in each of next 8 sts, (1 dc, ch 1, 1 dc) all in ch-1 sp, 1 dc in each of next 16 (16, 18, 18, 18, 18) sts, (1 dc, ch 1, 1 dc) all in ch-1 sp, 1 dc in each of next 8 sts, (1 dc, ch 1, 1 dc) all in ch-1 sp, 1 dc in each st to end, 2 dc in top of turning ch (inc).
Row 2: Ch 3, turn, 1 dc in first st, a dc in each st to first ch-1 sp, (1 dc, ch 1, 1 dc) all in ch-1 sp, *1 dc in each st to next ch-1 sp, (1 dc, ch 1, 1 dc) all in ch-1 sp. Repeat from * twice more, ending with 1 dc in each st, 2 dc in top of turning ch.

Repeat Row 2 till there are 64 (66, 68, 72, 76, 80) sts in back section.

Continue as for front, back, and sleeves of Women's Classic Knitting Worsted Sweaters—Crew Neck Cardigan.

Finishing:
Sew underarm seams. *For Zipper:* With right side facing you, starting at bottom right corner, work 2 rows sc around entire front and neck edges. Sew in zipper up to where V shaping starts. *For Buttonholes:* With right side facing you, work 3 rows sc around entire front and neck edges, place buttonholes evenly spaced on the 2nd row, between bottom of garment and start of V shaping. Make buttonholes on the right for girls, on the left for boys. To make buttonholes, ch 2, sk 2. On the 3rd row, make 2 sc in the ch-2 sp.

Crew Neck Pullover

Women's Sizes: Directions are for size 8. Changes for 10, 12, 14, 16, and 18 are in parentheses.
Materials: 16 (20, 20, 20, 24, 24) oz knitting worsted
Aluminium Hook: #6 or G
Gauge: 4 sts = 1 inch

Yoke:
Ch 44 (44, 48, 48, 48, 48) loosely, join to form a ring.
Foundation Row: Ch 3 (ch-3 always counts as first dc), 1 dc in each of next 5 chs, (1 dc, ch 1, 1 dc) all in next ch (sleeve), 1 dc in each of next 14 (14, 16, 16, 16, 16) chs, (1 dc, ch 1, 1 dc) all in next ch (front), 1 dc in each of next 6 chs, (1 dc, ch 1, 1 dc) all in next ch (sleeve), 1 dc in each of next 14 (14, 16, 16, 16, 16) chs, (1 dc, ch 1, 1 dc) all in next ch (back), join with a slst to starting ch-3.
Row 1: Ch 3, *1 dc in each st to ch-1 sp, (1 dc, ch 1, 1 dc) all in ch-1 sp. Repeat from * 3 times more, join with a slst to top of starting ch.

Repeat Row 1 till there are 64 (66, 68, 72, 76, 80) sts on back section.

Front and Back:
On next row, ch 3, sk sleeve section, work across front section, ch 2, sk other sleeve section, work back section, ch 2, join to top of starting ch-3. Working round and round, starting each rnd with ch-3, and ending with a slst to join, work till body is 15 (15, 16, 16, 17, 17) inches from underarm, end off.

Sleeves:
Join yarn at underarm ch, ch 3, work 1 dc in each st around sleeve, work 1 dc on the underarm ch, join with a slst. Working round and round, dec 1 st at the underarm, every 4th row 4 (4, 5, 5, 6, 6) times. Work even till 16 (16, 17, 17, 17, 17) inches from underarm, end off.

Finishing:
Sew underarm seams. Work 4 rows sc around neck opening.

WOMEN'S CLASSIC BULKY YARN SWEATERS

CREW NECK CARDIGAN

Women's Sizes: Directions are for size 8. Changes for 10, 12, 14, 16, and 18 are in parentheses.
Materials: 40 (42, 44, 46, 48, 50) oz bulky yarn
Aluminum Hook: #10½ or K
Gauge: 5 sts = 2 inches

Yoke:
Ch 41 (41, 44, 44, 47, 47) loosely.
Foundation Row: 1 dc in 3rd ch from hook, 1 dc in each of next 5 (5, 6, 6, 6, 6) chs, (1 dc, ch 1, 1 dc) all in next ch (front), 1 dc in each of next 5 (5, 5, 5, 6, 6) chs, (1 dc, ch 1, 1 dc) all in next ch (sleeve), 1 dc in each of next 12 (12, 13, 13, 14, 14) chs, (1 dc, ch 1, 1 dc) all in next ch (back), 1 dc in each of next 5 (5, 5, 5, 6, 6) chs, (1 dc, ch 1, 1 dc) all in next ch (sleeve), 1 dc in each of last 6 (6, 7, 7, 7, 7) chs (front).
Row 1: Ch 3, turn (ch-3 always counts as first dc), sk first st, 1 dc in each of next 6 (6, 7, 7, 7, 7) sts, (1 dc, ch 1, 1 dc) all in ch-1 sp (inc), 1 dc in each of next 7 (7, 7, 7, 8, 8) sts, (1 dc, ch 1, 1 dc) all in ch-1 sp (inc), 1 dc in each of next 14 (14, 15, 15, 16, 16) sts, (1 dc, ch 1, 1 dc) all in ch-1 sp (inc), 1 dc in each of next 7 (7, 7, 7, 8, 8) sts, (1 dc, ch 1, 1 dc) all in ch-1 sp (inc), 1 dc in each of last 6 (6, 7, 7, 7, 7) sts, 1 dc in top of turning ch.
Row 2: Ch 3, turn, 1 dc in each st to first ch-1 sp, (1 dc, ch 1, 1 dc) all in ch-1 sp. Repeat from * twice more, ending with 1 dc in each st, 1 dc in top of turning ch.

Repeat Row 2 till there are 40 (42, 44, 46, 48, 50) sts in back section.

Front and Back:
Work across front to first ch-1 sp, ch 2, sk sleeve section, work across back section, ch 2, sk other sleeve section, work across front section. Continue pat as established, omitting incs and working 2 dc on the added ch at underarm. Work entire body section till 16 (16, 17, 17, 17, 17) inches from underarm, end off.

Sleeves:
Join yarn at underarm, ch 3, work 1 dc in each st around sleeve section, work 2 dc on ch at underarm. Ch 3, turn. Working back and forth in pat as established, dec 1 st each side every 5th row, 4 (4, 4, 4, 5, 5) times. Work even till 15 (15, 16, 16, 17, 17) inches or desired length, end off.

Finishing:
Sew underarm seams. *For Zipper:* With right side facing you, starting at bottom right corner, work 2 rows sc around entire front and neck edges, making 3 sc in each corner st at neck. Sew in zipper. *For Buttonholes:* With right side facing you, work 3 rows sc around entire front and neck edges, making 3 sc in each corner st at neck and placing buttonholes evenly spaced on the 2nd row. Make buttonholes on the right for girls, on the left for boys. To make buttonholes, ch 2, sk 2. On the 3rd row, make 2 sc in the ch-2 sp.

V NECK CARDIGAN

Women's Sizes: Directions are for size 8. Changes for 10, 12, 14, 16, and 18 are in parentheses.
Materials: 40 (42, 44, 46, 48, 50) oz bulky yarn
Aluminum Hook: #10½ or K
Gauge: 5sts = 2 inches

Yoke:
Ch 31 (31, 32, 32, 35, 35) loosely.
Foundation Row: (1 dc, ch 1, 1 dc) all in 3rd ch from hook (front), 1 dc in each of next 5 (5, 5, 5, 6, 6) chs, (1 dc, ch 1, 1 dc) all in next ch (sleeve), 1 dc in each of next 12 (12, 13, 13, 14, 14) chs, (1 dc, ch 1, 1 dc) all in next ch (back), 1 dc in each of next 5 (5, 5, 5, 6, 6) chs, (1 dc, ch 1, 1 dc) all in next ch (sleeve), 1 dc in last ch (front).
Row 1: Ch 3, turn (ch-3 always counts as first dc) 1 dc in first st (inc), 1 dc in each st to first ch-1 sp, (1 dc, ch 1, 1 dc) all in ch-1 sp (inc), 1 dc in each of next 7 (7, 7, 7, 8, 8) sts, (1 dc, ch 1, 1 dc) all in ch-1 sp (inc), 1 dc in each of next 14 (14, 15, 15, 16, 16) sts, (1 dc, ch 1, 1 dc) all in ch-1 sp (inc), 1 dc in each of next 7 (7, 7, 7, 8, 8) sts, (1 dc, ch 1, 1 dc) all in ch-1 sp (inc), 1 dc in each st to end, 2 dc in top of turning ch (inc).
Row 2: Ch 3, turn, 1 dc in first st, 1 dc in each st to first ch-1 sp, (1 dc, ch 1, 1 dc) all in ch-1 sp, *1 dc in each st to next ch-1 sp, (1 dc, ch 1, 1 dc) all in ch-1 sp. Repeat from * twice more, ending with 1 dc in each st, 2 dc in top of turning ch.

Repeat Row 2 till there are 40 (42, 44, 46, 48, 50) sts in back section.

Continue as for front, back, and sleeves of Women's Classic Bulky Yarn Sweaters—Crew Neck Cardigan.

Finishing:
Sew underarm seams. *For Zipper:* With right side facing you, starting at bottom right corner, work 2 rows sc around entire front and neck edges. Sew in zipper up to where V shaping starts. *For Buttonholes:* With right side facing you, work 3 rows sc around entire front and neck edges, place buttonholes evenly spaced on the 2nd row, between bottom of garment and start of V Shaping. Make buttonholes on the right for girls, on the left for boys. To make buttonholes, ch 2, sk 2. On the 3rd row, make 2 sc in the ch-2 sp.

CREW NECK PULLOVER

Women's Sizes: Directions are for size 8. Changes for
10, 12, 14, 16, and 18 are in parentheses.
Materials: 40 (42, 44, 46, 48, 50) oz bulky yarn
Aluminum Hook: #10½ or K
Gauge: 5 sts = 2 inches

Yoke:

Ch 38 (38, 40, 40, 44, 44) loosely, join to form a ring.
Foundation Row: Ch 3 (ch-3 always counts as first dc),
1 dc in each of next 4 (4, 4, 4, 5, 5) chs, (1 dc, ch 1,
1 dc) all in next ch (sleeve), 1 dc in each of next 12 (12,
13, 13, 14, 14) chs, (1 dc, ch 1, 1 dc) all in next ch
(front), 1 dc in each of next 5 (5, 5, 5, 6, 6) chs, (1 dc,
ch 1, 1 dc) all in next ch (sleeve), 1 dc in each of next 12
(12, 13, 13, 14, 14) chs, (1 dc, ch 1, 1 dc) all in next ch
(back), join with a slst to starting ch-3.
Row 1: Ch 3, *1 dc in each st to ch-1 sp, (1 dc, ch 1,
1 dc) all in ch-1 sp. Repeat from * 3 times more, join
with a slst to top of starting ch.
   Repeat Row 1 till there are 40 (42, 44, 46, 48, 50)
sts in back section.

Front and Back:

On next row, ch 3, sk sleeve section, work across front
section, ch 2, sk other sleeve section, work back section,
ch 2, join to top of starting ch-3. Working round and
round, starting each rnd with a ch-3, and ending with
a slst to join, work till body is 16 (16, 17, 17, 17, 17)
inches from underarm.

Sleeves:

Join yarn at underarm, ch 3, work 1 dc in each st around
sleeve, work 1 dc on the underarm ch, join with a slst.
Working round and round, dec 1 st at the underarm,
every 5th row, 4 (4, 4, 4, 5, 5) times. Work even till 15
(15, 16, 16, 17, 17) inches from underarm, end off.

Finishing:

Sew underarm seams. Work 4 rows sc around neck
opening.

MEN'S CLASSIC SPORT WEIGHT
SWEATERS

CREW NECK CARDIGAN

Men's Sizes: Directions are for size 36. Changes for 38,
40, 42, 44, and 46 are in parentheses.
Materials: 16 (18, 18, 18, 20, 22) oz sport weight yarn
Aluminum Hook: #4 or E
Gauge: 5 sts = 1 inch

Yoke:

Ch 73 (73, 73, 77, 77, 77) loosely.
Foundation Row: 1 dc in 3rd ch from hook, 1 dc in
each of next 10 (10, 10, 11, 11, 11) chs, (1 dc, ch 1, 1
dc) all in next ch (front), 1 dc in each of next 11 chs,
(1 dc, ch 1, 1 dc) all in next ch (sleeve), 1 dc in each of
next 22 (22, 22, 24, 24, 24) chs, (1 dc, ch 1, 1 dc) all in
next ch (back), 1 dc in each of next 11 chs, (1 dc, ch 1,
1 dc) all in next ch (sleeve), 1 dc in each of last 11 (11,
11, 12, 12, 12) chs (front).
Row 1: Ch 3, turn (ch-3 always counts as first dc), sk
first st, 1 dc in each of next 11 (11, 11, 12, 12, 12) sts,
(1 dc, ch 1, 1 dc) all in ch-1 sp (inc), 1 dc in each of next
13 sts, (1 dc, ch 1, 1 dc) all in ch-1 sp (inc), 1 dc in each
of next 24 (24, 24, 26, 26, 26) sts, (1 dc, ch 1, 1 dc) all
in ch-1 sp (inc), 1 dc in each of next 13 sts, (1 dc, ch 1,
1 dc) all in ch-1 sp (inc), 1 dc in each of last 12 (12, 12,
13, 13, 13) sts (last st is in top of turning ch).
Row 2: Ch 3, turn, 1 dc in each st to first ch-1 sp, (1 dc,
ch 1, 1 dc) all in ch-1 sp, *1 dc in each st to next ch-1
sp, (1 dc, ch 1, 1 dc) all in ch-1 sp. Repeat from * twice
more, ending with 1 dc in each st, 1 dc in top of turning
ch.
   Repeat Row 2 till there are 86 (90, 94, 98, 104, 108)
sts in back section.

Front and Back:

Work across front to first ch-1 sp, ch 3, sk sleeve section,
work across back section, ch 3, sk other sleeve section,
work across front section. Continue in pat as established,
omitting incs and working 3 dc on the added ch at underarm. Work entire body section till 16 (16, 17, 17, 18,
18) inches from underarm, end off.

Sleeves:

Join yarn at underarm, ch 3, work 1 dc in each st around
sleeve section, work 1 dc on ch at underarm. Ch 3, turn.
Working back and forth in pat as established, dec 1 st
each side, every 4th row, 5 (5, 6, 6, 7, 7) times. Work
even till 18½ (18½, 19, 19, 19½, 19½) inches, end off.

Finishing:
Sew underarm seams. *For Zipper:* With right side facing you, starting at bottom right corner, work 2 rows sc around entire front and neck edges, making 3 sc in each corner st at neck. Sew in zipper. *For Buttonholes:* With right side facing you, work 5 rows sc around entire front and neck edges, making 3 sc in each corner st at neck and placing buttonholes evenly spaced on the 3rd row. Make buttonholes on the right for girls, on the left for boys. To make buttonholes, ch 2, sk 2 sts. On the 4th row, make 2 sc in the ch-2 sp.

V NECK CARDIGAN

Men's Sizes: Directions are for size 36. Changes for 38, 40, 42, 44, and 46 are in parentheses.
Materials: 16 (18, 18, 18, 20, 22) oz sport weight yarn
Aluminum Hook: #4 or E
Gauge: 5 sts = 1 inch

Yoke:
Ch 55 (55, 55, 57, 57, 57) loosely.

Foundation Row: 1 dc in 3rd ch from hook, (1 dc, ch 1, 1 dc) all in next ch (front), 1 dc in each of next 11 chs, (1 dc, ch 1, 1 dc) all in next ch (sleeve), 1 dc in each of next 22 (22, 22, 24, 24, 24) chs, (1 dc, ch 1, 1 dc) all in next ch (back), 1 dc in each of next 11 chs, (1 dc, ch 1, 1 dc) all in next ch (sleeve), 1 dc in next ch, 1 dc in last ch (front).
Row 1: Ch 3, turn (ch-3 always counts as first dc), 1 dc in first st (inc), 1 dc in each st to first ch-1 sp, (1 dc, ch 1, 1 dc) all in ch-1 sp (inc), 1 dc in each of next 13 sts, (1 dc, ch 1, 1 dc) all in ch-1 sp (inc), 1 dc in each of next 24 (24, 24, 26, 26, 26) sts, (1 dc, ch 1, 1 dc) all in ch-1 sp (inc), 1 dc in each of next 13 sts, (1 dc, ch 1, 1 dc) all in ch-1 sp (inc), 1 dc in each of last 2 sts, 2 dc in top of turning ch (inc).
Row 2: Ch 3, turn, 1 dc in first ch-1 sp, (1 dc, ch 1, 1 dc) all in ch-1 sp, *1 dc in each st to next ch-1 sp, (1 dc, ch 1, 1 dc) all in ch-1 sp. Repeat from * twice more, ending with 1 dc in each st, 2 dc in top of turning ch.
   Repeat Row 2 till there are 86 (90, 94, 98, 104, 108) dc in back section.
   Continue as for front, back, and sleeves of Men's Classic Sport Weight Sweaters—Crew Neck Cardigan.

Finishing:
Sew underarm seams. *For Zipper:* With right side facing you, starting at bottom right corner, work 2 rows sc around entire front and neck edges. Sew in zipper up to where V shaping starts. *For Buttonholes:* With right side facing you, work 5 rows sc around entire front and neck edges, place buttonholes evenly spaced on the 3rd row, between bottom of garment and start of V shaping. Make buttonholes on the right for girls, on the left for boys. To make buttonholes, ch 2, sk 2 sts. On the 4th row, make 2 sc in the ch-2 sp.

CREW NECK PULLOVER

Men's Sizes: Directions are for size 36. Changes for 38, 40, 42, 44, and 46 are in parentheses.
Materials: 16 (18, 18, 18, 20, 22) oz sport weight yarn
Aluminum Hook: #4 or E
Gauge: 5 sts = 1 inch

Yoke:
Ch 70 (70, 70, 74, 74, 74) loosely, join to form a ring.
Foundation Row: Ch 3 (counts as first dc), 1 dc in each of next 10 chs, (1 dc, ch 1, 1 dc) all in next ch (sleeve), 1 dc in each of next 22 (22, 22, 24, 24, 24) chs, (1 dc, ch 1, 1 dc) all in next ch (front), 1 dc in each of next 11 chs, (1 dc, ch 1, 1 dc) all in next ch (sleeve), 1 dc in each of next 22 (22, 22, 24, 24, 24) chs. (1 dc, ch 1, 1 dc) all in next ch (back), join with a slst to starting ch-3.
Row 1: Ch 3, *1 dc in each st to ch-1 sp, (1 dc, ch 1, 1 dc) all in ch-1 sp. Repeat from * 3 times more, join with a slst to top of starting ch.
   Repeat Row 1 till there are 86 (90, 94, 98, 104, 108) sts on back section.

Front and Back:
On next row, ch 3, sk sleeve section, work across front section, ch 3, sk other sleeve section, work back section, ch 3, join to top of starting ch-3. Working round and round, starting each rnd with a ch-3, and ending with a slst to join, work till body is 16 (16, 17, 17, 18, 18) inches from underarm, end off.

Sleeves:
Join yarn at underarm, ch 3, work 1 dc in each st around sleeve, work 1 dc on the underarm ch, join with a slst. Working round and round, dec 1 st at the underarm, every 4th row, 5 (5, 5, 5, 6, 6) times. Work even till 18½ (18½, 19, 19, 19½, 19½) inches from underarm, end off.

Finishing:
Sew underarm seams. Work 4 rows sc around neck opening.

MEN'S CLASSIC KNITTING WORSTED SWEATERS

CREW NECK CARDIGAN

Men's Sizes: Directions are for size 36. Changes for 38, 40, 42, 44, and 46 are in parentheses.
Materials: 24 (24, 28, 28, 32, 32) oz knitting worsted
Aluminum Hook: #6 or G
Gauge: 4 sts = 1 inch

Yoke:
Ch 63 (63, 67, 67, 71, 71) loosely.
Foundation Row: 1 dc in 3rd ch from hook, 1 dc in each of next 9 (9, 10, 10, 11, 11) chs, (1 dc, ch 1, 1 dc) all in next ch (front), 1 dc in each of next 8 chs, (1 dc, ch 1, 1 dc) all in next ch (sleeve), 1 dc in each of next 20 (20, 22, 22, 24, 24) chs, (1 dc, ch 1, 1 dc) all in next ch (back), 1 dc in each of next 8 chs, (1 dc, ch 1, 1 dc) all in next ch (sleeve), 1 dc in each of last 10 (10, 11, 11, 12, 12) chs.
Row 1: Ch 3, turn (ch-3 always counts as first dc), sk first st, 1 dc in each of next 10 (10, 11, 11, 12, 12) sts, (1 dc, ch 1, 1 dc) all in ch-1 sp (inc), 1 dc in each of next 10 sts, (1 dc, ch 1, 1 dc) all in ch-1 sp (inc), 1 dc in each of next 22 (22, 24, 24, 26, 26) sts, (1 dc, ch 1, 1 dc) all in ch-1 sp (inc), 1 dc in each of next 10 sts, (1 dc, ch 1, 1 dc) all in ch-1 sp (inc), 1 dc in each of last 11 (11, 12, 12, 13, 13) sts (last st is turning ch).
Row 2: Ch 3, turn, 1 dc in each st to first ch-1 sp, (1 dc, ch 1, 1 dc) all in ch-1 sp, *1 dc in each st to next ch-1 sp, (1 dc, ch 1, 1 dc) all in ch-1 sp. Repeat from * twice more, ending with 1 dc in each st, 1 dc in top of turning ch.
   Repeat Row 2 till there are 72 (76, 80, 84, 88, 90) sts in back section.

Front and Back:
Work across front to first ch-1 sp, ch 3, sk sleeve section, work across back section, ch 3, sk other sleeve section, work across front section. Continue in pat as established, omitting incs and working 3 dc on the added ch at underarm. Work entire body section till 16 (16, 17, 17, 18, 18) inches from underarm, end off.

Sleeves:
Join yarn at underarm, ch 3, work 1 dc in each st around sleeve section, work 1 dc on ch at underarm. Ch 3, turn. Working back and forth in pat as established, dec 1 st each side, every 4th row, 5 (5, 5, 5, 6, 6) times. Work even till 18½ (18½, 19, 19, 19½, 19½) inches, end off.

Finishing:
Sew underarm seams. *For Zipper:* With right side facing you, starting at bottom right corner, work 2 rows sc around entire front and neck edges, making 3 sc in each corner st at neck. Sew in zipper. *For Buttonholes:* With right side facing you, work 5 rows sc around entire front and neck edges, making 3 sc in each corner st at neck and placing buttonholes evenly spaced on the 3rd row. Make buttonholes on the right for girls, on the left for boys. To make buttonholes, ch 2, sk 2 sts. On the 4th row, make 2 sc in the ch-2 sp.

V NECK CARDIGAN

Men's Sizes: Directions are for size 36. Changes for 38, 40, 42, 44, and 46 are in parentheses.
Materials: 24 (24, 28, 28, 32, 32) oz knitting worsted
Aluminum Hook: #6 or G
Gauge: 4 sts = 1 inch

Yoke:
Ch 47 (47, 49, 49, 51, 51) loosely.
Foundation Row: 1 dc in 3rd ch from hook, 1 dc in next ch, (1 dc, ch 1, 1 dc) all in next ch (front), 1 dc in each of next 8 chs, (1 dc, ch 1, 1 dc) all in next ch (sleeve), 1 dc in each of next 20 (20, 22, 22, 24, 24) chs, (1 dc, ch 1, 1 dc) all in next ch (back), 1 dc in each of next 8 chs, (1 dc, ch 1, 1 dc) all in next ch (sleeve), 1 dc in each of last 2 chs (front).
Row 1: Ch 3, turn (ch-3 always counts as first dc), 1 dc in first st (inc), 1 dc in each st to ch-1 sp, (1 dc, ch 1, 1 dc) all in ch-1 sp (inc), 1 dc in each of next 10 sts, (1 dc, ch 1, 1 dc) all in ch-1 sp (inc), 1 dc in each of next 22 (22, 24, 24, 26, 26) sts, (1 dc, ch 1, 1 dc) all in the ch-1 sp (inc), 1 dc in each of next 10 sts, (1 dc, ch 1, 1 dc) all in the ch-1 sp (inc), 1 dc in each st to end, 2 dc in top of turning ch (inc).
Row 2: Ch 3, turn, 1 dc in first st, 1 dc in each st to first ch-1 sp, (1 dc, ch 1, 1 dc) all in ch-1 sp, *1 dc in each st to next ch-1 sp, (1 dc, ch 1, 1 dc) all in ch-1 sp. Repeat from * twice more, ending with 1 dc in each st, 2 dc in top of turning ch.
   Repeat Row 2 till there are 72 (76, 80, 84, 88, 92) dc in back section.
   Continue as for front, back, and sleeves of Men's Classic Knitting Worsted Sweaters—Crew Neck Cardigan.

Finishing:
Sew underarm seams. *For Zipper:* With right side facing you, starting at bottom right corner, work 2 rows sc around entire front and neck edges. Sew in zipper up to where V shaping starts. *For Buttonholes:* With right side facing you, work 5 rows sc around entire front and neck edges, place buttonholes evenly spaced on the 3rd row, between bottom of garment and start of V shaping. Make buttonholes on the right for girls, on the left for boys. To make buttonholes, ch 2, sk 2. On the 4th row, make 2 sc in the ch-2 sp.

CREW NECK PULLOVER

Men's Sizes: Directions are for size 36. Changes for 38, 40, 42, 44, and 46 are in parentheses.
Materials: 24 (24, 28, 28, 32, 32) oz knitting worsted
Aluminum Hook: #6 or G
Gauge: 4 sts = 1 inch

Yoke:

Ch 60 (60, 64, 64, 68, 68) loosely, join to form a ring.
Foundation Row: Ch 3 (ch-3 always counts as first dc), 1 dc in each of next 7 chs, (1 dc, ch 1, 1 dc) all in next ch (sleeve), 1 dc in each of next 20 (20, 22, 22, 24, 24) chs, (1 dc, ch 1, 1 dc) all in next ch (front), 1 dc in each of next 8 chs, (1 dc, ch 1, 1 dc) all in next ch (sleeve), 1 dc in each of next 20 (20, 22, 22, 24, 24) chs, (1 dc, ch 1, 1 dc) all in next ch (back), join with a slst to starting ch-3.
Row 1: Ch 3, *1 dc in each st to ch-1 sp, (1 dc, ch 1, 1 dc) all in ch-1 sp. Repeat from * 3 times more, join with a slst to top of starting ch.
  Repeat Row 1 till there are 72 (76, 80, 84, 88, 92) sts in back section.

Front and Back:

On next row ch 3, sk sleeve section, work across front section, ch 2, sk other sleeve section, work back section, ch 2, join to top of starting ch-3. Working round and round, starting each rnd with ch-3, and ending with a slst to join, work till body is 16 (16, 17, 17, 18, 18) inches from underarm, end off.

Sleeves:

Join yarn at underarm, ch 3, work 1 dc in each st around sleeve, work 1 dc on the underarm ch, join with a slst. Working round and round, dec 1 st at the underarm every 4th row, 5 (5, 6, 6, 6, 6) times. Work even till 18 (18½, 19, 19, 19½, 19½) inches, end off.

Finishing:

Sew underarm seams. Work 4 rows sc around neck.

MEN'S CLASSIC BULKY YARN SWEATERS

CREW NECK CARDIGAN

Men's Sizes: Directions are for size 36. Changes for 38, 40, 42, 44, and 46 are in parentheses.
Materials: 44 (46, 48, 50, 52, 52) oz bulky yarn
Aluminum Hook: #10½ or K
Gauge: 5 sts = 2 inches

Yoke:

Ch 47 (47, 51, 51, 55, 55) loosely.
Foundation Row: 1 dc in 3rd ch from hook, 1 dc in each of next 6 (6, 7, 7, 8, 8) chs, (1 dc, ch 1, 1 dc) all in the next ch (front), 1 dc in each of next 6 chs, (1 dc, ch 1, 1 dc) all in next ch (sleeve), 1 dc in each of next 14 (14, 16, 16, 18, 18) chs, (1 dc, ch 1, 1 dc) all in next ch (back), 1 dc in each of next 6 chs, (1 dc, ch 1, 1 dc) all in next ch (sleeve), 1 dc in each of last 7 (7, 8, 8, 9, 9) chs (front).
Row 1: Ch 3, turn (ch-3 always counts as first dc), sk first st, 1 dc in each of next 7 (7, 8, 8, 9, 9) sts, (1 dc, ch 1, 1 dc) all in ch-1 sp (inc), 1 dc in each of next 8 sts, (1 dc, ch 1, 1 dc) all in ch-1 sp (inc), 1 dc in each of next 16 (16, 18, 18, 20, 20) sts, (1 dc, ch 1, 1 dc) all in ch-1 sp (inc), 1 dc in each of next 8 sts, (1 dc, ch 1, 1 dc) all in ch-1 sp (inc), 1 dc in each of last 8 (8, 9, 9, 10, 10) sts (last st is in top of turning ch).
Row 2: Ch 3, turn, 1 dc in each st to next ch-1 sp, (1 dc, ch 1, 1 dc) all in ch-1 sp, *1 dc in each st to next ch-1 sp, (1 dc, ch 1, 1 dc) all in ch-1 sp. Repeat from * twice more, ending with 1 dc in each st, 1 dc in top of turning ch.
  Repeat Row 2 till there are 50 (52, 54, 56, 58, 60) sts in back section.

Front and Back:

Work across front to first ch-1 sp, ch 2, sk sleeve section, work across back section, ch 2, sk other sleeve section, work across front section. Continue pat as established, omitting incs and working 3 dc on the added ch at underarm. Work entire body section till 16 (16, 17, 17, 18, 18) inches from underarm, end off.

Sleeves:

Join yarn at underarm, ch 3, work 1 dc in each st around sleeve section, work 2 dc on ch at underarm. Ch 3, turn. Working back and forth in pat as established, dec 1 st each side every 5th row, 5 (5, 6, 6, 6, 6) times. Work even till 18½ (18½, 19, 19, 19½, 19½) inches, end off.

Finishing:

Sew underarm seams. *For Zipper:* With right side facing you, starting at bottom right corner, work 2 rows sc around entire front and neck edges, making 3 sc in each corner st at neck. Sew in zipper. *For Buttonholes:* With right side facing you, work 3 rows sc around entire front and neck edges, making 3 sc in each corner st at neck and placing buttonholes evenly spaced on the 2nd row. Make buttonholes on the right for girls, on the left for boys. To make buttonholes, ch 2, sk 2. On the 3rd row, make 2 sc in the ch-2 sp.

V NECK CARDIGAN

Men's Sizes: Directions are for size 36. Changes for 38, 40, 42, 44, and 46 are in parentheses.
Materials: 44 (46, 48, 50, 52, 52) oz bulky yarn
Aluminum Hook: #10½ or K
Gauge: 5 sts = 2 inches

Yoke:

Ch 35 (35, 37, 37, 39, 39) loosely.
Foundation Row: (1 dc, ch 1, 1 dc) all in 3rd ch from hook (front), 1 dc in each of next 6 chs, (1 dc, ch 1, 1 dc) all in next ch (sleeve), 1 dc in each of next 14 (14, 16, 16, 18, 18) chs, (1 dc, ch 1, 1 dc) all in next ch (back), 1 dc in each of next 6 chs, (1 dc, ch 1, 1 dc) all in next ch (sleeve), (1 dc, ch 1, 1 dc) all in next ch, 1 dc in last ch (front).
Row 1: Ch 3, turn (ch-3 always counts as first dc), 1 dc in first st (inc), 1 dc in each st to first ch-1 sp, (1 dc, ch 1, 1 dc) all in ch-1 sp (inc), 1 dc in each of next 8 sts, (1 dc, ch 1, 1 dc) all in ch-1 sp (inc), 1 dc in each of next 16 (16, 18, 18, 20, 20) sts, (1 dc, ch 1, 1 dc) all in ch-1 sp (inc), 1 dc in each of next 8 sts, (1 dc, ch 1, 1 dc) all in ch-1 sp (inc), 1 dc in each st to end, 2 dc in top of turning ch (inc).
Row 2: Ch 3, turn, 1 dc in first st, 1 dc in each st to first ch-1 sp, (1 dc, ch 1, 1 dc) all in ch-1 sp, *1 dc in each st to next ch-1 sp, (1 dc, ch 1, 1 dc) all in ch-1 sp. Repeat from * twice more, ending with 1 dc in each st, 2 dc in top of turning ch.

Repeat Row 2 till there are 50 (52, 54, 56, 58, 60) dc in back section.

Continue as for front, back, and sleeves of Men's Classic Bulky Yarn Sweaters—Crew Neck Cardigan.

Finishing:

Sew underarm seams. *For Zipper:* With right side facing you, starting at bottom right corner, work 2 rows sc around entire front and neck edges. Sew in zipper up to where V shaping starts. *For Buttonholes:* With right side facing you, work 3 rows sc around entire front and neck edges place buttonholes evenly spaced on the 3rd row, between bottom of garment and start of V shaping. Make buttonholes on the right for girls, on the left for boys. To make buttonholes, ch 2, sk 2. On the 3rd row, make 2 sc in the ch-2 sp.

CREW NECK PULLOVER

Men's Sizes: Directions are for size 36. Changes for 38, 40, 42, 44, and 46 are in parentheses.
Materials: 44 (44, 48, 50, 52, 52) oz bulky yarn
Aluminum Hook: #10½ or K
Gauge: 5 sts = 2 inches

Yoke:

Ch 44 (44, 48, 48, 52, 52) loosely, join to form a ring.
Foundation Row: Ch 3 (ch-3 always counts as first dc), 1 dc in each of next 5 chs, (1 dc, ch 1, 1 dc) all in next ch (sleeve), 1 dc in each of next 14 (14, 16, 16, 18, 18) chs, (1 dc, ch 1, 1 dc) all in next ch (front), 1 dc in each of next 6 chs, (1 dc, ch 1, 1 dc) all in next ch (sleeve), 1 dc in each of next 14 (14, 16, 16, 18, 18) chs, (1 dc, ch 1, 1 dc) all in next ch (back), join with a slst to starting ch-3.
Row 1: Ch 3, *1 dc in each st to ch-1 sp, (1 dc, ch 1, 1 dc) all in ch-1 sp. Repeat from * 3 times more, join with a slst to top of starting ch.

Repeat Row 1 till there are 50 (52, 54, 56, 58, 60) sts in back section.

Front and Back:

On next row, ch 3, sk sleeve section, work across front section, ch 3, sk other sleeve section, work back section, ch 2, join to top of starting ch-3. Working round and round, starting each rnd with ch-3, and ending with a slst to join, work till body is 16 (16, 17, 17, 18, 18) inches from underarm, end off.

Sleeves:

Join yarn at underarm, ch 3, work 1 dc in each st around sleeve, work 1 dc on the underarm ch, join with a slst. Working round and round, dec 1 st at the underarm every 5th row, 5 (5, 6, 6, 6, 6) times. Work even till 18½ (18½, 19, 19, 19½, 19½) inches from underarm, end off.

Finishing:

Sew underarm seams. Work 4 rows sc around neck opening.

Figure 17. Except for the slits at the sides and the seed stitch at the borders, this knitted T top is a classic crew neck cardigan knitted from the bottom up. Slits are easy to make and there will be some more examples of them in Part III. Yarn: Frostlon Petite by Spinnerin.

5. T Tops Knitted from Bottom to Top or from Side Over

This type of sweater is a comfortable, loose-fitting, easy-to-wear garment. The more relaxed atmosphere of today's living accounts for the popularity of this style. T tops are usually worn casually, over lightweight sweaters or shirts, as a topper for slacks, or countless other alternatives.

Whether you knit the T top from the bottom up or from the side over, the basic shape is not altered. The only reason for choosing one approach over the other is for the placement of a pattern or stripe. For example, if you wanted horizontal stripes, you would work from the bottom up, changing colors as you worked. If you wanted vertical stripes, however, you would work from the side over. See Figures 4 through 9 on pages 7 and 10 for schematic diagrams.

The sewing and finishing required on a T top is minimal, which makes it great fun to make. See Figures 17, 18, 19, and 20 for examples of these classic knitted T tops. Remember that you can make any of these sweaters in virtually any size, even though the instructions may not be given in the chapter. See page 16 for these instructions and for details on how to make V necks or turtleneck pullovers.

INFANTS' CLASSIC SPORT WEIGHT SWEATERS

CREW NECK CARDIGAN

Infants' Sizes: Directions are for 6 months. Changes for 1, 2, and 3 are in parentheses.
Materials: 4 (6, 8, 10) oz sport weight yarn
Needles: #5; crochet hook #3
Gauge: 6 sts = 1 inch; 6 rows = 1 inch

Front, Back, and Sleeves:
Starting at back, cast on 60 (64, 66, 68) sts. K each row in garter st for 6 rows, then work k 1 row, p 1 row in stockinette st till 6½ (7, 7½, 8) inches from beg. At beg of next 2 rows, cast on 30 (33, 36, 39) sts (sleeves). Continue in stockinette st on all sts for 3½ (3¾, 4, 4½) inches. Work across 50 (54, 57, 60) sts, join new ball of yarn, bind off center 20 (22, 24, 26) sts (neck opening), work rem 50 (54, 57, 60) sts. Working both sides at once, each with a separate ball of yarn, work for ½ inch more. On next row, work across 50 (54, 57, 60) sts, cast on 10 (11, 12, 13) sts, on other side cast on 10 (11, 12, 13) sts, and continue across last 50 (54, 57, 60) sts. Still working both sides at once, each with a separate ball of yarn, work till sleeve section measures 7½ (8, 8½, 9) inches. Bind off 30 (33, 36, 39) sts each outside edge. Continue front to correspond to back.

Finishing:
Sew underarm seams. *For Zipper:* With right side facing you, starting at bottom right corner, work 2 rows sc around entire front and neck edges, making 3 sc in each corner st at neck. Sew in zipper. *For Buttonholes:* With right side facing you, work 5 rows sc around entire front and neck edges, making 3 sc in each corner st at neck and placing buttonholes evenly spaced on the 3rd row. Make buttonholes on the right for girls, on the left for boys. To make buttonholes, ch 2, sk 2 sts. On the 4th row, make 2 sc in the ch-2 sp.

V NECK CARDIGAN

Infants' Sizes: Directions are for 6 months. Changes for 1, 2, and 3 are in parentheses.
Materials: 4 (6, 8, 10) oz sport weight yarn
Needles: #5; crochet hook #3
Gauge: 6 sts = 1 inch; 6 rows = 1 inch

Front, Back, and Sleeves:
Starting at back, cast on 60 (64, 66, 68) sts. K each row in garter st for 6 rows, then k 1 row, p 1 row in stockinette st till 6½ (7, 7½, 8) inches from beg. At beg of next 2 rows, cast on 30 (33, 36, 39) sts (sleeves). Continue in stockinette st on all sts for 3½ (3¾, 4, 4½) inches. Work across 50 (54, 57, 60) sts, join new ball of yarn, bind off center 20 (22, 24, 26) sts (neck opening), work rem 50 (54, 57, 60) sts. Working both sides at once, each with a separate ball of yarn, work for ½ inch more. Continue working both sides at once, 1 st at each neck edge, every other row, 10 (11, 12, 13) times. When sleeve section measures 7½ (8, 8½, 9) inches, bind off 30 (33, 36, 39) sts each outside edge.

Finishing:
Sew underarm seams. *For Zipper:* With right side facing you, starting at bottom right corner, work 2 rows sc around entire front and neck edges. Sew in zipper up to where V shaping starts. *For Buttonholes:* With right side facing you, work 5 rows sc around entire front and neck edges, place buttonholes evenly spaced on the 3rd row, between bottom of garment and start of V shaping. Make buttonholes on the right for girls, on the left for boys. To make buttonholes, ch 2, sk 2. On the 4th row, make 2 sc in the ch-2 sp.

CREW NECK PULLOVER

Infants' Sizes: Directions are for 6 months. Changes for 1, 2, and 3 are in parentheses.
Materials: 4 (6, 8, 10) oz sport weight yarn
Needles: #5; crochet hook #3
Gauge: 6 sts = 1 inch; 6 rows = 1 inch

Front, Back, and Sleeves:
Starting at back, cast on 60 (64, 66, 68) sts. K each row in garter st for 6 rows, then work k 1 row, p 1 row in stockinette st till 6½ (7, 7½, 8) inches from beg. At beg of next 2 rows, cast on 30 (33, 36, 39) sts (sleeves). Continue in stockinette st on all sts for 3½ (3¾, 4, 4¼) inches. Work across 50 (54, 57, 60) sts, join new ball of yarn, bind off center 20 (22, 24, 26) sts (neck open-ing), work rem 50 (54, 57, 60) sts. Working both sides at once, each with a separate ball of yarn, work for ½ inch more. On next row, work across 50 (54, 57, 60) sts, cast on 20 (22, 24, 26) sts, break off 2nd ball of yarn, and, continuing with same yarn, k across rem 50 (54, 57, 60) sts. Continue all as 1 piece, working till sleeve section measures 7½ (8, 8½, 9) inches. At beg of next 2 rows, bind off 30 (33, 36, 39) sts. Continue front to correspond to back.

Finishing:
Sew underarm seams. Work 1 row sc around bottom of sleeves and around neck edge.

Figure 18. Although slit at the sides and bordered with seed stitch, the sweater shown is still a classic version of the crew neck pullover T top knitted from the bottom up. Yarn: Frostlon Petite by Spinnerin.

INFANTS' CLASSIC KNITTING
WORSTED SWEATERS

CREW NECK CARDIGAN

Infants' Sizes: Directions are for 6 months. Changes for
1, 2, and 3 are in parentheses.
Materials: 4 (6, 8, 8) oz knitting worsted
Needles: #8; crochet hook #5
Gauge: 5 sts = 1 inch; 5 rows = 1 inch

Front, Back, and Sleeves:
Starting at back, cast on 48 (50, 52, 54) sts. K each row
in garter st for 6 rows, then work k 1 row, p 1 row in
stockinette st till 6½ (7, 7½, 8) inches from beg. At
beg of next 2 rows, cast on 25 (27, 30, 32) sts (sleeves).
Continue in stockinette st on all sts for 3½ (3¾, 4, 4½)
inches. Work across 39 (42, 45, 48) sts, join new ball
of yarn, bind off center 20 (20, 22, 22) sts (neck opening), work rem 39 (42, 45, 48) sts. Working both sides
at once, each with a separate ball of yarn, work for ½
inch more. On next row, work across 39 (42, 45, 48)
sts, cast on 10 (10, 11, 11) sts. On other side cast on
10 (10, 11, 11) sts, and continue across last 39 (42, 45,
48) sts. Still working both sides at once, each with a
separate ball of yarn, work till sleeve section measures
7½ (8, 8½, 9) inches. Bind off 25 (27, 30, 32) sts each
outside edge. Continue front to correspond to back.

Finishing:
Sew underarm seams. *For Zipper:* With right side facing
you, starting at bottom right corner, work 2 rows sc
around entire front and neck edges, making 3 sc in
each corner st at neck. Sew in zipper. *For Buttonholes:*
With right side facing you, work 3 rows sc around
entire front and neck edges, making 3 sc in each corner
st at neck and placing buttonholes evenly spaced on
the 2nd row. Make buttonholes on the right for girls,
on the left for boys. To make buttonholes, ch 2, sk 2.
On the 3rd row, make 2 sc in the ch-2 sp.

V NECK CARDIGAN

Infants' Sizes: Directions are for 6 months. Changes for
1, 2, and 3 are in parentheses.
Materials: 4 (6, 8, 8) oz knitting worsted
Needles: #8; crochet hook #5
Gauge: 5 sts = 1 inch; 5 rows = 1 inch

Front, Back, and Sleeves:
Starting at back, cast on 48 (50, 52, 54) sts. K each row
in garter st for 6 rows, then k 1 row, p 1 row in stockinette st till 6½ (7, 7½, 8) inches from beg. At beg of
next 2 rows, cast on 25 (27, 30, 32) sts (sleeves). Continue in stockinette st on all sts for 3½ (3¾, 4, 4¼)
inches. Work across 39 (42, 45, 48) sts, join new ball
of yarn, bind off center 20 (20, 22, 22) sts (neck opening), work rem 39 (42, 45, 48) sts. Working both sides
at once, each with a separate ball of yarn, work for
½ inch more. Continue working both sides at once, inc
1 st at each neck edge, every other row, 10 (10, 11, 11)
times. When sleeve section measures 7½ (8, 8½, 9)
inches, bind off 25 (27, 30, 32) sts each outside edge.

Finishing:
Sew underarm seams. *For Zipper:* With right side
facing you, starting at bottom right corner, work 2
rows sc around entire front and neck edges. Sew in
zipper up to where V shaping starts. *For Buttonholes:*
With right side facing you, work 3 rows sc around entire
front and neck edges, place buttonholes evenly spaced
on the 2nd row, between bottom of garment and start
of V shaping. Make buttonholes on the right for girls,
on the left for boys. To make buttonholes, ch 2, sk 2.
On the 3rd row, make 2 sc in the ch-2 sp.

CREW NECK PULLOVER

Infants' Sizes: Directions are for 6 months. Changes for
1, 2, and 3 are in parentheses.
Materials: 4 (6, 8, 8) oz knitting worsted
Needles: #8; crochet hook #5
Gauge: 5 sts = 1 inch; 5 rows = 1 inch

Front, Back, and Sleeves:
Starting at back, cast on 48 (50, 52, 54) sts. K each row
in garter st for 6 rows, then work k 1 row, p 1 row in
stockinette st till 6½ (7, 7½, 8) inches from beg. At
beg of next 2 rows, cast on 25 (27, 30, 32) sts (sleeves).
Continue in stockinette st on all sts for 3½ (3¾, 4, 4¼)
inches. Work across 39 (42, 45, 48) sts, join new ball
of yarn, bind off center 20 (20, 22, 22) sts (neck opening), work rem 39 (42, 45, 48) sts. Working both sides
at once, each with a separate ball of yarn, work for ½
inch more. On next row, work across 39 (42, 45, 48)
sts, cast on 20 (20, 22, 22) sts, break off 2nd ball of
yarn, and, continuing with same yarn, k across rem
39 (42, 45, 48) sts. Continue all as 1 piece, working
till sleeve section measures 7½ (8, 8½, 9) inches. At
beg of next 2 rows, bind off 25 (27, 30, 32) sts. Continue front to correspond to back.

Finishing:
Sew underarm seams. Work 1 sc around bottom of
sleeves and around neck edge.

CHILDREN'S CLASSIC SPORT WEIGHT SWEATERS

CREW NECK CARDIGAN

Children's Sizes: Directions are for size 4. Changes for 6, 8, 10, 12, and 14 are in parentheses.
Materials: 10 (10, 12, 12, 14, 14) oz sport weight yarn
Needles: #5; crochet hook #3
Gauge: 6 sts = 1 inch; 6 rows = 1 inch

Front, Back, and Sleeves:
Starting at back, cast on 70 (76, 82, 88, 94, 100) sts. K each row in garter st for 10 rows, then k 1 row, p 1 row in stockinette st till 10 (11, 12, 13, 14, 15) inches from beg. At beg of next 2 rows, cast on 63 (66, 69, 72, 75, 78) sts (sleeves). Continue in stockinette on all sts for 4 (4½, 5, 5½, 6, 6½) inches. Work across 82 (88, 92, 98, 102, 108) sts, join new ball of yarn, bind off center 32 (32, 36, 36, 40, 40) sts, (neck opening) work rem 82 (88, 92, 98, 102, 108) sts. Working both sides at once, each with a separate ball of yarn, work for 1½ (1½, 1½, 2, 2, 2) inches more. On next row, work across 82 (88, 92, 98, 102, 108) sts, cast on 16 (16, 18, 18, 20, 20) sts, on other side cast on 16 (16, 18, 18, 20, 20) sts, and continue across last 82 (88, 92, 98, 102, 108) sts. Still working both sides at once, each with a separate ball of yarn, work till sleeve section measures 9½ (10½, 11½, 13, 14, 15) inches. Bind off 63 (66, 69, 72, 75, 78) sts each outside edge. Continue front to correspond to back.

Finishing:
Sew underarm seams. *For Zipper:* With right side facing you, starting at bottom right corner, work 2 rows sc around entire front and neck edges, making 3 sc in each corner st at neck. Sew in zipper. *For Buttonholes:* With right side facing you, work 5 rows sc around entire front and neck edges, making 3 sc in each corner st at neck and placing buttonholes evenly spaced on the 3rd row. Make buttonholes on the right for girls, on the left for boys. To make buttonholes, ch 2, sk 2 sts. On the 4th row, make 2 sc in the ch-2 sp.

V NECK CARDIGAN

Children's Sizes: Directions are for size 4. Changes for 6, 8, 10, 12, and 14 are in parentheses.
Materials: 10 (10, 12, 12, 14, 14) oz sport weight yarn
Needles: #5; crochet hook #3
Gauge: 6 sts = 1 inch; 6 rows = 1 inch

Front, Back, and Sleeves:
Starting at back, cast on 70 (76, 82, 88, 94, 100) sts. K each row in garter st for 10 rows, then k 1 row, p 1 row in stockinette st till 10 (11, 12, 13, 14, 15) inches from beg. At beg of next 2 rows, cast on 63 (66, 69, 72, 75, 78) sts (sleeves). Continue in stockinette st on all sts for 4 (4½, 5, 5½, 6, 6½) inches. Work across 82 (88, 92, 98, 102, 108) sts, join new ball of yarn, bind off center 32 (33, 36, 36, 40, 40) sts, work rem 82 (88, 92, 98, 102, 108) sts. Working both sides at once, each with a separate ball of yarn, work for 1½ (1½, 1½, 2, 2, 2) inches more. Continue working both sides at once, each with a separate ball of yarn, inc 1 st at each neck edge, every other row, 16 (16, 18, 18, 20, 20) times. When sleeve section measures 9½ (10½, 11½, 13, 14, 15) inches, bind off 63 (66, 69, 72, 75, 78) sts each outside edge.

Finishing:
Sew underarm seams. *For Zipper:* With right side facing you, starting at bottom right corner, work 2 rows sc around entire front and neck edges. Sew in zipper up to where V shaping starts. *For Buttonholes:* With right side facing you, work 5 rows sc around entire front and neck edges, place buttonholes evenly spaced on the 3rd row, between bottom of garment and start of V shaping. Make buttonholes on the right for girls, on the left for boys. To make buttonholes, ch 2, sk 2. On the 4th row, make 2 sc in the ch-2 sp.

CREW NECK PULLOVER

Children's Sizes: Directions are for size 4. Changes for
6, 8, 10, 12, and 14 are in parentheses.
Materials: 10 (10, 12, 12, 14, 14) oz sport weight yarn
Needles: #5
Gauge: 6 sts = 1 inch; 6 rows = 1 inch

Front, Back, and Sleeves:
Starting at back, cast on 70 (76, 82, 88, 94, 100) sts.
K each row in garter st for 10 rows, then k 1 row,
p 1 row in stockinette st till 10 (11, 12, 13, 14, 15)
inches from beg. At beg of next 2 rows, cast on 63
(66, 69, 72, 75, 78) sts (sleeves). Continue in stockinette st on all sts for 4 (4½, 5, 5½, 6, 6½) inches.
Work across 82 (88, 92, 98, 102, 108) sts, join new
ball of yarn, bind off center 32 (32, 36, 36, 40, 40)
sts (neck opening), work rem 82 (88, 92, 98, 102, 108)
sts. Working both sides at once, each with a separate
ball of yarn, work for 1½ (1½, 1½, 2, 2, 2) inches more.
On next row, work across 82 (88, 92, 98, 102, 108)
sts, cast on 32 (32, 36, 36, 40, 40) sts, break off 2nd
ball of yarn, and, continuing with same yarn, k across
rem 82 (88, 92, 98, 102, 108) sts. Continue as 1 piece,
working till 9½ (10½, 11½, 13, 14, 15) inches. At beg
of next 2 rows, bind off 63 (66, 69, 72, 75, 78) sts.
Continue front to correspond to back.

Finishing:
Sew underarm seams. Work 1 row sc around bottom
of sleeves and around neck edge.

CHILDREN'S CLASSIC KNITTING
WORSTED SWEATERS

CREW NECK CARDIGAN

Children's Sizes: Directions are for size 4. Changes for
6, 8, 10, 12, and 14 are in parentheses.
Materials: 12 (12, 14, 16, 16, 20) oz knitting worsted
Needles: #8; crochet hook #5
Gauge: 5 sts = 1 inch; 5 rows = 1 inch

Front, Back, and Sleeves:
Starting at back, cast on 56 (60, 64, 66, 70, 74) sts.
K each row in garter st for 10 rows, then k 1 row,
p 1 row in stockinette st till 10 (11, 12, 13, 14, 15)
inches from beg. At beg of next 2 rows, cast on 53
(56, 59, 62, 65, 68) sts (sleeves). Continue in stockinette st on all sts for 4 (4½, 5, 5½, 6, 6½) inches. Work
across 69 (74, 79, 82, 86, 91) sts, join new ball of yarn,
bind off center 24 (24, 24, 26, 28, 28) sts (neck opening), work rem 69 (74, 79, 82, 86, 91) sts. Working both
sides at once, each with a separate ball of yarn, work
for 1½ (1½, 1½, 2, 2, 2) inches more. On next row, work
across 69 (74, 79, 82, 86, 91) sts, cast on 12 (12, 12,
13, 14, 14) sts, on other side cast on 12 (12, 12, 13,
14, 14) sts, and continue across last 69 (74, 79, 82, 86,
91) sts. Still working both sides at once, each with a
separate ball of yarn, work till sleeve section measures
9½ (10½, 11½, 13, 14, 15) inches. Bind off 53 (56, 59,
62, 65, 68) sts each outside edge. Continue front to
correspond to back.

Finishing:
Sew underarm seams. *For Zipper:* With right side
facing you, starting at bottom right corner, work 2
rows sc around entire front and neck edges, making
3 sc in each corner st at neck. Sew in zipper. *For Buttonholes:* With right side facing you, work 5 rows sc around
entire front and neck edges, making 3 sc in each corner
st at neck and placing buttonholes evenly spaced on the
3rd row. Make buttonholes on the right for girls, on the
left for boys. To make buttonholes, ch 2, sk 2 sts. On
the 4th row, make 2 sc in the ch-2 sp.

V NECK CARDIGAN

Children's Sizes: Directions are for size 4. Changes for
6, 8, 10, 12, and 14 are in parentheses.
Materials: 12 (12, 14, 16, 16, 20) oz knitting worsted
Needles: #8; crochet hook #5
Gauge: 5 sts = 1 inch; 5 rows = 1 inch

Front, Back, and Sleeves:

Starting at back, cast on 56 (60, 64, 66, 70, 74) sts. K each row in garter st for 10 rows, then k 1 row, p 1 row in stockinette st till 10 (11, 12, 13, 14, 15) inches from beg. At beg of next 2 rows, cast on 53 (56, 59, 62, 65, 68) sts (sleeves). Continue in stockinette st on all sts for 4 (4½, 5, 5½, 6, 6½) inches. Work across 69 (74, 79, 82, 86, 91) sts, join new ball of yarn, bind off center 24 (24, 24, 26, 28, 28) sts (neck opening), work rem 69 (74, 79, 82, 86, 91) sts. Working both sides at once, each with a separate ball of yarn, work for 1½ (1½, 1½, 2, 2, 2) inches more. Continue working both sides at once, each with a separate ball of yarn, inc 1 st at each neck edge, every other row, 12 (12, 12, 13, 14, 14) times. When sleeve section measures 9½ (10½, 11½, 13, 14, 15) inches, bind off 53 (56, 59, 62, 65, 68) sts each outside edge.

Finishing:

Sew underarm seams. *For Zipper:* With right side facing you, starting at bottom right corner, work 2 rows sc around entire front and neck edges. Sew in zipper up to where V shaping starts. *For Buttonholes:* With right side facing you, work 5 rows sc around entire front and neck edges, place buttonholes evenly spaced on the 3rd row, between bottom of garment and start of V shaping. Make buttonholes on the right for girls, on the left for boys. To make buttonholes, ch 2, sk 2. On the 4th row, make 2 sc in the ch-2 sp.

CREW NECK PULLOVER

Children's Sizes: Directions are for size 4. Changes for size 6, 8, 10, 12, and 14 are in parentheses.
Materials: 12 (12, 14, 16, 16, 20) oz knitting worsted
Needles: #8; crochet hook #5
Gauge: 5 sts = 1 inch; 5 rows = 1 inch

Front, Back, and Sleeves:

Starting at back, cast on 56 (60, 64, 66, 70, 74) sts. K each row in garter st for 10 rows, then k 1 row, p 1 row in stockinette st till 10 (11, 12, 13, 14, 15) inches from beg. At beg of next 2 rows, cast on 53 (56, 59, 62, 65, 68) sts (sleeves). Continue in stockinette st on all sts for 4 (4½, 5, 5½, 6, 6½) inches. Work across 69 (74, 79, 82, 86, 91) sts, join new ball of yarn, bind off center 24 (24, 24, 26, 28, 28) sts (neck opening), work rem 69 (74, 79, 82, 86, 91) sts. Working both sides at once, each with a separate ball of yarn, work for 1½ (1½, 1½, 2, 2, 2) inches more. On next row, work across 69 (74, 79, 82, 86, 91) sts, cast on 24 (24, 24, 26, 28, 28) sts, break off 2nd ball of yarn, and, continuing with same yarn, k across rem 69 (74, 79, 82, 86, 91) sts. Continue all as 1 piece, working till 9½ (10½, 11½, 13, 14, 15) inches. At beg of next 2 rows, bind off 53 (56, 59, 62, 65, 68) sts. Continue front to correspond to back.

Finishing:

Sew underarm seams. Work 1 row sc around bottom of sleeves and around neck edge.

CHILDREN'S CLASSIC BULKY YARN SWEATERS

CREW NECK CARDIGAN

Children's Sizes: Directions are for size 4. Changes for 6, 8, 10, 12, and 14 are in parentheses.
Materials: 20 (22, 24, 26, 28, 30) oz bulky yarn
Needles: #10½; crochet hook K
Gauge: 3½ sts = 1 inch

Front, Back, and Sleeves:

Starting at back, cast on 40 (44, 48, 52, 56, 60) sts. K each row in garter st for 6 rows, then k 1 row, p 1 row in stockinette st till 10 (11, 12, 13, 14, 15) inches from beg. At beg of next 2 rows, cast on 36 (38, 40, 42, 44, 46) sts (sleeves). Continue in stockinette st on all sts for 4 (4½, 5, 5½, 6, 6½) inches. Work across 48 (52, 55, 59, 62, 66) sts, join new ball of yarn, bind off center 16 (16, 18, 18, 20, 20) sts (neck opening), work rem 48 (52, 55, 59, 62, 66) sts. Working both sides at once, each with a separate ball of yarn, work for 1½ (1½, 1½, 2, 2, 2) inches more. On next row, work across 48 (52, 55, 59, 62, 66) sts, cast on 8 (8, 9, 9, 10, 10) sts, on other side cast on 8 (8, 9, 9, 10, 10) sts, and continue across last 48 (52, 55, 59, 62, 66) sts. Still working both sides at once, each with a separate ball of yarn, work till sleeve section measures 9½ (10½, 11½, 13, 14, 15) inches. Bind off 36 (38, 40, 42, 44, 46) sts each outside edge. Continue front to correspond to back.

Finishing:

Sew underarm seams. *For Zipper:* With right side facing you, starting at bottom right corner, work 2 rows sc around entire front and neck edges, making 3 sc in each corner st at neck. Sew in zipper. *For Buttonholes:* With right side facing you, work 3 rows sc around entire front and neck edges, making 3 sc in each corner st at neck and placing buttonholes evenly spaced on the 2nd row. Make buttonholes on the right for girls, on the left for boys. To make buttonholes, ch 2, sk 2. On the 3rd row, make 2 sc in the ch-2 sp.

V NECK CARDIGAN

Children's Sizes: Directions are for size 4. Changes for 6, 8, 10, 12, and 14 are in parentheses.
Materials: 20 (22, 24, 26, 28, 30) oz bulky yarn
Needles: #10½; crochet hook K
Gauge: 3½ sts = 1 inch; 4 rows = 1 inch

Front, Back, and Sleeves:

Starting at back, cast on 40 (44, 48, 52, 56, 60) sts. K each row in garter st for 6 rows, then k 1 row, p 1 row in stockinette st till 10 (11, 12, 13, 14, 15) inches from beg. At beg of next 2 rows, cast on 36 (38, 40, 42, 44, 46) sts (sleeves). Continue in stockinette st on all sts for 4 (4½, 5, 5½, 6, 6½) inches. Work across 48 (52, 55, 59, 62, 66) sts, join new ball of yarn, bind off center 16 (16, 18, 18, 20, 20) sts (neck opening), work rem 48 (52, 55, 59, 62, 66) sts. Working both sides at once, each with a separate ball of yarn, work for 1½ (1½, 1½, 2, 2, 2) inches more. Continue working both sides at once, each with a separate ball of yarn, inc 1 st at each neck edge, every other row, 8 (8, 9, 9, 10, 10) times. When sleeve section measures 9½ (10½, 11½, 13, 14, 15) inches, bind off 36 (38, 40, 42, 44, 46) sts each outside edge.

Finishing:

Sew underarm seams. *For Zipper*: With right side facing you, starting at bottom right corner, work 2 rows sc around entire front and neck edges. Sew in zipper up to where V shaping starts. *For Buttonholes*: With right side facing you, work 3 rows sc around entire front and neck edges, place buttonholes evenly spaced on the 2nd row, between bottom of garment and start of V shaping. Make buttonholes on the right for girls, on the left for boys. To make buttonholes, ch 2, sk 2. On the 3rd row, make 2 sc in the ch-2 sp.

Figure 19. The classic V neck raglan cardigan in this photograph has a rugged look. This is partly due to the yarn used, but mostly due to the oversized buttons. Remember that buttons, too, can completely transform the look of your sweater. Yarn: Nantuck by Columbia-Minerva.

Figure 20. A classic pullover with V neck. Rolled-up sleeves can be done as shown or they can be knitted with a turning ridge and reversed stitches as you'll see in projects in Part III. Yarn: Nantuck by Columbia-Minerva.

CREW NECK PULLOVER

Children's Sizes: Directions are for size 4. Changes for 6, 8, 10, 12, and 14 are in parentheses.
Materials: 20 (22, 24, 26, 28, 30) oz bulky yarn
Needles: #10½; crochet hook K
Gauge: 3½ sts = 1 inch; 4 rows = 1 inch

Front, Back, and Sleeves:

Starting at back, cast on 40 (44, 48, 52, 56, 60) sts. K each row in garter st for 6 rows, then k 1 row, p 1 row in stockinette st till 10 (11, 12, 13, 14, 15) inches from beg. At beg of next 2 rows, cast on 36 (38, 40, 42, 44, 46) sts (sleeves). Continue in stockinette st on all sts for 4 (4½, 5, 5½, 6, 6½) inches. Work across 48 (52, 55, 59, 62, 66) sts, join new ball of yarn, bind off center 16 (16, 18, 18, 20, 20) sts (neck opening), work rem 48 (52, 55, 59, 62, 66) sts. Working both sides at once, each side with separate ball of yarn, work for 1½ (1½, 1½, 2, 2, 2) inches more. On next row, work across 48 (52, 55, 59, 62, 66) sts, cast on 16 (16, 18, 18, 20, 20) sts, break off 2nd ball of yarn, and, continuing with same yarn, k across rem 48 (52, 55, 59, 62, 66) sts. Continue all as 1 piece, working till 9½ (10½, 11½, 13, 14, 15) inches. At beg of next 2 rows, bind off 36 (38, 40, 42, 44, 46) sts. Continue front to correspond to back.

Finishing:

Sew underarm seams. Work 1 row sc around bottom of sleeves and around neck edges.

WOMEN'S CLASSIC SPORT WEIGHT SWEATERS

CREW NECK CARDIGAN

Women's Sizes: Directions are for size 8. Changes for 10, 12, 14, 16, and 18 are in parentheses.
Materials: 14 (14, 16, 16, 18, 18) oz sport weight yarn
Needles: #5; crochet hook #3
Gauge: 6 sts = 1 inch; 6 rows = 1 inch

Front, Back, and Sleeves:
Starting at back, cast on 96 (102, 108, 112, 118, 124) sts. K each row in garter st for 10 rows, then k 1 row, p 1 row in stockinette st till 15 (15, 16, 16, 17, 17) inches from beg. At beg of next 2 rows, cast on 80 (80, 86, 86, 92, 92) sts (sleeves). Continue in stockinette st on all sts for 6 (6, 6½, 6½, 7, 7) inches. Work across 108 (111, 118, 120, 127, 130) sts, join new ball of yarn, bind off center 40 (40, 44, 44, 48, 48) sts (neck opening), work rem 108 (111, 118, 120, 127, 130) sts. Working both sides at once, each with a separate ball of yarn, work for 3 inches more. On next row, work across 108 (111, 118, 120, 127, 130) sts, cast on 20 (20, 22, 22, 24, 24) sts, on other side cast on 20 (20, 22, 22, 24, 24) sts, and continue across last 108 (111, 118, 120, 127, 130) sts. Still working both sides at once, each with a separate ball of yarn, work till sleeve section measures 15 (15, 16, 16, 17, 17) inches. Bind off 80 (80, 86, 86, 92, 92) sts each outside edge. Continue front to correspond to back.

Finishing:
Sew underarm seams. *For Zipper*: With right side facing you, starting at bottom right corner, work 2 rows sc around entire front and neck edges, making 3 sc in each corner st at neck. Sew in zipper. *For Buttonholes*: With right side facing you, work 5 rows sc around entire front and neck edges, making 3 sc in each corner st at neck and placing buttonholes evenly spaced on the 3rd row. Make buttonholes on the right for girls, on the left for boys. To make buttonholes, ch 2, sk 2. On the 4th row, make 2 sc in the ch-2 sp.

V NECK CARDIGAN

Women's Sizes: Directions are for size 8. Changes for 10, 12, 14, 16, and 18 are in parentheses.
Materials: 14 (14, 16, 16, 18, 18) oz sport weight yarn
Needles: #5; crochet hook #3
Gauge: 6 sts = 1 inch; 6 rows = 1 inch

Front, Back, and Sleeves:
Starting at back, cast on 96 (102, 108, 112, 118, 124) sts. K each row in garter st for 10 rows, then k 1 row, p 1 row in stockinette st till 15 (15, 16, 16, 17, 17) inches from beg. At beg of next 2 rows, cast on 80 (80, 86, 86, 92, 92) sts (sleeves). Continue in stockinette st on all sts for 6 (6, 6½, 6½, 7, 7) inches. Work across 108 (111, 118, 120, 127, 130) sts, join new ball of yarn, bind off center 40 (40, 44, 44, 48, 48) sts (neck opening), work rem 108 (111, 118, 120, 127, 130) sts. Working both sides at once, each with a separate ball of yarn, work for 3 inches more. Continue working both sides at once, each with a separate ball of yarn, inc 1 st at each neck edge, every 4th row, 20 (20, 22, 22, 24, 24) times. When sleeve section measures 15 (15, 16, 16, 17, 17) inches, bind off 80 (80, 86, 86, 92, 92) sts each outside edge.

Finishing
Sew underarm seams. *For Zipper*: With right side facing you, starting at bottom right corner, work 2 rows sc around entire front and neck edges. Sew in zipper up to where V shaping starts. *For Buttonholes*: With right side facing you, work 5 rows sc around entire front and neck edges, place buttonholes evenly spaced on the 3rd row, between bottom of garment and start of V shaping. Make buttonholes on the right for girls, on the left for boys. To make buttonholes, ch 2, sk 2. On the 4th row, make 2 sc in the ch-2 sp.

CREW NECK PULLOVER

Women's Sizes: Directions are for size 8. Changes for 10, 12, 14, 16, and 18 are in parentheses.
Materials: 14 (14, 16, 16, 18, 18) oz sport weight yarn
Needles: #5; crochet hook #3
Gauge: 6 sts = 1 inch; 6 rows = 1 inch

Front, Back, and Sleeves:
Starting at back, cast on 96 (102, 108, 112, 118, 124) sts. K each row in garter st for 10 rows, then k 1 row, p 1 row in stockinette st till 15 (15, 16, 16, 17, 17) inches from beg. At beg of next 2 rows, cast on 80 (80, 86, 86, 92, 92) sts (sleeves). Continue in stockinette st on all sts for 6 (6, 6½, 6½, 7, 7) inches. Work across 108 (111, 118, 120, 127, 130) sts, join new ball of yarn, bind off center 40 (40, 44, 44, 48, 48) sts (neck opening), work rem 108 (111, 118, 120, 127, 130) sts. Working both sides at once, each with separate ball of yarn, work for 3 inches more. On next row, work across 108 (111, 118, 120, 127, 130) sts, cast on 40 (40, 44, 44, 48, 48) sts, break off 2nd ball of yarn, and, continuing with same yarn, k across rem 108 (111, 118, 120, 127, 130) sts. Continue all as 1 piece, working till 15 (15, 16, 16, 17, 17) inches. At beg of next 2 rows, bind off 80 (80, 86, 86, 92, 92) sts. Continue front to correspond to back.

Finishing:
Sew underarm seams. Work 1 row sc around bottom of sleeves and around neck edge.

WOMEN'S CLASSIC KNITTING WORSTED SWEATERS

CREW NECK CARDIGAN

Women's Sizes: Directions are for size 8. Changes for 10, 12, 14, 16, and 18 are in parentheses.
Materials: 16 (20, 20, 20, 24, 24) oz knitting worsted
Needles: #8; crochet hook #5
Gauge: 5 sts = 1 inch; 5 rows = 1 inch

Front, Back, and Sleeves:
Starting at back, cast on 78 (82, 86, 90, 94, 98) sts. K each row in garter st for 10 rows, then k 1 row, p 1 row in stockinette st till 15 (15, 16, 16, 17, 17) inches from beg. At beg of next 2 rows, cast on 70 (70, 74, 74, 78, 78) sts (sleeves). Continue in stockinette st for 6 (6, 6½, 6½, 7, 7) inches. Work across 95 (97, 100, 102, 106, 108) sts, join new ball of yarn, bind off center 28 (28, 34, 34, 38, 38) sts (neck opening), work rem 95 (97, 100, 102, 106, 108) sts. Working both sides at once, each with a separate ball of yarn, work for 3 inches more. On next row, work across 95 (97, 100, 102, 106, 108) sts, cast on 14 (14, 17, 17, 19, 19) sts, on other side cast on 14 (14, 17, 17, 19, 19) sts, and continue across last 95 (97, 100, 102, 106, 108) sts. Still working both sides at once, each with a separate ball of yarn, work till sleeve section measures 15 (15, 16, 16, 17, 17) inches. Bind off 70 (70, 74, 74, 78, 78) sts each outside edge. Continue front to correspond to back.

Finishing:
Sew underarm seams. *For Zipper*: With right side facing you, starting at bottom right corner, work 2 rows sc around entire front and neck edges, making 3 sc in each corner st at neck. Sew in zipper. *For Buttonholes*: With right side facing you, work 5 rows sc around entire front and neck edges, making 3 sc in each corner st at neck and placing buttonholes evenly spaced on the 3rd row. Make buttonholes on the right for girls, on the left for boys. To make buttonholes, ch 2, sk 2 sts. On the 4th row, make 2 sc in the ch-2 sp.

V NECK CARDIGAN

Women's Sizes: Directions are for size 8. Changes for 10, 12, 14, 16, and 18 are in parentheses.
Materials: 16 (20, 20, 20, 24, 24) oz knitting worsted
Needles: #8; crochet hook #5
Gauge: 5 sts = 1 inch; 5 rows = 1 inch

Front, Back, and Sleeves:
Starting at back, cast on 78 (82, 86, 90, 94, 98) sts. K each row in garter st for 10 rows, then k 1 row, p 1 row in stockinette st till 15 (15, 16, 16, 17, 17) inches from beg. At beg of next 2 rows, cast on 70 (70, 74, 74, 78, 78) sts (sleeves). Continue in stockinette st on all sts for 6 (6, 6½, 6½, 7, 7) inches. Work across 95 (97, 100, 102, 106, 108) sts, join new ball of yarn, bind off center 28 (28, 34, 34, 38, 38) sts (neck opening), work rem 95 (97, 100, 102, 106, 108) sts. Working both sides at once, each with a separate ball of yarn, work for 3 inches more. Continue working both sides at once, each with a separate ball of yarn, inc 1 st at each neck edge, every 4th row, 14 (14, 17, 17, 19, 19) times. When sleeve section measures 15 (15, 16, 16, 17, 17) inches, bind off 70 (70, 74, 74, 78, 78) sts each outside edge.

Finishing:
Sew underarm seams. *For Zipper*: With right side facing you, starting at bottom right corner, work 2 rows sc around entire front and neck edges. Sew in zipper up to where V shaping starts. *For Buttonholes*: With right side facing you, work 5 rows sc around entire front and neck edges, place buttonholes evenly spaced on the 3rd row, between bottom of garment and start of V shaping. Make buttonholes on the right for girls, on the left for boys. To make buttonholes, ch 2, sk 2. On the 4th row, make 2 sc in the ch-2 sp.

CREW NECK PULLOVER

Women's Sizes: Directions are for size 8. Changes for 10, 12, 14, 16, and 18 are in parentheses.
Materials: 16 (20, 20, 20, 24, 24) oz knitting worsted.
Needles: #8; crochet hook #5
Gauge: 5 sts = 1 inch; 5 rows = 1 inch

Front, Back, and Sleeves:
Starting at back, cast on 78 (82, 86, 90, 94, 98) sts. K each row in garter st for 10 rows, then k 1 row, p 1 row in stockinette st till 15 (15, 16, 16, 17, 17) inches from beg. At beg of next 2 rows, cast on 70 (70, 74, 74, 78, 78) sts (sleeves). Continue in stockinette st on all sts for 6 (6, 6½, 6½, 7, 7) inches. Work across 95 (97, 100, 102, 106, 108) sts, join new ball of yarn, bind off center 28 (28, 34, 34, 38, 38) sts (neck opening), work rem 95 (97, 100, 102, 106, 108) sts. Working both sides at once, each with a separate ball of yarn, work for 3 inches more. On next row, work across 95 (97, 100, 102, 106, 108) sts, cast on 28 (28, 34, 34, 38, 38) sts, break off 2nd ball of yarn, and, continuing with same yarn, k across rem 95 (97, 100, 102, 106, 108) sts. Continue all as 1 piece, working till 15 (15, 16, 16, 17, 17) inches from beg of sleeve. At beg of next 2 rows, bind off 70 (70, 74, 74, 78, 78) sts. Continue front to correspond to back.

Finishing:
Sew underarm seams. Work 1 row sc around bottom of sleeves and around neck edge.

WOMEN'S CLASSIC BULKY YARN SWEATERS

CREW NECK CARDIGAN

Women's Sizes: Directions are for size 8. Changes for 10, 12, 14, 16, and 18 are in parentheses.
Materials: 40 (42, 44, 46, 50, 50) oz bulky yarn
Needles: 10½; crochet hook K
Gauge: 3½ sts = 1 inch; 4 rows = 1 inch

Front, Back, and Sleeves:
Starting at back, cast on 56 (60, 62, 66, 70, 74) sts. K each row in garter st for 6 rows, then k 1 row, p 1 row in stockinette st till 15 (15, 16, 16, 17, 17) inches from beg. At beg of next 2 rows, cast on 48 (48, 50, 50, 52, 52) sts (sleeves). Continue in stockinette st on all sts for 6 (6, 6½, 6½, 7, 7) inches. Work across 66 (68, 70, 72, 75, 77) sts, join new ball of yarn, bind off center 20 (20, 22, 22, 24, 24) sts (neck opening), work rem 66 (68, 70, 72, 75, 77) sts. Working both sides at once, each with a separate ball of yarn, work for 3 inches more. On next row, work across 66 (68, 70, 72, 75, 77) sts, cast on 10 (10, 11, 11, 12, 12) sts, on other side cast on 10 (10, 11, 11, 12, 12) sts, and continue across last 66 (68, 70, 72, 75, 77) sts. Still working both sides at once, each with a separate ball of yarn, work till sleeve section measures 15 (15, 16, 16, 17, 17) inches. Bind off 48 (48, 50, 50, 52, 52) sts each outside edge. Continue front to correspond to back.

Finishing:
Sew underarm seams. *For Zipper*: With right side facing you, starting at bottom right corner, work 2 rows sc around entire front and neck edges, making 3 sc in each corner st at neck. Sew in zipper. *For Buttonholes*: With right side facing you, work 3 rows sc around entire front and neck edges, making 3 sc in each corner st at neck and placing buttonholes evenly spaced on the 2nd row. Make buttonholes on the right for girls, on the left for boys. To make buttonholes, ch 2, sk 2. On the 3rd row, make 2 sc in the ch-2 sp.

V NECK CARDIGAN

Women's Sizes: Directions are for size 8. Changes for 10, 12, 14, 16, and 18 are in parentheses.
Materials: 40 (42, 44, 46, 50, 50) oz bulky yarn
Needles: #10½; crochet hook K
Gauge: 3½ sts = 1 inch; 4 rows = 1 inch

Front, Back, and Sleeves:
Starting at back, cast on 56 (60, 62, 66, 70, 74) sts. K each row in garter st for 6 rows, then k 1 row, p 1 row in stockinette st till 15 (15, 16, 16, 17, 17) inches from beg. At beg of next 2 rows, cast on 48 (48, 50, 50, 52, 52) sts (sleeves). Continue in stockinette st on all sts for 6 (6, 6½, 6½, 7, 7) sts, work across 66 (68, 70, 72, 75, 77) sts join new ball of yarn, bind off center 20 (20, 22, 22, 24, 24) sts (neck opening), work rem 66 (68, 70, 72, 75, 77) sts. Working both sides at once, each with a separate ball of yarn, work for 3 inches more. Continue working both sides at once, each with a separate ball of yarn, inc 1 st at each neck edge, every 4th row, 10 (10, 11, 11, 12, 12) times. When sleeve section measures 15 (15, 16, 16, 17, 17) inches bind off 48 (48, 50, 50, 52, 52) sts each outside edge.

Finishing:
Sew underarm seams. *For Zipper*: With right side facing you, starting at bottom right corner, work 2 rows sc around entire front and neck edges. Sew in zipper up to where V shaping starts. *For Buttonholes*: With right side facing you, work 3 rows sc around entire front and neck edges, place buttonholes evenly spaced on the 2nd row, between bottom of garment and start of V shaping. Make buttonholes on the right for girls, on the left for boys. To make buttonholes, ch 2, sk 2. On the 3rd row, make 2 sc in the ch-2 sp.

CREW NECK PULLOVER

Women's Sizes: Directions are for size 8. Changes for 10, 12, 14, 16, 18 are in parentheses.
Materials: 40 (42, 44, 46, 50, 50) oz bulky yarn
Needles: #10½; crochet hook K
Gauge: 3½ sts = 1 inch; 4 rows = 1 inch

Front, Back and Sleeves:
Starting at back, cast on 56 (60, 62, 66, 70, 74) sts. K each row in garter st for 6 rows, then k 1 row, p 1 row in stockinette st till 15 (15, 16, 16, 17, 17) inches from beg. At beg of next 2 rows, cast on 48 (48, 50, 50, 52, 52) sts (sleeves). Continue in stockinette st on all sts till 6 (6, 6½, 6½, 7, 7) inches. Work across 66 (68, 70, 72, 75, 77) sts, join new ball of yarn, bind off center 20 (20, 22, 22, 24, 24) sts (neck opening), work rem 66 (68, 70, 72, 75, 77) sts. Working both sides at once, each side with a separate ball of yarn, work for 3 inches more. On next row, work across 66 (68, 70, 72, 75, 77) sts, cast on 20 (20, 22, 22, 24, 24) sts, break off 2nd ball of yarn, and, continuing with same yarn, k across rem 66 (68, 70, 72, 75, 77) sts. Continue all as 1 piece, working till 15 (15, 16, 16, 17, 17) inches from beg of sleeve. At beg of next 2 rows, bind off 48 (48, 50, 50, 52, 52) sts. Continue front to correspond to back.

Finishing:
Sew underarm seams. Work 1 row sc around bottom of sleeves and around neck edge.

MEN'S CLASSIC SPORT WEIGHT SWEATERS

CREW NECK CARDIGAN

Men's Sizes: Directions are for size 36. Changes for 38, 40, and 42 are in parentheses.
Materials: 16 (16, 18, 18) oz sport weight yarn
Needles: #5; crochet hook #3
Gauge: 6 sts = 1 inch; 6 rows = 1 inch

Front, Back, and Sleeves:
Starting at back, cast on 114 (118, 124, 130) sts. K each row in garter st for 10 rows, then k 1 row, p 1 row in stockinette st till 17 (17, 18, 18) inches from beg. At beg of next 2 rows, cast on 86 (86, 92, 92) sts (sleeves). Continue in stockinette st on all sts for 6½ (6½, 7, 7) inches. Work across 121 (123, 130, 133) sts, join new ball of yarn, bind off center 44 (44, 48, 48) sts (neck opening), work rem 121 (123, 130, 133) sts. Working both sides at once, each with a separate ball of yarn, work for 3 inches more. On next row, work across 121, (123, 130, 133) sts, cast on 22 (22, 24, 24) sts, on other side cast on 22 (22, 24, 24) sts, and continue across last 121 (123, 130, 133) sts. Still working both sides at once, each with a separate ball of yarn, work till sleeve section measures 16 (16, 17, 17) inches. Bind off 86 (86, 92, 92) sts each outside edge. Continue front to correspond to back.

Finishing:
Sew underarm seams. *For Zipper:* With right side facing you, starting at bottom right corner, work 2 rows sc around entire front and neck edges, making 3 sc in each corner st at neck. Sew in zipper. *For Buttonholes:* With right side facing you, work 5 rows sc around entire front and neck edges, making 3 sc in each corner st at neck and placing buttonholes evenly spaced on the 3rd row. Make buttonholes on the right for girls, on the left for boys. To make buttonholes, ch 2, sk 2 sts. On the 4th row, make 2 sc in the ch-2 sp.

V NECK CARDIGAN

Men's Sizes: Directions are for size 36. Changes for 38, 40, and 42 are in parentheses.
Materials: 16 (16, 18, 18) oz sport weight yarn
Needles: #5; crochet hook #3
Gauge: 6 sts = 1 inch; 6 rows = 1 inch

Front, Back, and Sleeves:
Starting at back, cast on 114 (118, 124, 130) sts. K each row in garter st for 10 rows, then k 1 row, p 1 row in stockinette st till 17 (17, 18, 18) inches from beg. At beg of next 2 rows, cast on 86 (86, 92, 92) sts (sleeves). Continue in stockinette st on all sts for 6½ (6½, 7, 7) inches. Work across 121 (123, 130, 133) sts, join new ball of yarn, bind off center 44 (44, 48, 48) sts (neck opening), work rem 121 (123, 130, 133) sts. Working both sides at once, each with a separate ball of yarn, work for 3 inches more. Continue working both sides at once, each with a separate ball of yarn, inc 1 st each neck edge, every 4th row, 22 (22, 24, 24) times. When sleeve section measures 16 (16, 17, 17) inches, bind off 86 (86, 92, 92) sts each outside edge.

Finishing:
Sew underarm seams. *For Zipper:* With right side facing you, starting at bottom right corner, work 2 rows sc around entire front and neck edges. Sew in zipper up to where V shaping starts. *For Buttonholes:* With right side facing you, work 5 rows sc around entire front and neck edges, place buttonholes evenly spaced on the 3rd row, between bottom f garment and start of V shaping. Make buttonholes on tne right for girls, on the left for boys. To make buttonholes, ch 2, sk 2. On the 4th row, make 2 sc in the ch-2 sp.

CREW NECK PULLOVER

Men's Sizes: Directions are for size 36. Changes for 38, 40, and 42 are in parentheses.
Materials: 16 (16, 18, 18) oz sport weight yarn
Needles: #5; crochet hook #3
Gauge: 6 sts = 1 inch; 6 rows = 1 inch

Front, Back, and Sleeves:
Starting at back, cast on 114 (118, 124, 130) sts. K each row in garter st for 10 rows, then k 1 row, p 1 row in stockinette st till 17 (17, 18, 18) inches from beg. At beg of next 2 rows, cast on 86 (86, 92, 92) sts (sleeves). Continue in stockinette st on all sts for 6½ (6½, 7, 7) inches. Work across 121 (123, 130, 133) sts, join new ball of yarn, bind off center 44 (44, 48, 48) sts (neck opening), work rem 121 (123, 130, 133) sts. Working both sides at once, each with a separate ball of yarn, work for 3 inches. On next row, work across 121 (123, 130, 133) sts, cast on 44, (44, 48, 48) sts, break off 2nd ball of yarn, and, continuing with same yarn, k across rem 121 (123, 130, 133) sts. Continue all as 1 piece, working till 16 (16, 17, 17) inches. At beg of next 2 rows, bind off 86 (86, 92, 92) sts. Continue front to correspond to back.

MEN'S CLASSIC KNITTING WORSTED SWEATERS

CREW NECK CARDIGAN

Men's Sizes: Directions are for size 36. Changes for 38, 40, and 42 are in parentheses.
Materials: 20 (20, 24, 24) oz knitting worsted
Needles: #8; crochet hook #5
Gauge: 5 sts = 1 inch; 5 rows = 1 inch

Front, Back, and Sleeves:
Starting at back, cast on 90 (94, 98, 102) sts. K each row in garter st for 10 rows, then work k 1 row, p 1 row in stockinette st till 17 (17, 18, 18) inches from beg. At beg of next 2 rows, cast on 74 (74, 78, 78) sts (sleeves). Continue in stockinette st on all sts for 6½ (6½ 7, 7) inches. Work across 100 (102, 107, 109) sts, join new ball of yarn, bind off center 38 (38, 40, 40) sts (neck opening), work rem 100 (102, 107, 109) sts. Working both sides at once, each with a separate ball of yarn, work for 3 inches more. On next row, work across 100 (102, 107, 109) sts, cast on 19 (19, 20, 20) sts, and continue across last 100 (102, 107, 109) sts. Still working both sides at once, each with a separate ball of yarn, work till sleeve section measures 16 (16, 17, 17) inches. Bind off 74 (74, 78, 78) sts each outside edge. Continue front to correspond to back.

Finishing:
Sew underarm seams. *For Zipper:* With right side facing you, starting at bottom right corner, work 2 rows sc around entire front and neck edges, making 3 sc in each corner st at neck. Sew in zipper. *For Buttonholes:* With right side facing you, work 5 rows sc around entire front and neck edges, making 3 sc in each corner st at neck and placing buttonholes evenly spaced on the 3rd row. Make buttonholes on the right for girls, on the left for boys. To make buttonholes, ch 2, sk 2 sts. On the 4th row, make 2 sc in the ch-2 sp.

V NECK CARDIGAN

Men's Sizes: Direction are for size 36. Changes for 38, 40, and 42 are in parentheses.
Materials: 20 (20, 24, 24) oz knitting worsted
Needles: #8; crochet hook #5
Gauge: 5 sts = 1 inch; 5 rows = 1 inch

Front, Back, and Sleeves:
Starting at back, cast on 90 (94, 98, 102) sts. K each row in garter st for 10 rows, then k 1 row, p 1 row in stockinette st till 17 (17, 18, 18) inches from beg. At beg of next 2 rows, cast on 74 (74, 78, 78) sts (sleeves). Continue in stockinette st on all sts for 6½ (6½, 7, 7) inches. Work across 100 (102, 107, 109) sts, join new ball of yarn, bind off center 38 (38, 40, 40) sts (neck opening), work rem 100 (102, 107, 109) sts. Working both sides at once, each with a separate ball of yarn, work for 3 inches more. Continue working both sides at once, each with a separate ball of yarn, inc 1 st at each neck edge, every 4th row 19 (19, 20, 20) times. When sleeve section measures 16 (16, 17, 17) inches, bind off 74 (74, 78, 78) sts each outside edge.

Finishing:
Sew underarm seams. *For Zipper:* With right side facing you, starting at bottom right corner, work 2 rows sc around entire front and neck edges. Sew in zipper up to where V shaping starts. *For Buttonholes:* With right side facing you, work 5 rows sc around entire front and neck edges, place buttonholes evenly spaced on the 3rd row, between bottom of garment and start of V shaping. Make buttonholes on the right for girls, on the left for boys. To make buttonholes, ch 2, sk 2. On the 4th row, make 2 sc in the ch-2 sp.

CREW NECK PULLOVER

Men's Sizes: Directions are for size 36. Changes for 38, 40, and 42 are in parentheses.
Materials: 20 (20, 24, 24) oz knitting worsted
Needles: #8; crochet hook #5
Gauge: 5 sts = 1 inch; 5 rows = 1 inch

Front, Back, and Sleeves:
Starting at back, cast on 90 (94, 98, 102) sts. K each row in garter st for 10 rows, then k 1 row, p 1 row in stockinette st till 17 (17, 18, 18) inches from beg. At beg of next 2 rows, cast on 74 (74, 78, 78) sts (sleeves). Continue in stockinette st on all sts for 6½ (6½, 7, 7) inches. Work across 100 (102, 107, 109) sts, join new ball of yarn, bind off center 38 (38, 40, 40) sts (neck opening), work rem 100 (102, 107, 109) sts. Working both sides at once, each with a separate ball of yarn, work for 3 inches more. On next row, work across 100 (102, 107, 109) sts, cast on 38 (38, 40, 40) sts, break off 2nd ball of yarn, and, continuing with same yarn, k across rem 100 (102, 107, 109) sts. Continue all as 1 piece, working till 16 (16, 17, 17) inches from beg of sleeve. At beg of next 2 rows, bind off 74 (74, 78, 78) sts. Continue front to correspond to back.

Finishing:
Sew underarm seams. Work 1 row sc around bottom of sleeves and around neck edge.

MEN'S CLASSIC BULKY YARN SWEATERS

CREW NECK CARDIGAN

Men's Sizes: Directions are for size 36. Changes for 38, 40, and 42 are in parentheses.
Materials: 44 (46, 50, 52) oz bulky yarn
Needles: #10½; crochet hook K
Gauge: 3½ sts = 1 inch; 4 rows = 1 inch

Front, Back, and Sleeves:
Starting at back, cast on 62 (66, 70, 74) sts. K each row in garter st for 6 rows, then k 1 row, p 1 row in stockinette st till 17 (17, 18, 18) inches from beg. At beg of next 2 rows, cast on 50 (50, 52, 52) sts (sleeves). Continue in stockinette st on all sts for 6½ (6½, 7, 7) inches. Work across 70 (72, 75, 77) sts, join new ball of yarn, bind off center 22 (22, 24, 24) sts (neck opening), work rem 70 (72, 75, 77) sts. Working both sides at once, each with a separate ball of yarn, work for 3 inches more. On next row, work across 70 (72, 75, 77) sts, cast on 11, (11, 12, 12) sts, on other side cast on 11 (11, 12, 12) sts, and continue across last 70 (72, 75, 77) sts. Still working both sides at once, each with a separate ball of yarn, work till sleeve section measures 16 (16, 17, 17) inches. Bind off 50 (50, 52, 52) sts each outside edge. Continue front to correspond to back.

Finishing:
Sew underarm seams. *For Zipper:* With right side facing you, starting at bottom right corner, work 2 rows sc around entire front and neck edges, making 3 sc in each corner st at neck. Sew in zipper. *For Buttonholes:* With right side facing you, work 3 rows sc around entire front and neck edges, making 3 sc in each corner st at neck and placing buttonholes evenly spaced on the 2nd row. Make buttonholes on the right for girls, on the left for boys. To make buttonholes, ch 2, sk 2. On the 3rd row, make 2 sc in the ch-2 sp.

V NECK CARDIGAN

Men's Sizes: Directions are for size 36. Changes for 38, 40, and 42 are in parentheses.
Materials: 44 (46, 50, 52) oz bulky yarn
Needles: #10½; crochet hook K
Gauge: 3½ sts = 1 inch; 4 rows = 1 inch

Front, Back, and Sleeves:
Starting at back, cast on 62 (66, 70, 74) sts. K each row in garter st for 6 rows, then k 1 row, p 1 row in stockinette st till 17 (17, 18, 18) inches from beg. At beg of next 2 rows, cast on 50 (50, 52, 52) sts (sleeves). Continue in stockinette st on all sts for 6½ (6½, 7, 7) inches, join new ball of yarn, bind off center 22 (22, 24, 24) sts (neck opening), work rem 70 (72, 75, 77) sts. Working both sides at once, each with a separate ball of yarn, work for 3 inches more. Continue working both sides at once, each with a separate ball of yarn, inc 1 st at each neck edge, every 4th row, 11 (11, 12, 12) times. When sleeve section measures 16 (16, 17, 17) inches, bind off 50 (50, 52, 52) sts each outside edge.

Finishing:
Sew underarm seams. *For Zipper:* With right side facing you, starting at bottom right corner, work 2 rows sc around entire front and neck edges. Sew in zipper up to where V shaping starts. *For Buttonholes:* With right side facing you, work 3 rows sc around entire front and neck edges, place buttonholes evenly spaced on the 2nd row, between bottom of garment and start of V shaping. Make buttonholes on the right for girls, on the left for boys. To make buttonholes, ch 2, sk 2. On the 3rd row, make 2 sc in the ch-2 sp.

CREW NECK PULLOVER

Men's Sizes: Directions are for size 36. Changes for 38, 40, and 42 are in parentheses.
Materials: 44 (46, 50, 52) oz bulky yarn
Needles: #10½; crochet hook K
Gauge: 3½ sts = 1 inch; 4 rows = 1 inch

Front, Back, and Sleeves:
Starting at back, cast on 62 (66, 70, 74) sts. K each row in garter st for 6 rows, then k 1 row, p 1 row in stockinette st till 17 (17, 18, 18) inches from beg. At beg of next 2 rows, cast on 50 (50, 52, 52) sts (sleeves). Continue in stockinette st on all sts till 6½ (6½, 7, 7) inches. Work across 70 (72, 75, 77) sts, join new ball of yarn, bind off center 22 (22, 24, 24) sts (neck opening), work rem 70 (72, 75, 77) sts. Working both sides at once, each side with a separate ball of yarn, work for 3 inches more. On next row, work across 70 (72, 75, 77) sts, cast on 22 (22, 24, 24) sts, break off 2nd ball of yarn, and, continuing with same yarn, k across rem 70 (72, 75, 77) sts. Continue all as 1 piece, working till 16 (16, 17, 17) inches from beg of sleeve. At beg of next 2 rows, bind off 74 (74, 78, 78) sts. Continue front to correspond to back.

Finishing:
Sew underarm seams. Work 1 row sc around bottom of sleeves and around neck edge.

6. T Tops Crocheted from Bottom to Top or from Side Over

Figure 21. The crocheted version of the crew neck cardigan T top knit from the bottom up. Yarn: Nantuck by Columbia-Minerva.

Crocheted T tops are, happily, very easy to make. They're even easier than knitted T tops, believe it or not. These styles, which can be seen in Figures 21 through 24 are attractive and contemporary. As with knitted T tops, the method you choose—from the top down or from the side over—will not change the shape of the garment. Here again, pattern and color placement will be the determining factors with regard to which method you use. See Figures 4 through 9 on pages 7 and 10 for schematic diagrams.

Remember to be faithful to the gauge. If you cannot maintain the gauge, change your hook size. Also, if your crocheted chain is too tight, work it on a larger hook and then switch back to the correct size. If your chain is too tight at the end of the row, chain 4 instead of 3 when turning. That will help. One more thing: make sure your edges are not pulling.

See page 16 if you are interested in teen or women's large sizes or if you want to make a V neck or turtleneck pullover.

INFANTS' SPORT WEIGHT SWEATERS

CREW NECK CARDIGAN

Infants' Sizes: Directions are for 6 months. Changes for 1, 2, and 3 are in parentheses.
Materials: 4 (6, 8, 10) oz sport weight yarn
Aluminum Hook: #4 or E
Gauge: 5 sts = 1 inch

Back, Front, and Sleeves:
Starting at back, ch 50 (52, 54, 56) loosely.
Foundation Row: 1 dc in 3rd ch from hook, 1 dc in each ch to end of row, ch 3, turn (ch-3 always counts as first dc).
Row 1: Sk first st, 1 dc in each st to end of row, 1 dc in top of turning ch, ch 3, turn.

Repeat Row 1 till 6½ (7, 7½, 8) inches from beg. Ch 28 (30, 33, 36) (sleeve), 1 sc in 2nd ch from hook, 1 sc in each of next 26 (28, 31, 33) chs. 1 sc in each of next 48 (50, 52, 54) sts, ch 28 (30, 33, 36) (sleeve) turn. Make 1 dc in 3rd ch from hook, 1 dc in each ch and each st to end of row, 1 dc in top of turning ch. Continue to repeat Row 1 for 3½ (3¾, 4, 4¼) inches from the added ch. Work across 42 (45, 48, 52) sts, ch 3, turn (neck opening). Work back and forth on these sts for 1½ inches, ending at neck edge. Ch 13 (13, 14, 14) (front), 1 dc in 3rd ch from hook, 1 dc in each ch and each st to end of row. Continue in pat as established till sleeve section measures 7½ (8, 8½, 9) inches, ending at front edge. Ch 3, turn, 1 dc in 2nd st, 1 dc in each of next 22 (23, 24, 25) sts, ch 3, turn. Work back and forth on these sts only till same length as back, end off. Sk center 20 (20, 22, 22) sts at neck opening, join yarn, and work other front side to correspond, end off.

Finishing:
Sew underarm seams. *For Zipper:* With right side facing you, starting at bottom right corner, work 2 rows sc around entire front and neck edges, making 3 sc in each corner st at neck. Sew in zipper. *For Buttonholes:* With right side facing you, work 5 rows sc around entire front and neck edges, making 3 sc in each corner st at neck and placing buttonholes evenly spaced on the 3rd row. Make buttonholes on the right for girls, on the left for boys. To make buttonholes, ch 2, sk, 2 sts. On the 4th row, make 2 sc in the ch-2 sp.

V NECK CARDIGAN

Infants' Sizes: Directions are for 6 months. Changes for 1, 2, and 3 are in parentheses.
Materials: 4 (6, 8, 10) oz sport weight yarn
Aluminum Hook: #4 or E
Gauge: 5 sts = 1 inch

Front, Back, and Sleeves:
Starting at back, ch 50 (52, 54, 56) loosely.
Foundation Row: 1 dc in 3rd ch from hook, 1 dc in each ch to end of row, ch 3, turn (ch-3 always counts as first dc).
Row 1: Sk first st, 1 dc in each st to end of row, 1 dc in top of turning ch, ch 3, turn.

Repeat Row 1 till 6½ (7, 7½, 8) inches from beg. Ch 28 (30, 33, 36) (sleeve), 1 sc in 2nd ch from hook, 1 sc in each of next 26 (28, 31, 33) chs, 1 dc in each of next 48 (50, 52, 54) sts, ch 29 (31, 34, 36) (sleeve), turn. Make 1 dc in 3rd ch from hook, 1 dc in each ch and each st to end of row, 1 dc in top of turning ch. Continue to repeat Row 1 for 3½ (3¾, 4, 4¼) inches from the added ch. Work across 40 (44, 48, 52) sts, ch 3, turn (neck opening). Work back and forth on these sts for 1½ inches, ending at neck edge. Continue in pat till sleeve section measures 7½ (8, 8½, 9) inches, *and at the same time* inc 1 st at neck edge, every row, 10 (10, 11, 11) times, ending at front edge. Ch 3, turn, 1 dc in 2nd st, 1 dc in each of next 22 (23, 24, 25) sts, ch 3, turn. Work back and forth on these sts only till same length as back, end off. Sk center 20 (20, 22, 22) sts at neck opening, join yarn, and work other side to correspond, end off.

Finishing:
Sew underarm seams. *For Zipper:* With right side facing you, starting at bottom right corner, work 2 rows sc around entire front and neck edges. Sew in zipper up to where V shaping starts. *For Buttonholes:* With right side facing you, work 5 rows sc around entire front and neck edges, place buttonholes evenly spaced on the 3rd row, between bottom of garment and start of V shaping. Make buttonholes on the right for girls, on the left for boys. To make buttonholes, ch 2, sk 2. On the 4th row, make 2 sc in the ch-2 sp.

CREW NECK PULLOVER

Infants' Sizes: Directions are for 6 months. Changes for 1, 2, and 3 are in parentheses.
Materials: 4 (6, 8, 10) oz sport weight yarn
Aluminum Hook: #4 or E
Gauge: 5 sts = 1 inch

Front, Back, and Sleeves:
Starting at back, ch 50 (52, 54, 56) loosely.
Foundation Row: 1 dc in 3rd ch from hook, 1 dc in each ch to end of row, ch 3 turn (ch-3 always counts as first dc).
Row 1: Sk first st, 1 dc in each st to end of row, 1 dc in top of turning ch, ch 3, turn.

Repeat Row 1 till 6½ (7, 7½, 8) inches from beg. Ch 28 (30, 33, 36) (sleeve) 1 sc in 2nd ch from hook, 1 sc in each of next 26 (28, 31, 33) chs, 1 sc in each of next 48 (50, 52, 54) sts, ch 28 (30, 33, 36) (sleeve), turn. Make 1 dc in 3rd ch from hook, 1 dc in each ch and each st to end of row, 1 dc in top of turning ch. Continue to repeat Row 1 till 3½ (3¾, 4, 4¼) inches from the added ch. Work across 42 (45, 48, 52) sts, ch 3 turn (neck opening). Work back and forth on these sts for 1½ inches, ending at neck edge, break yarn. Sk center 20 (20, 22, 22) sts at neck opening, join yarn and work rem 42 (45, 48, 52) sts for 1½ inches. With same yarn, ch 20 (20, 22, 22) and join to other side. Continue as one piece till sleeve section measures 7½ (8, 8½, 9) inches, break yarn. Work center 48 (50, 52, 54) sts, sk 28 (30, 33, 36) sts each side till same length as back, end off.

Finishing:
Sew underarm seams. Work 1 row sc around bottom, neck, and sleeves.

INFANTS' CLASSIC KNITTING WORSTED SWEATERS

CREW NECK CARDIGAN

Infants' Sizes: Directions are for 6 months. Changes for 1, 2, and 3 are in parentheses.
Materials: 4 (6, 8, 8) oz knitting worsted
Aluminum Hook: #6 or G
Gauge: 4 sts = 1 inch

Front, Back, and Sleeves:
Starting at back, ch 42 (44, 46, 48) loosely.
Foundation Row: 1 dc in 3rd ch from hook, 1 dc in each ch to end of row, ch 3, turn (ch-3 always counts as first dc).
Row 1: Sk first st, 1 dc in each st to end of row, 1 dc in top of turning ch, ch 3, turn.

Repeat Row 1 till 6¼ (7, 7½, 8) inches from beg. Ch 20 (22, 24, 26) (sleeve), 1 sc in 2nd ch from hook, 1 sc in each of next 18 (20, 22, 24) chs, 1 sc in each of next 40 (42, 44, 46) sts, ch 20 (22, 24, 26) (sleeve), turn, make 1 dc in 3rd ch from hook, 1 dc in each ch and each st to end of row, 1 dc in top of turning ch. Continue to repeat Row 1 for 3½ (3¾, 4, 4½) inches from the added ch. Work across 31 (33, 37, 37) sts, ch 3, turn (neck opening). Work back and forth on these sts for 2 more rows, ending at neck edge. Ch 10 (11, 11, 11) (front), 1 dc in 3rd ch from hook, 1 dc in each ch and each st to end of row. Continue in pat as established till sleeve section measures 7½ (8, 8½, 9) inches, ending at front edge. Ch 3, turn, 1 dc in 2nd st, 1 dc in each of next 18 (19, 20, 21) sts, ch 3, turn. Work back and forth on these sts only till same length as back, end off. Sk center 18 (18, 18, 20) sts at neck opening, join yarn and work other front side to correspond, end off.

Finishing:
Sew underarm seams. *For Zipper:* With right side facing you, starting at bottom right corner, work 2 rows sc around entire front and neck edges, making 3 sc in each corner st at neck. Sew in zipper. *For Buttonholes:* With right side facing you, work 3 rows sc around entire front and neck edges, making 3 sc in each corner st at neck and placing buttonholes evenly spaced on the 2nd row. Make buttonholes on the right for girls, on the left for boys. To make buttonholes, ch 2, sk 2. On the 3rd row, make 2 sc in the ch-2 sp.

V Neck Cardigan

Infants' Sizes: Directions are for 6 months. Changes for 1, 2, and 3 are in parentheses.
Materials: 4 (6, 8, 8) oz knitting worsted
Aluminum Hook: #6 or G
Gauge: 4 sts = 1 inch

Front, Back, and Sleeves:
Starting at back, ch 42 (44, 46, 48) loosely.
Foundation Row: 1 dc in 3rd ch from hook, 1 dc in each ch to end of row, ch 3, turn (ch-3 always counts as first dc).
Row 1: Sk first st, 1 dc in each st to end of row, 1 dc in top of turning ch, ch 3, turn.

Repeat Row 1 till 6½ (7, 7½, 8) inches from beg. Ch 20 (22, 24, 26) (sleeve), 1 sc in 2nd ch from hook, 1 sc in each of next 18 (20, 22, 24) chs, 1 sc in each of next 40 (42, 44, 46) sts, ch 20 (22, 24, 26) (sleeve), turn. Make 1 dc in 3rd ch from hook, 1 dc in each ch and each st to end of row, 1 dc in top of turning ch. Continue to repeat Row 1 for 3½ (3¾, 4, 4½) inches from the added ch. Work across 31 (33, 37, 37) sts, ch 3, turn, (neck opening). Work back and forth on these sts for 2 more rows, ending at neck edge. Continue in pat till sleeve section measures 7½ (8, 8½, 9) inches, *and at the same time* inc 1 st at neck edge, every row, 7 (8, 8, 9) times and ending at front edge. Ch 3, turn, 1 dc in 2nd st, 1 dc in each of next 18 (19, 20, 21) sts, ch 3, turn. Work back and forth on these sts only till same length as back, end off. Sk center 18 (18, 18, 20) sts at neck opening, join yarn, and work other front side to correspond, end off.

Figure 22. The crocheted crew neck pullover T top crocheted from the bottom up. Yarn: Columbia-Minerva Bulky Yarn.

Finishing:

Sew underarm seams. *For Zipper:* With right side facing you, starting at bottom right corner, work 2 rows sc around entire front and neck edges. Sew in zipper up to where V shaping starts. *For Buttonholes:* With right side facing you, work 3 rows sc around entire front and neck edges, place buttonholes evenly spaced on the 2nd row, between bottom of garment and start of V shaping. Make buttonholes on the right for girls, on the left for boys. To make buttonholes, ch 2, sk 2. On the 3rd row, make 2 sc in the ch-2 sp.

CREW NECK PULLOVER

Infants' Sizes: Directions are for 6 months. Changes for 1, 2, and 3 are in parentheses.
Materials: 4 (6, 8, 8) oz knitting worsted
Aluminum Hook: #6 or G
Gauge: 4 sts = 1 inch

Front, Back, and Sleeves:
Starting at back, ch 42 (44, 46, 48) loosely.
Foundation Row: 1 dc in 3rd ch from hook, 1 dc in each ch to end of row, ch 3, turn (ch-3 always counts as first dc).
Row 1: Sk first st, 1 dc in each st to end of row, 1 dc in top of turning ch, ch 3, turn.

Repeat Row 1 till 6½ (7, 7½, 8) inches from beg. Ch 20 (22, 24, 26) (sleeve), 1 sc in 2nd ch from hook, 1 sc in each of next 18 (20, 22, 24) chs, 1 sc in each of next 40 (42, 44, 46) sts, ch 20 (22, 24, 26) (sleeve), turn. Make 1 dc in 3rd ch from hook, 1 dc in each ch and each st to end of row, 1 dc in top of turning ch. Continue to repeat Row 1 for 3½ (3¾, 4, 4½) inches from the added ch. Work across 31 (33, 37, 37) sts, ch 3, turn, (neck opening). Work back and forth on these sts for 2 more rows, ending at neck edge, break yarn. Sk center 18 (18, 18, 20) sts at neck opening, join yarn and work rem 31 (33, 37, 37) sts for 3 rows. With same yarn, ch 14 (15, 15, 17) and join to other side. Continue as 1 piece till sleeve section measures 7½ (8, 8½, 9) inches, break yarn. Work center 40 (42, 44, 46) sts, sk 20 (22, 24, 26) sts at each side till same length as back, end off.

Finishing:
Sew underarm seams. Work 1 row sc around bottom, neck, and sleeves.

CHILDREN'S CLASSIC SPORT WEIGHT SWEATERS

CREW NECK CARDIGAN

Children's Sizes: Directions are for size 4. Changes for 6, 8, 10, 12, and 14 are in parentheses.
Materials: 10 (10, 12, 12, 14, 14) oz sport weight yarn
Aluminum Hook: #4 or E
Gauge: 5 sts = 1 inch

Front, Back, and Sleeves:
Starting at back, ch 58 (62, 66, 72, 76, 80) loosely.
Foundation Row: 1 dc in 3rd ch from hook, 1 dc in each ch to end of row, ch 3, turn (ch-3 always counts as first dc).
Row 1: Sk first st, 1 dc in each st to end of row, 1 dc in top of turning ch, ch 3, turn.

Repeat Row 1 till 9½ (10½, 11½, 12½, 13½, 14) inches from beg. Ch 39 (41, 43, 45, 47, 49) (sleeve), 1 sc in 2nd ch from hook, 1 sc in each of the next 37 (39, 41, 43, 45, 47) chs, 1 sc in each of next 56 (60, 64, 70, 74, 78) sts, ch 39 (41, 43, 45, 47, 50) (sleeve), turn. Make 1 dc in 3rd ch from hook , 1dc in each ch and each st to end of row, 1 dc in top of turning ch. Continue to repeat Row 1 for 4 (4½, 5, 5½, 6, 6½) inches from the added ch. Work across 54 (58, 60, 64, 68, 72) sts, ch 3, turn (neck opening). Work back and forth on these sts for 1½ (1½, 1½, 2, 2, 2) inches more, ending at neck edge. Ch 16 (16, 17, 17, 18, 18) (front), 1 dc in 3rd ch from hook, 1 dc in each ch and each st to end of row. Continue in pat as established till sleeve section measures 9½ (10½, 11½, 13, 14, 15) inches, ending at front edge. Ch 3, turn, 1 dc in 2nd st, 1 dc in each of next 26 (28, 30, 32, 35, 40) sts, ch 3, turn. Work back and forth on these sts only till same length as back, end off. Sk center 26 (26, 30, 30, 30, 30) sts at neck opening, join yarn and work other front side to correspond, end off.

Finishing:
Sew underarm seams. *For Zipper:* With right side facing you, starting at bottom right corner, work 2 rows sc around entire front and neck edges, making 3 sc in each corner st at neck. Sew in zipper. *For Buttonholes:* With right side facing you, work 5 rows sc around entire front and neck edges, making 3 sc in each corner st at neck and placing buttonholes evenly spaced on the 3rd row. Make buttonholes on the right for girls, on the left for boys. To make buttonholes, ch 2, sk 2 sts. On the 4th row, make 2 sc in the ch-2sp.

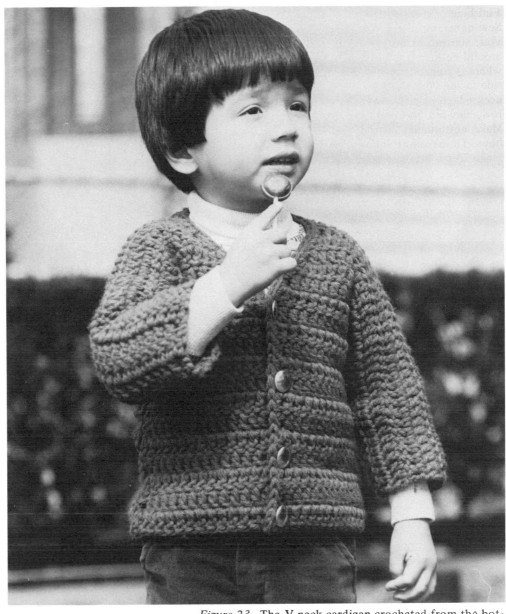

Figure 23. The V neck cardigan crocheted from the bottom up. Yarn: Columbia-Minerva Bulky Yarn.

V Neck Cardigan

Children's Sizes: Directions are for size 4. Changes for 6, 8, 10, 12, and 14 are in parentheses.
Materials: 10 (10, 12, 12, 14, 14) oz sport weight yarn
Aluminum Hook: #4 or E
Gauge: 5 sts = 1 inch

Front, Back, and Sleeves:
Starting at back, ch 58 (62, 66, 72, 76, 80) loosely.
Foundation Row: 1 dc in 3rd ch from hook, 1 dc in each ch to end of row, ch 3, turn (ch-3 always counts as first dc).
Row 1: Sk first st, 1 dc in each st to end of row, 1 dc in top of turning ch, ch 3, turn. Repeat Row 1 till 9½ (10½, 11½, 12½, 13½, 14) inches from beg. Ch 39 (41, 43, 45, 47, 49) (sleeve), 1 sc in 2nd ch from hook, 1 sc in each of the next 37 (39, 41, 43, 45, 47) chs, 1 sc in each of next 56 (60, 64, 70, 74, 78) sts, ch 39 (41, 43, 45, 47, 50) (sleeve), turn. Make 1 dc in 3rd ch from hook, 1 dc in each ch and each st to end of row, 1 dc in top of turning ch. Continue to repeat Row 1 for 4 (4½, 5, 5½, 6, 6½) inches from the added ch. Work across 54 (58, 60, 64, 68, 72) sts, ch 3, turn (neck opening). Work back and forth on these sts for 1½ (1½, 1½, 2, 2, 2) inches more, ending at neck edge. Continue in pat till sleeve section measures 9½ (10½, 11½, 13, 14, 15) inches, *and at the same time* inc 1 st at neck edge, every row, 13 (13, 14, 14, 15, 15) times and ending at front edge. Ch 3, turn, 1 dc in 2nd st, 1 dc in each of next 26 (28, 30, 32, 35, 40) sts, ch 3, turn. Work back and forth on these sts only till same length as back, end off.

Finishing:
Sew underarm seams. *For Zipper:* With right side facing you, starting at bottom right corner, work 2 rows sc around entire front and neck edges. Sew in zipper up to where V shaping starts. *For Buttonholes:* With right side facing you, work 5 rows sc around entire front and neck edges, place buttonholes evenly spaced on the 3rd row, between bottom of garment and start of V shaping. Make buttonholes on the right for girls, on the left for boys. To make buttonholes, ch 2, sk 2. On the 4th row, make 2 sc in the ch-2 sp.

CREW NECK PULLOVER

Children's Sizes: Directions are for size 4. Changes for 6, 8, 10, 12, and 14 are in parentheses.
Materials: 10 (10, 12, 12, 14, 14) oz sport weight yarn
Aluminum Hook: #4 or E
Gauge: 5 sts = 1 inch

Front, Back, and Sleeves:
Starting at back, ch 58 (62, 66, 68, 72, 76) loosely.

Foundation Row: 1 dc in 4th ch from hook, 1 dc in each ch to end of row, ch 3, turn (ch-3 always counts as first dc).
Row 1: Sk first st, 1 dc in each st to end of row, 1 dc in top of turning ch, ch 3, turn.
   Repeat Row 1 till 9½ (10½, 11½, 12½, 13½, 14) inches from beg. Ch 39 (41, 43, 45, 47, 50) (sleeve), 1 sc in 2nd ch from hook, 1 sc in each of next 37 (39, 41, 43, 45, 47) chs, 1 sc in each of next 56 (60, 64, 66, 70, 74) sts, ch 39 (41, 43, 45, 47, 50) (sleeve), turn. Make 1 dc in 3rd ch from hook, 1 dc in each ch and each st to end of row, 1 dc in top of turning ch. Continue to repeat Row 1 for 4 (4½, 5, 5½, 6, 6½) inches from the added ch. Work across 53 (58, 60, 63, 66, 70) sts, ch 3, turn, (neck opening). Work back and forth on these sts for 1½ (1½, 1½, 2, 2, 2) inches more, ending at neck edge, break yarn. Sk the center 26 (26, 28, 28, 30, 30) sts at neck opening, join yarn, and work rem 53 (58, 60, 63, 66, 70) sts for 1½ (1½, 1½, 2, 2, 2) inches. With same yarn, ch 26 (26, 28, 28, 30, 30) and join to other side. Continue as 1 piece till sleeve section measures 9½ (10½, 11½, 13, 14, 15) inches, break yarn. Work center 56 (60, 64, 66, 70, 74) sts, sk 36 (38, 40, 42, 44, 47) each side till same length as back, end off.

Finishing:
Sew underarm seams. Work 1 row sc around bottom, neck, and sleeves.

CHILDREN'S CLASSIC KNITTING WORSTED SWEATERS

CREW NECK CARDIGAN

Children's Sizes: Directions are for size 4. Changes for 6, 8, 10, 12, and 14 are in parentheses.
Materials: 12 (12, 14, 16, 16, 20) oz knitting worsted
Aluminum Hook: #6 or G
Gauge: 4 sts = 1 inch

Front, Back, and Sleeves:
Starting at back, ch 50 (52, 54, 58, 62, 66) loosely.
Foundation Row: 1 dc in 3rd ch from hook, 1 dc in each ch to end of row, ch 3, turn (ch-3 always counts as first dc).
Row 1: Sk first st, 1 dc in each st to end of row, 1 dc in top of turning ch, ch 3, turn.
   Repeat Row 1 till 9½ (10½ 11½, 12½, 13½, 14) inches from beg. Ch 28 (30, 32, 34, 36, 38) (sleeve), 1 sc in 2nd ch from hook, 1 sc in each of the next 26 (28, 30, 32, 34, 36) chs, 1 sc in each of next 48 (50, 52, 56, 60, 64) sts, ch 28 (30, 32, 34, 36, 38) (sleeve), turn. Make 1 dc in 3rd ch from hook, 1 dc in each ch and each st to end of row, 1 dc in top of turning ch. Continue to repeat Row 1 for 4 (4½, 5, 5½, 6, 6½) inches from the added ch. Work across 41 (46, 48, 52, 55, 59) sts, ch 3, turn (neck opening). Work back and forth on these sts for 1½ (1½, 1½, 2, 2, 2) inches more, ending at neck edge. Ch 12 (12, 13, 13, 14, 14) (front), 1 dc in 3rd ch from hook, 1 dc in each ch and each st to end of row. Continue in pat as established till sleeve section measures 9½ (10½, 11½, 13, 14, 15) inches, ending at front edge. Ch 3, turn, 1 dc in 2nd st, 1 dc in each of next 22 (23, 24, 26, 28, 30) sts, ch 3, turn. Work back and forth on these sts only till same length as back, end off. Sk center 18 (18, 20, 20, 22, 22) sts at neck opening, join yarn, and work other front side to correspond, end off.

Finishing:
Sew underarm seams. *For Zipper:* With right side facing you, starting at bottom right corner, work 2 rows sc around entire front and neck edges, making 3 sc in each corner st at neck. Sew in zipper. *For Buttonholes:* With right side facing you, work 5 rows sc around entire front and neck edges, making 3 sc in each corner st at neck and placing buttonholes evenly spaced on the 3rd row. Make buttonholes on the right for girls, on the left for boys. To make buttonholes, ch 2, sk 2 sts. On the 4th row, make 2 sc in the ch-2 sp.

V NECK CARDIGAN

Children's Sizes: Directions are for size 4. Changes for 6, 8, 10, 12, and 14 are in parentheses.
Materials: 12 (12, 14, 16, 16, 20) oz knitting worsted
Aluminum Hook: #6 or G
Gauge: 4 sts = 1 inch

Front, Back, and Sleeves:
Starting at back, ch 50 (52, 54, 58, 62, 66) loosely.
Foundation Row: 1 dc in 4th ch from hook, 1 dc in each ch to end of row, ch 3, turn (ch-3 always counts as first dc).
Row 1: Sk first st, 1 dc in each st to end of row, 1 dc in top of turning ch, ch 3, turn.

Repeat Row 1 till 9½ (10½, 11½, 12½, 13½, 14) inches from beg. Ch 28 (30, 32, 34, 36, 38) (sleeve), 1 sc in 2nd ch from hook, 1 sc in each of the next 26 (28, 30, 32, 34, 36) chs, 1 sc in each of the next 48 (50, 52, 56, 60, 64) sts, ch 28 (30, 32, 34, 36, 38) (sleeve), turn. Make 1 dc in 3rd ch from hook, 1 dc in each ch and each st to end to row, 1 dc in top of turning ch. Continue to repeat Row 1 for 4 (4½ 5, 5½, 6, 6½) inches from the added ch. Work across 41 (46, 48, 52, 55, 59) sts, ch 3, turn (neck opening). Work back and forth on these sts for 1½ (1½, 1½, 2, 2, 2) inches more, ending at neck edge. Continue in pat till sleeve section measures 9½ (10½, 11½, 13, 14, 15) inches, *and at the same time* inc 1 st at neck edge, every row, 9 (9, 10, 10, 11, 11) times, ending at front edge. Ch 3, turn, 1 dc in 2nd st, 1 dc in each of next 22 (23, 24, 26, 28, 30) sts, ch 3, turn. Work back and forth on these sts only till same length as back, end off. Sk center 18 (18, 20, 20, 22, 22) sts at neck opening, join yarn and work to correspond to other side, end off.

Finishing:
Sew underarm seams. *For Zipper:* With right side facing you, starting at bottom right corner, work 2 rows sc around entire front and neck edges. Sew in zipper up to where V shaping starts. *For Buttonholes:* With right side facing you, work 5 rows sc around entire front and neck edges, place buttonholes evenly spaced on the 3rd row, between bottom of garment and start of V shaping. Make buttonholes on the right for girls, on the left for boys. To make buttonholes, ch 2, sk 2. On the 4th row, make 2 sc in the ch-2 sp.

CREW NECK PULLOVER

Children's Sizes: Directions are for size 4. Changes for 6, 8, 10, 12, and 14 are in parentheses.
Materials: 12 (12, 14, 16, 16, 20) oz knitting worsted
Aluminum Hook: #6 or G
Gauge: 4 sts = 1 inch

Front, Back, and Sleeves:
Starting at back, ch 50 (52, 54, 58, 62, 66) loosely.
Foundation Row: 1 dc in 3rd ch from hook, 1 dc in each ch to end of row, ch 3, turn (ch-3 always counts as first dc).
Row 1: Sk first st, 1 dc in each st to end of row, 1 dc in top of turning ch, ch 3, turn.

Repeat Row 1 till 9½ (10½, 11½, 12½, 13½, 14) inches from beg. Ch 28 (30, 32, 34, 36, 38) (sleeve), 1 sc in 2nd ch from hook, 1 sc in each of next 26 (28, 30, 32, 34, 36) chs, 1 sc in each of next 48 (50, 52, 56, 60, 64) sts, ch 28 (30, 32, 34, 36 38) (sleeve), turn. Make 1 dc in 3rd ch from hook, 1 dc in each ch and each st to end of row, 1 dc in top of turning ch. Continue to repeat Row 1 till 4 (4½, 5, 5½, 6, 6½) inches from the added ch. Work across 41 (46, 48, 52, 55, 59) sts, ch 3, turn (neck opening). Work back and forth on these sts for 1½ (1½, 1½, 2, 2, 2) inches more, ending at neck edge, break yarn. Sk the center 18 (18, 20, 20, 22, 22) sts at neck opening, join yarn and work rem 41 (46, 48, 52, 55, 59) sts for 1½ (1½, 1½, 2, 2, 2) inches. With same yarn, ch 18 (18, 20, 20, 22, 22) and join to other side. Continue as 1 piece till sleeve section measures 9½ (10½, 11½, 13, 14, 15) inches, break yarn. Work on center 48 (50, 52, 56, 60, 64) sts, sk 28 (30, 32, 34, 36, 38) sts each side till same length as back, end off.

Finishing:
Sew underarm seams. Work 1 row sc around bottom, neck, and sleeves.

CHILDREN'S CLASSIC BULKY YARN SWEATERS

CREW NECK CARDIGAN

Children's Sizes: Directions are for size 4. Changes for 6, 8, 10, 12, and 14 are in parentheses.
Materials: 20 (22, 24, 26, 28, 30) oz bulky yarn
Aluminum Hook: #10½ or K
Gauge: 5 sts = 2 inches

Front, Back, and Sleeves:
Starting at back, ch 33 (35, 37, 39, 41, 43) loosely.
Foundation Row: 1 dc in 4th ch from hook, 1 dc in each ch to end of row, ch 3, turn (ch-3 always counts as first dc).
Row 1: Sk first st, 1 dc in each st to end of row, 1 dc in top of turning ch, ch 3, turn.

Repeat Row 1 till 9½ (10½, 11½, 12½, 13½, 14) inches from beg. Ch 20 (22, 24, 24, 26, 26) (sleeve), 1 sc in 2nd ch from hook, 1 sc in each of the next 18 (20, 22, 22, 24, 24) chs, 1 sc in each of next 30 (32, 34, 36, 38, 40) sts, ch 20 (22, 24, 24, 26, 26) (sleeve), turn. Make 1 dc in 4th ch from hook, 1 dc in each ch and each st to end of row, 1 dc in top of turning ch. Continue to repeat Row 1 for 4 (4½, 5, 5½, 6, 6½) inches from the added ch. Work across 28 (31, 33, 34, 36, 37) sts, ch 3, turn (neck opening). Work back and forth on these sts for 1½ (1½, 1½, 2, 2, 2) inches more, ending at neck edge. Ch 10 (10, 11, 11, 12, 12) (front), 1 dc in 4th ch from hook, 1 dc in each ch and each st to end of row. Continue in pat as established till sleeve section measures 9½ (10½, 11½, 13, 14, 15) inches, ending at front edge. Ch 3, turn, 1 dc in 2nd st, 1 dc in each of next 13 (14, 15, 16, 17, 18) sts, ch 3, turn. Work back and forth on these sts only till same length as back, end off. Sk center 14 (14, 16, 16, 18, 18) sts at neck opening, join yarn, and work other front side to correspond, end off.

Finishing:
Sew underarm seams. *For Zipper:* With right side facing you, starting at bottom right corner, work 2 rows sc around entire front and neck edges, making 3 sc in each corner st at neck. Sew in zipper. *For Buttonholes:* With right side facing you, work 3 rows sc around entire front and neck edges, making 3 sc in each corner st at neck and placing buttonholes evenly spaced on the 2nd row. Make buttonholes on the right for girls, on the left for boys. To make buttonholes, ch 2, sk 2. On the 3rd row, make 2 sc in the ch-2 sp.

V NECK CARDIGAN

Children's Sizes: Directions are for size 4. Changes for 6, 8, 10, 12, and 14 are in parentheses.
Materials: 20 (22, 24, 26, 28, 30) oz bulky yarn
Aluminum Hook: #10½ or K
Gauge: 5 sts = 2 inches

Front, Back, and Sleeves:
Starting at back, ch 33 (35, 37, 39, 41, 43) loosely.
Foundation Row: 1 dc in 4 ch from hook, 1 dc in each ch to end of row, ch 3, turn (ch-3 always counts as first dc).
Row 1: Sk first st, 1 dc in each st to end of row, 1 dc in top of turning ch, ch 3, turn.

Repeat Row 1 till 9½ (10½, 11½, 12½, 13½, 14) inches from beg. Ch 20 (22, 24, 24, 26, 26) (sleeve), 1 sc in 2nd ch from hook, 1 sc in each of the next 18 (20, 22, 22, 24, 24) chs, 1 sc in each of next 30 (32, 34, 36, 38, 40) sts, ch 20 (22, 24, 24, 26, 26) (sleeve), turn. Make 1 dc in 4th ch from hook, 1 dc in each ch and each st to end of row, 1 dc in top of turning ch. Continue to repeat Row 1 for 4 (4½, 5, 5½, 6, 6½) inches from the added ch. Work across 28 (31, 33, 34, 36, 37) sts, ch 3, turn (neck opening). Work back and forth on these sts for 1½ (1½, 1½, 2, 2, 2) inches more, ending at neck edge. Continue in pat till sleeve section measures 9½ (10½, 11½, 13, 14, 15) inches, *and at the same time* inc 1 st at neck edge, every row, 7 (7, 8, 8, 9, 9) times, and ending at front edge. Ch 3, turn, 1 dc in 2nd st, 1 dc in each of next 13 (14, 15, 16, 17, 18) sts, ch 3, turn. Work back and forth on these sts only till same length as back, end off. Sk center 14 (14, 16, 16, 18, 18) sts at neck opening, join yarn and work to correspond, end off.

Finishing:
Sew underarm seams. *For Zipper:* With right side facing you, starting at bottom right corner, work 2 rows sc around entire front and neck edges. Sew in zipper up to where V shaping starts. *For Buttonholes:* With right side facing you, work 3 rows sc around entire front and neck edges, place buttonholes evenly spaced on the 2nd row, between bottom of garment and start of V shaping. Make buttonholes on the right for girls, on the left for boys. To make buttonholes, ch 2, sk 2. On the 3rd row, make 2 sc in the ch-2 sp.

CREW NECK PULLOVER

Children's Sizes: Directions are for size 4. Changes for 6, 8, 10, 12, and 14 are in parentheses.
Materials: 20 (22, 24, 26, 28, 30) oz bulky yarn
Aluminum Hook: #10½ or K
Gauge: 5 sts = 2 inches

Front, Back, and Sleeves:
Starting at back, ch 33 (35, 37, 39, 41, 43) loosely.
Foundation Row: 1 dc in 4th ch from hook, 1 dc in each ch to end of row, ch 3, turn (ch-3 always counts as first dc).
Row 1: Sk first st, 1 dc in each st to end of row, 1 dc in top of turning ch, ch 3, turn.

Repeat Row 1 till 9½ (10½, 11½ 12½, 13½, 14) inches from beg. Ch 20 (22, 24, 24, 26, 26) (sleeve), 1 sc in 2nd ch from hook, 1 sc in each of next 18 (20, 22, 22, 24, 24) chs, 1 sc in each of next 30 (32, 34, 36, 38, 40) sts, ch 20 (22, 24, 24, 26, 26) (sleeve), turn. Make 1 dc in 4th from hook, 1 dc in each ch and each st to end of row, 1 dc in top of turning ch. Continue to repeat Row 1 till 4 (4½, 5, 5½, 6, 6½) inches from the ch. Work across 28 (31, 33, 34, 36, 37) sts, ch 3, turn (neck opening). Work back and forth on these sts for 1½ (1½, 1½, 2, 2, 2) inches more, ending at neck edge, break yarn. Sk the center 14 (14, 16, 16, 18, 18) sts at neck opening, join yarn, and work rem 28 (31, 33, 34, 36, 37) sts for 1½ (1½, 1½, 2, 2, 2) inches. With same yarn, ch 14 (14, 16, 16, 18, 18) and join to other side. Continue as 1 piece till sleeve section measures 9½ (10½, 11½, 13, 14, 15) inches, break yarn. Work on center 30 (32, 34, 36, 38, 40) sts, sk 20 (22, 24, 24, 26, 26) sts each side till same length as back, end off.

Finishing:
Sew underarm seams. Work 1 row sc around bottom, neck, and sleeves.

Figure 24. The crocheted V neck pullover crocheted from the bottom up. Yarn: Columbia-Minerva Bulky Yarn.

WOMEN'S CLASSIC SPORT WEIGHT SWEATERS

CREW NECK CARDIGAN

Women's Sizes: Directions are for size 8. Changes for 10, 12, 14, 16, and 18 are in parentheses.
Materials: 14 (14, 16, 16, 18, 18) oz sport weight yarn
Aluminum Hook: #4 or E
Gauge: 5 sts = 1 inch

Front, Back, and Sleeves:
Starting at back, ch 80 (84, 88, 92, 96, 100) loosely.
Foundation Row: 1 dc in 3rd ch from hook, 1 dc in each ch to end of row, ch 3, turn (ch-3 always counts as first dc).
Row 1: Sk first st, 1 dc in each st to end of row, 1 dc in top of turning ch, ch 3, turn.
    Repeat Row 1 till 15 (15, 16, 16, 17, 17) inches from beg. Ch 62 (64, 66, 68, 70, 72) (sleeve), 1 sc in 2nd ch from hook, 1 sc in each of the next 60 (62, 64, 66, 68, 70) chs, 1 sc in each of next 78 (82, 86, 90, 94, 98) sts, ch 62 (64, 66, 68, 70, 72) (sleeve), turn. Make 1 dc in 3rd ch from hook, 1 dc in each ch and each st to end of row, 1 dc in top of turning ch. Continue to repeat Row 1 till 6 (6½, 6½, 6½, 7, 7½) inches from the added ch. Work across 85 (89, 92, 96, 99, 103) sts, ch 3, turn (neck opening). Work back and forth on these sts for 3 inches more, ending at neck edge. Ch 17 (17, 18, 18, 19, 19) (front), 1 dc in 3rd ch from hook, 1 dc in each ch and each st to end of row. Continue in pat as established till sleeve section measures 15 (15, 16, 16, 17, 17) inches from beg of sleeve, ending at front edge. Ch 3, turn, 1 dc in 2nd st, 1 dc in each of next 37 (39, 41, 43, 45, 47) sts, ch 3, turn. Work back and forth on these sts only till same length as back, end off. Sk center 28 (28, 30, 30, 32, 32) sts at neck opening, join yarn and work other front side to correspond, end off.

Finishing:
Sew underarm seams. *For Zipper:* With right side facing you, starting at bottom right corner, work 2 rows sc around entire front and neck edges, making 3 sc in each corner st at neck. Sew in zipper. *For Buttonholes:* With right side facing you, work 5 rows sc around entire front and neck edges, making 3 sc in each corner st at neck and placing buttonholes evenly spaced on the 3rd row. Make buttonholes on the right for girls, on the left for boys. To make buttonholes, ch 2, sk 2 sts. On the 4th row, make 2 sc in the ch-2 sp.

V NECK CARDIGAN

Women's Sizes: Directions are for size 8. Changes for sizes 10, 12, 14, 16, and 18 are in parentheses.
Materials: 14 (14, 16, 16, 18, 18) oz sport weight yarn
Aluminum Hook: #4 or E
Gauge: 5 sts = 1 inch

Front, Back, and Sleeves:
Starting at back, ch 80 (84, 88, 92, 96, 100) loosely.
Foundation Row: 1 dc in 3rd ch from hook, 1 dc in each ch to end of row, ch 3, turn (ch-3 always counts as first dc).
Row 1: Sk first st, 1 dc in each st to end of row, 1 dc in top of turning ch, ch 3, turn.
    Repeat Row 1 till 15 (15, 16, 16, 17, 17) inches from beg. Ch 62 (64, 66, 68, 70, 72) (sleeve), 1 sc in 2nd ch from hook, 1 sc in each of the next 60 (62, 64, 66, 68, 70) chs, 1 sc in each of next 78 (82, 86, 90, 94, 98) sts, ch 62 (64, 66, 68, 70, 72) (sleeve), turn. Make 1 dc in 3rd ch from hook, 1 dc in each ch and each st to end of row, 1 dc in top of turning ch. Continue to repeat Row 1 till 6 (6½, 6½, 6½, 7, 7½) inches from the added ch. Work across 85 (89, 92, 96, 99, 103) sts, ch 3, turn (neck opening). Work back and forth on these sts for 3 inches more, ending at neck edge. Continue in pat till sleeve section measures 15 (15, 16, 16, 17, 17) inches, *and at the same time,* inc 1 st at neck edge, every row, 14 (14, 15, 15, 16, 16) times, ending at front edge. Ch 3, turn, 1 dc in 2nd st, 1 dc in each of next 37 (39, 41, 43, 45, 47) sts, ch 3, turn. Work back and forth on these sts only till same length as back, end off. Sk center 28 (28, 30, 30, 32, 32) sts at neck opening, join yarn, and work to correspond, end off.

Finishing:
Sew underarm seams. *For Zipper:* With right side facing you, starting at bottom right corner, work 2 rows sc around entire front and neck edges. Sew in zipper up to where V shaping starts. *For Buttonholes:* With right side facing you, work 5 rows sc around entire front and neck edges, place buttonholes evenly spaced on the 3rd row, between bottom of garment and start of V shaping. Make buttonholes on the right for girls, on the left for boys. To make buttonholes, ch 2, sk 2. On the 4th row, make 2 sc in the ch-2 sp.

CREW NECK PULLOVER

Women's Sizes: Directions are for size 8. Changes for 10, 12, 14, 16, and 18 are in parentheses.
Materials: 14 (14, 16, 16, 18, 18) oz sport weight yarn
Aluminum Hook: #4 or E
Gauge: 5 sts = 1 inch

Front, Back, and Sleeves:
Starting at back, ch 80 (84, 88, 92, 96, 100) loosely.
Foundation Row: 1 dc in 3rd ch from hook, 1 dc in each ch to end of row, ch 3, turn (ch-3 always counts as first dc).
Row 1: Sk first st, 1 dc in each st to end of row, 1 dc in top of turning ch, ch 3, turn.

Repeat Row 1 till 15 (15, 16, 16, 17, 17) inches from beg. Ch 62 (64, 66, 68, 70, 72) (sleeve), make 1 sc in 2nd ch from hook, 1 sc in each of next 60 (62, 64, 66, 68, 70) (sleeve), turn. Make 1 dc in 3rd ch from hook, 1 dc in each ch and each st to end of row, 1 dc in top of turning ch. Continue to repeat Row 1 till 6 (6, 6½, 6½, 7, 7½) inches from the added ch. Work across 85 (89, 92, 96, 99, 103) sts, ch 3, turn (neck opening). Work back and forth on these sts for 3 inches more, ending at neck edge, break yarn. Sk center 28 (28, 30, 30, 32, 32) sts at neck opening, join yarn, and work rem 85 (89, 92, 96, 99, 103) sts for 3 inches. With same yarn ch 28 (28, 30, 30, 32, 32) and join to other side. Continue as 1 piece till sleeve section measures 15 (15, 16, 16, 17, 17) inches, break yarn. Work on center 78 (82, 86, 90, 94, 98) sts, sk 62 (64, 66, 68, 70, 72) sts each side till same length as back, end off.

Finishing:
Sew underarm seams. Work 2 rows sc around bottom, neck, and sleeves.

WOMEN'S CLASSIC KNITTING WORSTED SWEATERS

CREW NECK CARDIGAN

Women's Sizes: Directions are for size 8. Changes for 10, 12, 14, 16, and 18 are in parentheses.
Materials: 16 (20, 20, 20, 24, 24) oz knitting worsted
Aluminum Hook: #6 or G
Gauge: 4 sts = 1 inch

Front, Back, and Sleeves:
Starting at back, ch 66 (70, 74, 78, 82, 86) loosely.
Foundation Row: 1 dc in 3rd ch from hook, 1 dc in each ch to end of row, ch 3, turn (ch-3 always counts as first dc).
Row 1: Sk first st, 1 dc in each st to end of row, 1 dc in top of turning ch, ch 3, turn.

Repeat Row 1 till 15 (15, 16, 16, 17, 17) inches from beg. Ch 48 (50, 52, 54, 56, 58) (sleeve), 1 sc in 2nd ch from hook, 1 sc in each of the next 46 (48, 50, 52, 54, 56) chs, 1 sc in each of next 64 (68, 72, 76, 80, 84) sts, ch 48 (50, 52, 54, 56, 58) (sleeve), turn. Make 1 dc in 3rd ch from hook, 1 dc in each ch and each st to end of row, 1 dc in top of turning ch. Continue to repeat row 1 for 6 (6, 6½, 6½, 7, 7½) inches from the added ch. Work across 65 (69, 72, 76, 78, 82) sts, ch 3, turn (neck opening). Work back and forth on these sts for 3 inches more, ending at neck edge. Ch 18 (18, 19, 19, 21, 21) (front), 1 dc in 3rd ch from hook, 1 dc in each ch and each st to end of row. Continue in pat as established till sleeve section measures 15 (15, 16, 16, 17, 17) inches, ending at front edge. Ch 3, turn, 1 dc in 2nd st, 1 dc in each of next 30 (32, 34, 36, 38, 40) sts, ch 3, turn. Work back and forth on these sts only till same length as back, end off. Sk center 30 (30, 32, 32, 36, 36) sts at neck opening, join yarn, and work other front side to correspond, end off.

Finishing:
Sew underarm seams. *For Zipper:* With right side facing you, starting at bottom right corner, work 2 rows sc around entire front and neck edges, making 3 sc in each corner st at neck. Sew in zipper. *For Buttonholes:* With right side facing you, work 5 rows sc around entire front and neck edges, making 3 sc in each corner st at neck and placing buttonholes evenly spaced on the 3rd row. Make buttonholes on the right for girls, on the left for boys. To make buttonholes, ch 2, sk 2 sts. On the 4th row, make 2 sc in the ch-2 sp.

V NECK CARDIGAN

Women's Sizes: Directions are for size 8. Changes for 10 12, 14, 16, and 18 are in parentheses.
Materials: 20 (20, 20, 24, 24) oz knitting worsted
Aluminum Hook: #6 or G
Gauge: 4 sts = 1 inch

Front, Back, and Sleeves:
Starting at back, ch 66 (70, 74, 78, 82, 86) loosely.
Foundation Row: 1 dc in 3rd ch from hook, 1 dc in each ch to end of row, ch 3, turn (ch-3 always counts as first dc).
Row 1: Sk first st, 1 dc in each st to end of row, 1 dc in top of turning ch, ch 3, turn.

Repeat Row 1 till 15 (15, 16, 16, 17, 17) inches from beg. Ch 48 (50, 52, 54, 56, 58) (sleeve), 1 sc in 2nd ch from hook, 1 sc in each of the next 46 (48, 50, 52, 54, 56) chs, 1 sc in each of next 64 (68, 72, 76, 80, 84) sts, ch 48 (50, 52, 54, 56, 58) (sleeve), turn. Make 1 dc in 3rd ch from hook, 1 dc in each ch and each st to end of row, 1 dc in top of turning ch. Continue to repeat Row 1 for 6 (6½, 6½, 7, 7½) inches from the added ch. Work across 65 (69, 72, 76, 78, 82) sts, ch 3, turn (neck opening). Work back and forth on these sts for 3 inches more, ending at neck edge. Continue in pat till sleeve section measures 15 (15, 16, 16, 17, 17) inches, *and at the same time* inc 1 st at neck edge, every row, 15 (15, 16, 16, 18, 18) times. Ch 3, turn, 1 dc in 2nd st, 1 dc in each of next 30 (32, 34, 36, 38, 40) sts, ch 3, turn. Work back and forth on these sts till same length as back, end off. Sk center 30 (30, 32, 32, 36, 36) sts at neck opening, join yarn, and work other side to correspond, end off.

Finishing:
Sew underarm seams. *For Zipper*: With right side facing you, starting at bottom right corner, work 2 rows sc around entire front and neck edges. Sew in zipper up to where V shaping starts. *For Buttonholes*: With right side facing you, work 5 rows sc around entire front and neck edges, place buttonholes evenly spaced on the 3rd row, between bottom of garment and start of V shaping. Make buttonholes on the right for girls, on the left for boys. To make buttonholes, ch 2, sk 2. On the 4th row, make 2 sc in the ch-2 sp.

CREW NECK PULLOVER

Women's Sizes: Directions are for size 8. Changes for 10, 12, 14, 16, and 18 are in parentheses.
Materials: 16 (20, 20, 20, 24, 24) oz knitting worsted
Aluminum Hook: #6 or G
Gauge: 4 sts = 1 inch

Front, Back, and Sleeves:
Starting at back, ch 66 (70, 74, 78, 82, 86) loosely.
Foundation Row: 1 dc in 3rd ch from hook, 1 dc in each ch to end of row, ch 3, turn (ch-3 always counts as first dc).
Row 1: Sk the first st, 1 dc in each st to end of row, 1 dc in top of turning ch, ch 3, turn.

Repeat Row 1 till 15 (15, 16, 16, 17, 17) inches from beg. Ch 48 (50, 52, 54, 56, 58) (sleeve), 1 sc in 2nd ch from hook, 1 sc in each of next 46 (48, 50, 52, 54, 56) chs, 1 sc in each of next 64 (68, 72, 76, 80, 84) sts, ch 48 (50, 52, 54, 56, 58) (sleeve), turn. Make 1 dc in 3rd ch from hook, 1 dc in each ch and each st to end of row, 1 dc in top of turning ch. Continue to repeat Row 1 for 6 (6, 6½, 6½, 7, 7½) inches from the added ch. Work across 65 (69, 72, 76, 78, 82) sts, ch 3, turn (neck opening). Work back and forth on these sts for 3 inches more, ending at neck edge, break yarn. Sk center 30 (30, 32, 32, 36, 36) sts at neck opening, join yarn, and work rem 65 (69, 72, 76, 78, 82) sts for 3 inches. With same yarn, ch 30 (30, 32, 32, 36, 36) and join to other side. Continue as 1 piece till sleeve section measures 15 (15, 16, 16, 17, 17) inches, break yarn. Work on center 64 (68, 72, 76, 80, 84) sts, sk 48 (50, 52, 54, 56, 58) sts each side till same length as back, end off.

Finishing:
Sew underarm seams. Work 2 rows sc around bottom, neck, and sleeves.

WOMEN'S CLASSIC BULKY YARN SWEATERS

CREW NECK CARDIGAN

Women's Sizes: Directions are for size 8. Changes for 10, 12, 14, 16, and 18 are in parentheses.
Materials: 40 (42, 44, 46, 48, 50) oz bulky yarn
Aluminum Hook: #10½ or K
Gauge: 5 sts = 2 inches

Front, Back, and Sleeves:
Starting at back, ch 45 (47, 49, 51, 53, 55) loosely.

Foundation Row: 1 dc in 4th ch from hook, 1 dc in each ch to end of row, ch 3, turn (ch-3 always counts as first dc).
Row 1: Sk first st, 1 dc in each st to end of row, 1 dc in top of turning ch, ch 3, turn.

Repeat Row 1 till 15 (15, 16, 16, 17, 17) inches from beg. Ch 26 (26, 28, 28, 30, 30) (sleeve), make 1 sc in 2nd ch from hook, 1 sc in each of the next 24 (24, 26, 26, 28, 28) chs, 1 sc in each of next 42 (44, 46, 48, 50, 52) sts, ch 26 (26, 28, 28, 30, 30) (sleeve), turn. Make 1 dc in 4th ch from hook, 1 dc in each ch and each st to end of row, 1 dc in top of turning ch. Continue to repeat Row 1 for 6 (6, 6½, 6½, 7, 7½) inches from the added ch. Work across 37 (38, 40, 41, 43, 44) sts, ch 3, turn (neck opening). Work back and forth on these sts for 3 inches more, ending at neck edge. Ch 13 (13, 14, 14, 15, 15) (front), 1 dc in 4th ch from hook, 1 dc in each ch and each st to end of row. Continue in pat as established till sleeve section measures 15 (15, 16, 16, 17, 17) inches, ending at front edge. Ch 3, turn, 1 dc in 2nd st, 1 dc in each of next 19 (20, 21, 22, 23, 24) sts, ch 3, turn. Work back and forth on these sts only till same length as back, end off. Sk center 20 (20, 22, 22, 24, 24) sts at neck opening, join yarn, and work other front side to correspond, end off.

Finishing:
Sew underarms seams. *For Zipper*: With right side facing you, starting at bottom right corner, work 2 rows sc around entire front and neck edge, making 3 sc in each corner st at neck. Sew in zipper. *For Buttonholes*: With right side facing you, work 3 rows sc around entire front and neck edges, making 3 sc in each corner st at neck and placing buttonholes evenly spaced on the 2nd row. Make buttonholes on the right for girls, on the left for boys. To make buttonholes, ch 2, sk 2. On the 3rd row, make 2 sc in the ch-2 sp.

V NECK CARDIGAN

Women's Sizes: Directions are for size 8. Changes for 10, 12, 14, 16, and 18 are in parentheses.
Materials: 40 (42, 44, 46, 48, 50) oz bulky yarn
Aluminum Hook: #10½ or K
Gauge: 5 sts = 2 inches

Front, Back, and Sleeves:
Starting at back, ch 45 (47, 49, 51, 53, 55) loosely.
Foundation Row: 1 dc in 4th ch from hook, 1 dc in each ch to end of row, ch 3, turn (ch-3 always counts as first dc).
Row 1: Sk first st, 1 dc in each st to end of row, 1 dc in top of turning ch, ch 3, turn.

Repeat Row 1 till 15 (15, 16, 16, 17, 17) inches from beg. Ch 26 (26, 28, 28, 30, 30) (sleeve), 1 sc in 2nd ch from hook, 1 sc in each of the next 24 (24, 26, 26, 28, 28) chs, 1 sc in each of the next 42 (44, 46, 48, 50, 52) sts, ch 26 (26, 28, 28, 30, 30) (sleeve), turn. Make 1 dc in 4th ch from hook, 1 dc in each ch and each st to end of row, 1 dc in top of turning ch. Continue to repeat Row 1 for 6 (6, 6½, 6½, 7, 7½) inches from the added ch. Work across 37 (38, 40, 41, 43, 44) sts, ch 3, turn (neck opening). Work back and forth on these sts for 3 inches more, ending at neck edge. Continue in pat till sleeve section measures 15 (15, 16, 16, 17, 17) inches, ending at front edge, *and at the same time*, inc 1 st at neck edge, every row, 10 times. Ch 3, turn, 1 dc in 2nd st, 1 dc in each of next 19 (20, 21, 22, 23, 24) sts, ch 3, turn. Work back and forth in these sts only till same length as back, end off.

Finishing:
Sew underarm seams. *For Zipper*: With right side facing you, starting at bottom right corner, work 2 rows sc around entire front and neck edges. Sew in zipper up to where V shaping starts. *For Buttonholes*: With right side facing you, work 3 rows sc around entire front and neck edges, place buttonholes evenly spaced on the 2nd row, between bottom of garment and start of V shaping. Make buttonholes on the right for girls, on the left for boys. To make buttonholes, ch 2, sk 2. On the 3rd row, make 2 sc in the ch-2 sp.

CREW NECK PULLOVER

Women's Sizes: Directions are for size 8. Changes for 10, 12, 14, 16, and 18 are in parentheses.
Materials: 40 (42, 44, 46, 48, 50) oz bulky yarn
Aluminum Hook: #10½ or K
Gauge: 5 sts = 2 inches

Front, Back, and Sleeves:
Starting at back, ch 45 (47, 49, 51, 53, 55) loosely.
Foundation Row: 1 dc in 4th ch from hook, 1 dc in each ch to end of row, ch 3, turn (ch-3 always counts as first dc).
Row 1: Sk first st, 1 dc in each st to end of row, 1 dc in top of turning ch, ch 3, turn.
   Repeat Row 1 till 15 (15, 16, 16, 17, 17) inches from beg. Ch 26 (26, 28, 28, 30, 30) (sleeve), 1 sc in 2nd ch from hook, 1 sc in each of next 24 (24, 26, 26, 28, 28) ch, 1 sc in each of next 42 (44, 46, 48, 50, 52) sts, ch 26 (26, 28, 28, 30, 30) (sleeve), turn. Make 1 dc in 4th ch from hook, 1 dc in each ch and each st to end of row, 1 dc in top of turning ch. Continue to repeat Row 1 till 6 (6, 6½, 6½, 7, 7½) inches from the added ch. Work across 37 (38, 40, 41, 43, 44) sts, ch 3, turn (neck opening). Work back and forth on these sts for 3 inches more, ending at neck edge, break yarn. Sk the center 20 (20, 22, 22, 24, 24) sts at neck opening, join yarn, and work rem 37 (38, 40, 41, 43, 44) sts for 3 inches. With same yarn, ch 20 (20, 22, 22, 24, 24) and join to other side. Continue as 1 piece till sleeve section measures 15 (15, 16, 16, 17, 17) inches, break yarn. Work on center 42 (44, 46, 48, 50, 52) sts, sk 26 (26, 28, 28, 30, 30) sts each side till same length as back, end off.

Finishing:
Sew underarm seams. Work 2 rows sc around bottom, neck and sleeves.

MEN'S CLASSIC SPORT WEIGHT SWEATERS

CREW NECK CARDIGAN

Men's Sizes: Directions are for size 36. Changes for 38, 40, and 42 are in parentheses.
Materials: 16 (18, 18, 20) oz sport weight yarn
Aluminum Hook: #4 or E
Gauge: 5 sts = 1 inch

Front, Back, and Sleeves:
Starting at back, ch 96 (100, 104, 108) loosely.
Foundation Row: 1 dc in 3rd ch from hook, 1 dc in each ch to end of row, ch 3, turn (ch-3 always counts as first dc).
Row 1: Sk first st, 1 dc in each st to end of row, 1 dc in top of turning ch, ch 3, turn.
   Repeat Row 1 till 17 (17, 18, 18) inches from beg. Ch 70, (72, 72, 74) (sleeve), 1 sc in 2nd ch from hook, 1 sc in each of the next 68 (70, 70, 72) chs, 1 sc in each of next 94 (98, 102, 106) sts, ch 70 (72, 72, 74) (sleeve), turn. Make 1 dc in 3rd ch from hook, 1 dc in each ch and each st to end of row, 1 dc in top of turning ch. Continue to repeat Row 1 till 7 (7½, 8, 8½) inches from the added ch. Work across 99 (103, 105, 107) sts, ch 3, turn (neck opening). Work back and forth on these sts for 3½ inches more, ending at neck edge. Ch 17 (17, 18, 19) (front), 1 dc in 3rd ch from hook, 1 dc in each ch and each st to end of row. Continue in pat as established till sleeve section measures 17 (17, 18, 18) inches from beg of sleeve, ending at front edge. Ch 3, turn, 1 dc in 2nd st, 1 dc in each of next 45 (47, 49, 51) sts, ch 3, turn. Work back and forth on these sts only till same length as back, end off. Sk center 36 (36, 40, 40) sts at neck opening, join yarn, and work other front side to correspond, end off.

Finishing:
Sew underarm seams. *For Zipper:* With right side facing you, starting at bottom right corner, work 2 rows sc around entire front and neck edges, making 3 sc in each corner st at neck. Sew in zipper. *For Buttonholes:* With right side facing you, work 5 rows sc around entire front and neck edges, making 3 sc in each corner st at neck and placing buttonholes evenly spaced on the 3rd row. Make buttonholes on the right for girls, on the left for boys. To make buttonholes, ch 2, sk 2 sts. On the 4th row, make 2 sc in the ch-2 sp.

V Neck Cardigan

Men's Sizes: Directions are for size 36. Changes for 38, 40, and 42 are in parentheses.
Materials: 16 (18, 18, 20) oz sport weight yarn
Aluminum Hook: #4 or E
Gauge: 5 sts = 1 inch

Front, Back, and Sleeves:
Starting at back, ch 96 (100, 104, 108) loosely.
Foundation Row: 1 dc in 3rd ch from hook, 1 dc in each ch to end of row, ch 3, turn (ch-3 always counts as first dc).
Row 1: Sk first st, 1 dc in each st to end of row, 1 dc in top of turning ch, ch 3, turn.

Repeat Row 1 till 17 (17, 18, 18) inches from beg. Ch 70 (72, 72, 74) (sleeve), 1 sc in 2nd ch from hook, 1 sc in each of the next 68 (70, 70, 72) chs, 1 sc in each of next 94 (98, 102, 106) sts, ch 70 (72, 72, 74) (sleeve), turn. Make 1 dc in 3rd ch from hook, 1 dc in each ch and each st to end of row, 1 dc in top of turning ch. Continue to repeat Row 1 till 7 (7½, 8, 8½) inches from the added ch. Work across 99 (103, 105, 107) sts, ch 3, turn (neck opening). Work back and forth on these sts for 3½ inches more, ending at neck edge. Continue in pat till sleeve section measures 17 (17, 18, 18) inches, *and at the same time,* inc 1 st at neck edge, every row, 15 (15, 18, 19) times. Ch 3, turn, 1 dc in 2nd st, 1 dc in each of next 45 (47, 49, 51) sts, ch 3, turn. Work back and forth on these sts only till same length as back, end off. Sk center 32 (32, 34, 34) sts at neck opening, join yarn, and work other side to correspond, end off.

Finishing:
Sew underarm seams. *For Zipper:* With right side facing you, starting at bottom right corner, work 2 rows sc around entire front and neck edges. Sew in zipper up to where V shaping starts. *For Buttonholes:* With right side facing you, work 5 rows sc around entire front and neck edges, place buttonholes evenly spaced on the 3rd row, between bottom of garment and start of V shaping. Make buttonholes on the right for girls, on the left for boys. To make buttonholes, ch 2, sk 2. On the 4th row, make 2 sc in the ch-2 sp.

Crew Neck Pullover

Men's Sizes: Directions are for size 36. Changes for 38, 40, and 42 are in parentheses.
Materials: 16 (18, 18, 20) oz sport weight yarn
Aluminum Hook: #4 or E
Gauge: 5 sts = 1 inch

Front, Back, and Sleeves:
Starting at back, ch 96 (100, 104, 108) loosely.
Foundation Row: 1 dc in 3rd ch from hook, 1 dc in each ch to end of row, ch 3, turn (ch-3 always counts as first dc).
Row 1: Sk first st, 1 dc in each st to end of row, 1 dc in top of turning ch, ch 3, turn.

Repeat Row 1 till 17 (17, 18, 18) inches from beg. Ch 70 (72, 72, 74) (sleeve), make 1 sc in 2nd ch from hook, 1 sc in each of next 94 (98, 102, 106) sts, ch 70 (72, 72, 74) (sleeve), turn. Make 1 dc in 3rd ch from hook, 1 dc in each ch and each st to end of row, 1 dc in top of turning ch. Continue to repeat Row 1 till 7 (7½, 8, 8½) inches from the added ch. Work across 99 (103, 105, 107) sts, ch 3, turn (neck opening). Work back and forth on these sts for 3½ inches more, ending at neck edge, break yarn. Sk center 32 (32, 34, 34) sts at neck opening, join yarn, and work rem 99 (103, 105, 107) sts. With same yarn, ch 32 (32, 34, 34) and join to other side. Continue as 1 piece till sleeve section measures 17 (17, 18, 18) inches, break yarn. Work on center 94 (98, 102, 106) sts, sk 70 (72, 72, 74) sts each side till same length as back, end off.

Finishing:
Sew underarm seams. Work 2 rows sc around bottom, neck, and sleeves.

MEN'S CLASSIC KNITTING WORSTED SWEATERS

CREW NECK CARDIGAN

Men's Sizes: Directions are for size 36. Changes for 38, 40, and 42 are in parentheses.
Materials: 24 (24, 26, 28) oz knitting worsted
Aluminum Hook: #6 or G
Gauge: 4 sts = 1 inch

Front, Back, and Sleeves:
Starting at back, ch 82 (86, 90, 94) loosely.
Foundation Row: 1 dc in 3rd ch from hook, 1 dc in each ch to end of row, ch 3, turn (ch-3 always counts as first dc).
Row 1: Sk first st, 1 dc in each st to end of row, 1 dc in top of turning ch, ch 3, turn.

Repeat Row 1 till 17 (17, 18, 18) inches from beg. Ch 56 (58, 60, 62) (sleeve), 1 sc in 2nd ch from hook, 1 sc in each of the next 54 (56, 58, 60) chs, 1 sc in each of next 80 (84, 88, 92) sts, ch 56 (58, 60, 62) (sleeve), turn. Make 1 dc in 3rd ch from hook, 1 dc in each ch and each st to end of row, 1 dc in top of turning ch. Continue to repeat Row 1 for 7 (7½, 8, 8½) inches from the added ch. Work across 78 (82, 84, 86) sts, ch 3, turn (neck opening). Work back and forth on these sts for 3½ inches more, ending at neck edge. Ch 19 (19, 20, 22) (front), 1 dc in 3rd ch from hook, 1 dc in each ch and each st to end of row. Continue in pat as established till sleeve section measures 17 (17, 18, 18) inches, ending at front edge. Ch 3, turn, 1 dc in 2nd st, 1 dc in each of next 38 (40, 42, 44) sts, ch 3, turn. Work back and forth on these sts only till same length as back, end off. Sk center 36 (36, 38, 44) sts at neck opening, join yarn, and work other front side to correspond, end off.

Finishing:
Sew underarm seams. *For Zipper:* With right side facing you, starting at bottom right corner, work 2 rows sc around entire front and neck edges, making 3 sc in each corner st at neck. Sew in zipper. *For Buttonholes:* With right side facing you, work 5 rows sc around entire front and neck edges, making 3 sc in each corner st at neck and placing buttonholes evenly spaced on the 3rd row. Make buttonholes on the right for girls, on the left for boys. To make buttonholes, ch 2, sk 2. On the 4th row, make 2 sc in the ch-2 sp.

V NECK CARDIGAN

Men's Sizes: Directions are for size 36. Changes for 38, 40, and 42 are in parentheses.
Materials: 24 (24, 26, 28) oz knitting worsted
Aluminum Hook: #6 or G
Gauge: 4 sts = 1 inch

Front, Back, and Sleeves:
Starting at back, ch 82 (86, 90, 94) loosely.
Foundation Row: 1 dc in 3rd ch from hook, 1 dc in each ch to end of row, ch 3, turn (ch-3 always counts as first dc).
Row 1: Sk first st, 1 dc in each st to end of row, 1 dc in top of turning ch, ch 3, turn.

Repeat Row 1 till 17 (17, 18, 18) inches from beg. Ch 56 (58, 60, 62) (sleeve), 1 sc in 2nd ch from hook, 1 sc in each of the next 54 (56, 58, 60) chs, 1 sc in each of next 80 (84, 88, 92) sts, ch 56 (58, 60, 62) (sleeve), turn. Make 1 dc in 3rd ch from hook, 1 dc in each ch and each st to end of row, 1 dc in top of turning ch. Continue to repeat Row 1 for 7 (7½, 8, 8½) inches from the added ch. Work across 78 (82, 84, 86) sts, ch 3, turn (neck opening). Work back and forth on these sts for 3½ inches more, ending at neck edge. Continue in pat till sleeve section measures 17 (17, 18, 18) inches, *and at the same time*, inc 1 st at neck edge, every row, 17 (17, 18, 20) times. Ch 3, turn, 1 dc in 2nd st, 1 dc in each of next 38 (40, 42, 44) sts, ch 3, turn. Work back and forth on these sts till same length as back, end off. Sk center 36 (36, 38, 44) sts at neck opening, join yarn, and work to correspond, end off.

Finishing:
Sew underarm seams. *For Zipper:* With right side facing you, starting at bottom right corner, work 2 rows sc around entire front and neck edges. Sew in zipper up to where V shaping starts. *For Buttonholes:* With right side facing you, work 5 rows sc around entire front and neck edges, place buttonholes evenly spaced on the 3rd row, between bottom of garment and start of V shaping. Make buttonholes on the right for girls, on the left for boys. To make buttonholes, ch 2, sk 2. On the 4th row, make 2 sc in the ch-2 sp.

CREW NECK PULLOVER

Men's Sizes: Directions are for size 36. Changes for 38, 40, and 42 are in parentheses.
Materials: 24 (24, 26, 28) oz knitting worsted
Aluminum Hook: #6 or G
Gauge: 4 sts = 1 inch

Front, Back, and Sleeves:
Starting at back, ch 82 (86, 90, 94) loosely.
Foundation Row: 1 dc in 3rd ch from hook, 1 dc in each ch to end of row, ch 3, turn (ch-3 always counts as first dc).
Row 1: Sk the first st, 1 dc in each st to end of row, 1 dc in top of turning ch, ch 3, turn.

Repeat Row 1 till 17 (17, 18, 18) inches from beg. Ch 56 (58, 60, 62) (sleeve), 1 sc in 2nd ch from hook, 1 sc in each of next 54 (56, 58, 60) chs, 1 sc in each of next 80 (84, 88, 92) sts, ch 56 (58, 60, 62) (sleeve), turn. Make 1 dc in 3rd ch from hook, 1 dc in each ch and each st to end of row, 1 dc in top of turning ch. Continue to repeat Row 1 for 7 (7½, 8, 8½) inches from the added ch. Work across 78 (82, 84, 86) sts, ch 3, turn (neck opening). Work back and forth on these sts for 3½ inches more, ending at neck edge, break yarn. Sk center 36 (36, 38, 44) sts at neck opening, join yarn and work rem 78 (82, 84, 86) sts for 3 inches. With same yarn, ch 36 (36, 38, 40) and join to other side. Continue as 1 piece till sleeve section measures 17 (17, 18, 18), inches, break yarn. Work on center 80 (84, 88, 92) sts, sk 56 (58, 60, 62) sts on each side till same length as back, end off.

Finishing:
Sew underarm seams. Work 2 rows sc around bottom, neck, and sleeves.

MEN'S CLASSIC BULKY YARN SWEATERS

CREW NECK CARDIGAN

Men's Sizes: Directions are for size 36. Changes for 38, 40, and 42 are in parentheses.
Materials: 46 (48, 50, 52) oz bulky yarn
Aluminum Hook: #10½ or K
Gauge: 5 sts = 2 inches

Front, Back, and Sleeves:
Starting at back, ch 53 (55, 57, 59) loosely.
Foundation Row: 1 dc in 4th ch from hook, 1 sc in each ch to end of row, ch 3, turn (ch-3 always counts as first dc).
Row 1: Sk first st, 1 dc in each st to end of row, 1 dc in top of turning ch, ch 3, turn.

Repeat Row 1 till 17 (17, 18, 18) inches from beg. Ch 30 (30, 32, 32) (sleeve), make 1 sc in 2nd ch from hook, 1 sc in each of the next 28 (28, 30, 30) chs, 1 sc in each of next 50 (52, 54, 56) sts, ch 30 (30, 32, 32) (sleeve), turn. Make 1 dc in 4th ch from hook, 1 dc in each ch and each st to end of row, 1 dc in top of turning ch. Continue to repeat Row 1 for 7 (7½, 8, 8½) inches from the added ch. Work across 43 (44, 46, 46) sts, ch 3, turn (neck opening). Work back and forth on these sts for 3 inches more, ending at neck edge. Ch 15 (15, 16, 16) (front), 1 dc in 4th ch from hook, 1 dc in each ch and each st to end of row. Continue in pat as established till sleeve section measures 17 (17, 18, 18) inches, ending at front edge. Ch 3, turn, 1 dc in 2nd st, 1 dc in each of next 22 (23, 25, 26) sts, ch 3, turn. Work back and forth on these sts only till same length as back, end off. Sk center 24 (24, 26, 28) sts at neck opening, join yarn, and work other front side to correspond, end off.

Finishing:
Sew underarm seams. *For Zipper:* With right side facing you, starting at bottom right corner, work 2 rows sc around entire front and neck edges, making 3 sc in each corner st at neck. Sew in zipper. *For Buttonholes:* With right side facing you, work 3 rows sc around entire front and neck edges, making 3 sc in each corner st at neck and placing buttonholes evenly spaced on the 2nd row. Make buttonholes on the right for girls, on the left for boys. To make buttonholes, ch 2, sk 2. On the 3rd row, make 2 sc in the ch-2 sp.

V NECK CARDIGAN

Men's Sizes: Directions are for size 36. Changes for 38, 40, and 42 are in parentheses.
Materials: 46 (48, 50, 52) oz bulky yarn
Aluminum Hook: #10½ or K
Gauge: 5 sts = 2 inches

Front, Back, and Sleeves:
Starting at back, ch 53 (55, 57, 59) loosely.
Foundation Row: 1 dc in 4th ch from hook, 1 dc in each ch to end of row, ch 3, turn (ch-3 always counts as first dc).
Row 1: Sk first st, 1 dc in each st to end of row, 1 dc in top of turning ch, ch 3, turn.

Repeat Row 1 till 17 (17, 18, 18) inches from beg. Ch 30 (30, 32, 32) (sleeve), 1 sc in 2nd ch from hook, 1 sc in each of the next 28 (28, 30, 30) chs, 1 sc in each of the next 50 (52, 54, 56) sts, ch 30 (30, 32, 32) (sleeve), turn. Make 1 dc in 4th ch from hook, 1 dc in each ch and each st to end of row, 1 dc in top of turning ch. Continue to repeat Row 1 for 7 (7½, 8, 8½) inches from the added ch. Work across 43 (44, 46, 46) sts, ch 3, turn (neck opening). Work back and forth on these sts for 3½ inches more, ending at neck edge. Continue in pat till sleeve section measures 17 (17, 18, 18) inches, ending at front edge, *and at the same time,* inc 1 st neck edge, every row, 12 (12, 13, 13) times. Ch 3, turn, 1 dc in 2nd st, 1 dc in each of next 22 (23, 25, 26) sts, ch 3, turn. Work back and forth in these sts only till same length as back, end off. Sk center 24 (24, 26, 28) sts at neck opening, join yarn and work to correspond, end off.

Finishing:
Sew underarm seams. *For Zipper:* With right side facing you, starting at bottom right corner, work 2 rows sc around entire front and neck edges. Sew in zipper up to where V shaping starts. *For Buttonholes:* With right side facing you, work 3 rows sc around entire front and neck edges, place buttonholes evenly spaced on the 2nd row, between bottom of garment and start of V shaping. Make buttonholes on the right for girls, on the left for boys. To make buttonholes, ch 2, sk 2. On the 3rd row, make 2 sc in the ch-2 sp.

CREW NECK PULLOVER

Men's Sizes: Directions are for size 36. Changes for 38, 40, and 42 are in parentheses.
Materials: 46 (48, 50, 52) oz bulky yarn
Aluminum Hook: #10½ or K
Gauge: 5 sts = 2 inches

Front, Back, and Sleeves:
Starting at back, ch 53 (55, 57, 59) sts loosely.
Foundation Row: 1 dc in 4th ch from hook, 1 dc in each ch to end of row, ch 3, turn (ch-3 always counts as first dc).
Row 1: Sk first st, 1 dc in each st to end of row, 1 dc in top of turning ch, ch 3, turn.

Repeat Row 1 till 17 (17, 18, 18) inches from beg. Ch 30 (30, 32, 32) (sleeve), 1 sc in 2nd ch from hook, 1 sc in each of next 28 (28, 30, 30) chs, 1 sc in each of next 50 (52, 54, 56) sts, ch 30 (30, 32, 32) (sleeve), turn. Make 1 dc in 4th ch from hook, 1 dc in each ch and each st to end of row, 1 dc in top of turning ch. Continue to repeat Row 1 till 7 (7½, 8, 8½) inches from the added ch. Work across 43 (44, 46, 46) sts, ch 3, turn (neck opening). Work back and forth on these sts for 3½ inches more, ending at neck edge, break yarn. Sk the center 24 (24, 26, 28) sts at neck opening, join yarn, and work rem 43 (44, 46, 46) and join to other side. Continue as 1 piece till sleeve section measures 17 (17, 18, 18) inches, break yarn. Work on center 50 (52, 54, 56) sts, sk 30 (30, 32, 32) sts each side till same length as back, end off.

Finishing:
Sew underarm seams. Work 1 row sc around bottom, neck, and sleeves.

7. Knitted Raglans and T Tops

Figure 25. Stripes, hoods, and kangaroo pockets are simple variations of the classic. Hoods are made as extensions of the collar and then sewn together down the top. Note the center seam line on the top of the hoods. The pockets are made separately and then sewn on. Yarn: Nantuck by Columbia-Minerva.

Now that you've learned how to knit classics in one piece you're ready to move on to the variations and embellishments that follow.

One of the most interesting features of the knitted classic garment is that it can be changed rather simply into a high-fashion garment. One way to do this is with the addition of some high-fashion trick, such as oversized pockets, shawl collars, belts, or whatever is in vogue at present. Another way to create an entirely different look is to use one of the many interesting yarns that are available today. You may take a very simple sweater and either knit it in a plush, curly yarn, or stripe it, or use one of many patterns, thereby creating a truly original sweater. Just remember to use weights that are similar to the ones called for in the directions.

One variation of knitted raglans that I particularly like is the addition of interesting crocheted edges to a very simple sweater. This is achieved by eliminating all neck, bottom, and sleeve borders and then crocheting around the edges with an interesting border stitch.

Remember that any of these expanded styles can be adapted to any size. Now that you've learned the basic principles, you should have no trouble sizing and designing for yourself. So, if you see a project you'd like for yourself but it's given in a children's size only, go ahead and use your newfound knowledge to make it in your own size.

In general, the possibilities here are endless, with one exception. Patterns with definite top and bottom motifs do not adapt well to this style of knitting. But, all-over texture patterns, cables, stripes, yarn-over trellis patterns, and just about any high-fashion trick you can think of are all good choices.

CHILDREN'S WARM-UPS

The sweaters shown in Figure 25 are each variations of the Children's Classic Crew Neck Cardigan in Chapter 3. All three of the sweaters are zippered; two of the three are hooded; two of the three are striped; two of the three have pockets. If you'd like the striping effect, start the stripes after dividing the yoke. Make as many stripes as you like in widths of your choice. If you are making pockets, just make sure that the striping pattern is the same.

Children's Sizes: Decide whether you want to make the
Materials: sweater in sport weight, knitting wor-
Needles: sted or bulky yarn and refer to the ap-
Gauge: propriate directions in Chapter 3. Fol-
low size, materials, needles, and gauge specifications. If striping, estimate amount of contrasting color yarn (cc) needed and subtract that amount from the total amount of yarn.

Hood:
Using larger needles, add 10 sts to the cast on. Keeping 5 sts each side in garter st, k 1 row, p 1 row in stockinette st for 8½ (9, 9½, 10, 10½, 11) inches.

Yoke, Back, Front, and Sleeves:
Changing to smaller needles, follow directions, still keeping the 5 sts each side in garter st throughout. For striping effect, start stripes after dividing yoke.

Kangaroo Pockets (make 2):
With larger needles cast on 20 (20, 22, 22, 24, 24) sts. Work in stockinette st for 3 inches. If striping, be sure to make same stripes. At outside edges, bind off 8 sts, dec 1 st same edge, every other row, till 8 sts remain, bind off.

Finishing:
Sew underarm seams and hood seam. Work 1 row sc around front and hood edges, do not turn. Ch 1, work 1 row sc backwards over sts just worked, end off. Work same edging around pockets. Sew pockets in place and crochet a chain for hood, using doubled yarn. Weave chain in and out of garter st around front of hood. Sew in zipper.

Figure 26. All three of these sweaters feature cable patterns. Cables look complicated, but once you master the particular stitching sequence, the movements will start to flow and become rhythmic. The sweaters on the right and left, which are basically the same except for the turtleneck, are taught on page 93. Yarn: Nantuck by Columbia-Minerva.

BIG AND LITTLE CABLES

The sweaters on the right and left in Figure 26 and on the right in Figure 27 are cabled versions of the Classic Crew Neck Pullover in Chapter 3. These are explained below. (The sweater in the middle of Figure 26 is explained on page 94 and the sweater on the left in Figure 27 is explained on page 95). For adults, follow the cable pattern given below. For children, omit the rib of knit-4 in the center and work the cable pattern on 20, rather than 24 stitches.

Sizes: Do you want to make the sweater for an in-
Materials: fant, child, woman, or man? Which yarn do
Needles: you want to use, sport weight, knitting wor-

Gauge: sted, or bulky yarn? Once you've decided refer to the appropriate directions in Chapter 3 and follow sizes, materials, needles, and gauge specifications.

Center Cable Pat (for men and women, worked on 24 sts):
Row 1: K across.
Row 2: P 2, k 6, p 2, k 4, p 2, k 6, p 2.
Row 3: Repeat Row 1.
Row 4: P 2, *sl next 3 sts to dp needle, hold to back, k next 3 sts, k 3 held back,* p 2, k 4, p 2. Repeat between *s once, p 2.
Rows 5–7: Repeat Row 1.
Row 8: Repeat Row 2.
    Repeat these 8 rows for center cable pat.

Cable Pat for Sleeve (worked on 10 sts):
Row 1: K across.
Row 2: P 2, k 6, p 2.
Row 3: Repeat Row 1.
Row 4: P 2, sl next 3 sts to dp needle, hold to back, k next 3 sts, k 3 being held, p 2.
Row 5: Repeat Row 1.
Row 6: Repeat Row 2.
Row 7: Repeat Row 1.
Row 8: Repeat Row 2.
    Repeat these 8 rows for sleeve cable pat.

For crew necks, start as directed. For turtlenecks, cast on with larger needles. Work 4 or 5 inches, change to smaller needles, and continue as directed, centering cable pat on front, back, and sleeves.

HAT

The hat shown on the woman in Figure 26 and the man in Figure 27 is made with 2 oz knitting worsted and #5 and #8 needles. Directions for men's sizes are in parentheses. Directions for the hat worn on the boy appear on page 96.
    With #5 needles, cast on 100 (108) sts. K 1, p 1 in rib for 5 (5½) inches. Change to #8 needles and work cable pat as follows:
Row 1: K across.
Row 2: P 38 (42), k 2, p 6, k 2, p 4, k 2, p 6, k 2, p 38 (42).
Row 3: K 40 (44), sl next 3 sts to dp needle, hold to back of work, k next 3 sts, k 3 from dp needle, k 8, sl next 3 sts to dp needle, hold to back of work, k next 3 sts, k 3 from dp needle, k 40 (44).
Row 4: Repeat Row 2
Row 5: Repeat Row 1.
Row 6: Repeat Row 2.
Row 7: Repeat Row 1.
Row 8: Repeat Row 2.
    Repeat these 8 rows for cable pat for 4 (4½) inches, ending with a p row. Shape top as follows:
Row 1: *K 8, k 2 tog, repeat from * across row.
Row 2: P across.
Row 3: *k 7, k 2 tog, repeat from * across row.
Row 4: P across.
    Continue in this manner, dec every k row and always having 1 st less between decs, till about 18 sts rem. Break yarn, leaving a long end. Pull this yarn through rem sts, gather up, and sew seam, weaving ribbed section.

INFANT'S CUDDLE-UP

The jacket worn by the baby in Figure 26 is basically the Infants' Classic Knitting Worsted Crew Neck Cardigan taught in Chapter 3. While it has a cable pattern added to the front, as well as a hood and a zipper, it is essentially the same sweater.

Infants' Sizes: Directions are for 6 months. Changes for 1, 2, and 3 are in parentheses.
Materials: 4 (6, 7, 8) oz knitting worsted
Needles: #5 and #8; crochet hook #6 or G
Gauge: 5 sts = 1 inch

Hood:
With #8 needles, cast on 58 (58, 60, 60) sts. Work as follows:
Row 1: K 5, *p 2, k 1, yo, k 1, p 2, k 1, yo, k 1, p 2,* k across row to last 15 sts, repeat from * to * once, k 5.
Row 2: K 4, p 1, *k 2, p 3, k 2, p 3, k 2,* p across row to last 17 sts, repeat from * to * once, p 1, k 4.
Row 3: K 5, * p 2, sl 1, k 2, psso both k sts, p 2, sl 1, k 2, psso both k sts, p 2,* k across row to last 17 sts, repeat from * to * once, k 5.
Row 4: K 4, p 1, *k 2, p 2, k 2, p 2, k 2,* p across to last 15 sts, repeat from * to * once, p 1, k 4.
    Repeat the last 4 rows till 7½ (8, 8½, 9) inches from beg, ending with Row 4.
    Change to #5 needles, still keeping pat as established. K 1, p 1 in rib on center sts for 1 inch.

Yoke:
With #8 needles k 5, *p 2, k 1, yo, k 1, p 2, k 1, yo, k 1, p 2,* place marker (front), k 5 (5, 6, 6), place marker (sleeve), k 18, place marker (back), k 5 (5, 6, 6), place marker (sleeve). Repeat from * to * once, k 5 (front). Continue pat row 2, keeping pat as established and doing rem sts in stockinette st. Inc 1 st before and after each marker every k row. Work in this manner till there are 48 (50, 52, 54) sts on back section. End with a right side row.

Front, Back, and Sleeves:
Keeping pat as established, finish as for front, back, and sleeves of Infant's Classic Knitting Worsted Sweater— Crew Neck Cardigan.

Finishing:
Sew underarm seams. Work 1 row sc on each front edge and around hood and sew in zipper. Using doubled yarn, crochet a chain for hood and weave chain in and out of garter st at hood edge.

CHILD'S CABLED CARDIGAN

The cabled sweater worn by the boy in Figure 27 is based on the Classic Knitting Worsted Crew Neck Cardigan in Chapter 3.

Children's Sizes: Directions are for size 4. Changes for 6, 8, 10, 12, and 14 are in parentheses.
Materials: 12 (12, 12, 16, 16, 20) oz knitting worsted
Needles: #5 and #8; crochet hook #6 or G; regular cable needle;
Gauge: 5 sts = 1 inch

Figure 27. A cabled crew neck cardigan and turtleneck cable pullover. The pullover is the same one worn by the woman and boy in Figure 26. See page 93 for instructions. Yarn: Nantuck by Columbia-Minerva.

Yoke:

With #5 needles, cast on 69 (69, 69, 69, 73, 73) sts. K 1, p 1 in rib for 2 inches. Change to #8 needles and work as follows:

Marking row: K 3, p 6, k 3, p 0 (0, 0, 0, 1, 1) st, place marker (front), k 3, p 6, k 3, place marker (sleeve), p 0 (0, 0, 0, 1, 1) st, k 3, p 6, k 3, p 6, k 3, p 0 (0, 0, 0, 1, 1) st, place marker (back), k 3, p 6, k 3, place marker (sleeve), p 0 (0, 0, 0, 1, 1) st, k 3, p 6, k 3 (front). Continue as follows:

Row 1: K all across row, inc 1 st before and after each marker (8 incs).

Row 2: K 3, p 6, k 3, p 1 (1, 1, 1, 2, 2) sts, p 1, k 3, p 6, k 3, p 1, p 1 (1, 1, 1, 2, 2) sts, k 3, p 6, k 3, p 6, k 3, p 1 (1, 1, 1, 2, 2) sts, p 1, k 3, p 6, k 3, p 1, p 1 (1, 1, 1, 2, 2) sts, k 3, p 5, k 3.

Row 3: Repeat Row 1.

Row 4: K 3, p 6, k 3, p 2 (2, 2, 2, 3, 3) sts, p 2, k 3, p 6, k 3, p 2, p 2 (2, 2, 2, 3, 3) sts, p 2, k 3, p 6, k 3, p 2, p 2 (2, 2, 2, 3, 3) sts, k 3, p 6, k 3.

Row 5: Repeat Row 1, except twist cables on the ribs of k-6 as follows: sl first 3 sts to cable needle, hold to back of work, k next 3 sts, k sts from cable needle.

Row 6: K 3, p 6, k 3, p 3 (3, 3, 3, 4, 4) sts, p 3, k 3, p 6, k 3, p 3, p 3 (3, 3, 3, 4, 4) sts, k 3, p 6, k 3, p 6, k 3, p 3 (3, 3, 3, 4, 4) sts, p 3, k 3, p 6, k 3, p 3, p 3 (3, 3, 3, 4, 4) sts, k 3, p 6, k 3.

Row 7: Repeat Row 1.

Row 8: K 3, p 6, k 3, p 4 (4, 4, 4, 5, 5) sts, p 4, k 3, p 6, k 3, p 4, p 4 (4, 4, 4, 5, 5) sts, k 3, p 6, k 3, p 6, k 3, p 4 (4, 4, 4, 5, 5) sts, p 4, k 3, p 6, k 3, p 4, p 4 (4, 4, 4, 5, 5) sts, k 3, p 6, k 3.

Continue in this manner, repeating Rows 1–8, always keeping pat as established with new sts added in stockinette st. Work till there are 57, (61, 65, 67, 71, 75) sts on back section. End with a right side row.

Front, Back, and Sleeves:

P across to first marker, place sts just worked on holder, p to 3rd marker, place sts between 2nd and 3rd marker on holder, p to 4th marker, place rem sts not worked on holder. Mark this front and remove all other markers. Do not break yarn. You now have 2 sleeve sections left on needles. Working both at once and joining 2nd ball of yarn for 2nd sleeve, work as follows: Dec 1 st each side of each sleeve, every 1 inch, 7 (8, 9, 10, 11, 12) times. Work even till 10 (11, 12, 13, 14, 14½) inches or 2 inches less than desired length. Change to #5 needles, k 1, p 1 in rib for 2 inches. Bind off loosely in rib. Join yarn at underarm of marked front. P across this front section, turn, k same front, k back section, k other front section. Continue body in 1 piece, keeping pat as established and working till 9 (10, 11, 12, 13, 14) inches or 2 inches less than desired length. Change to #5 needles, k 1, p 1 in rib for 2 inches, bind off.

Finishing:

Sew underarm seams. Work 5 rows sc on each front edge as follows: Starting at bottom right front, work 1 row up front, ch 1, turn. Work 2nd row. On 3rd row make evenly spaced buttonholes. Work 2 more rows. Work other front to correspond. *For Buttonholes:* On 3rd row work 2 chs, sk 2 sts. On 4th row make 2 sc in each ch-2 sp.

HAT

The hat worn by the boy in Figures 26 and 27 is made with 2 oz knitting worsted on #5 and #8 needles.

With #5 needles, cast on 88 sts. K 1, p 1 in rib for 5 inches. Change to #8 needles and work stockinette st for 3½ inches more, ending with a p row. Shape top as follows:

Row 1: *K 6, k 2 tog, repeat from * across row.

Row 2: P across.

Row 3: *k 5, k 2 tog, repeat from * across row.

Row 4: P across.

Continue in this manner to dec every k row, always having 1 st less between decs, till 11 sts rem. Break yarn, leaving a long end. Pull this yarn through rem sts, gather up, and sew seam with same yarn, weaving ribbed section.

GIRL'S BACK-TO-SCHOOL COAT

Bulky yarn and large needles were used to make the coat in Figure 28, which was based on the Children's Classic Bulky Yarn Crew Neck Cardigan in Chapter 3. You will need 2 extra buttons for the back belt.

Children's Sizes: Directions are for size 4. Changes for 6, 8, 10, 12, and 14 are in parentheses.
Materials: 20 (22, 24, 26, 28, 30) oz bulky yarn
Needles: #10½; crochet hook #10½ or K
Gauge: 3½ sts = 1 inch

Cast on as directed and work in k 1, p 1 rib for 4¼ inches. Continue as directed till just before waistline border, but omit border. Continue in stockinette st, inc 1 st at each underarm, every 3 inches, 4 times. Work even till 1 inch less than desired length. Work garter st for 6 rows, bind off. Work garter st on bottom of sleeves also.

Belt:
Cast on 20 sts. Work in garter st for 2 inches, bind off.

Finishing:
Sew underarm seams. Sew belt in place and add 2 buttons. Crochet front border, starting buttonholes 6 inches from bottom.

Figure 28. Perfect for brisk autumn days, the bulky yarn coat in the photograph is an embellished version of a crew neck cardigan. Notice how the collar, longer length, and ornamental belt in the back completely transform the sweater. Yarn: Nantuck by Columbia-Minerva.

BIG, BOLD STRIPED PULLOVER

This is probably the simplest variation possible. The girl in Figure 29 is wearing a striped version of the Classic Crew Neck Pullover in Chapter 3. Start stripes after you have divided the yoke and then make even-sized, evenly spaced rows in a contrasting color (cc) of yarn. Be sure that the sleeve pattern matches the front and back. The effect may be accomplished with two or many colors. It's a great way to use up leftover yarn.

Sizes:
Materials:
Needles:
Gauge:

Do you want to make the sweater for an infant, child, woman or man? Which yarn do you want to use, sport weight, knitting worsted, or bulky yarn? Once you have decided, refer to the appropriate directions in Chapter 3 and follow sizes, materials, needles, and gauge specifications. Estimate the amount of yarn you will need for the stripes.

Cast on as directed and follow instructions till yoke is completed. Divide the inch measurement of the desired length to get striping pat. Finish as directed.

Figure 29. Everyone loves stripes and stripes are a very simple way to add pizzazz to a classic style. Yarn: Aspen by Brunswick.

GIRL'S SUNDAY BEST RAGLAN DRESS

Turning a sweater into a dress is simply a matter of lengthening. The dress shown in Figure 30 is based on the Classic Crew Neck Pullover in Chapter 3. By the way, cable patterns such as the one shown here, do require a bit more concentration, but are well worth the effort.

Children's Sizes: Decide whether you want to make
Materials: the dress in sport weight, knitting wor-
Needles: sted, or bulky yarn. Refer to the ap-
Gauge: propriate directions in Chapter 3 and follow sizes, materials, needles, and gauge specifications.

Cable Pat for Front (worked on 24 sts):
Row 1: P 2, k 4, p 2, k 8, p 2, k 4, p 2.
Rows 2–3: Repeat Row 1.
Row 4: P 2, sl next 2 sts to dp needle, hold to back, k next 2 sts, k 2 held back, p 2, k 8, p 2, sl next 2 sts to dp needle, hold to back, k next 2 sts, k 2 held back, p 2.
Rows 5–7: Repeat Row 1.
Row 8: P 2, sl next 2 sts to dp needle, hold to back, k next 2 sts, k 2 held back, p 2, sl next 2 sts to dp needle, hold to front, k next 2 sts, k 2 being held, sl next 2 sts to dp needle, hold to back, k next 2 sts, k 2 being held, p 2, sl next 2 sts to dp needle, hold to back, k next 2 sts, k 2 being held, p 2.
Repeat these 8 rows for front cable pat.

Cable Pat for Sleeve (worked on 8 sts):
Row 1: P 2, k 4, p 2.
Rows 2–3: Repeat Row 1.
Row 4: P 2, sl next 2 sts to dp needle, hold to back, k next 2 sts, k 2 being held, p 2.
Repeat these 4 rows for sleeve cable pat.

Cast on sts with larger needle, work in k 1, p 1 rib for 3 inches. Change to smaller needle, continue rib for 1 inch more. Continue as directed, centering front cable pat on front sts and sleeve cable pat on sleeve sts. Continue till waistline, change to smaller needles. K 1, p 1 in rib for 2 inches. On next row, inc 10 sts, evenly spaced all around. Change back to larger needles and continue in stockinette st till 1 inch less than desired length. Work garter st for 1 inch, bind off loosely.

Figure 30. A warm wintertime dress with cable pattern and turtleneck is easily accomplished following the directions for the classic crew neck pullover. Yarn: Brunswick.

GIRL'S SOFT LITTLE SWEATER

The mohair sweater in Figure 31 is a version of the Classic Crew Neck Cardigan in Chapter 3. Which yarn do you wish to use for this soft sweater? A mohair blend yarn was used, but any worsted yarn will do, as long as the gauge is correct.

Children's Sizes: Directions are for size 4. Changes for 6, 8, 10, 12, and 14 are in parentheses.
Materials: 6 oz (8, 10, 10, 12, 12) mohair blend in main color (mc); 2 oz mohair blend in contrasting color (cc)
Needles: #5 and #8; crochet hook #5
Gauge: 5 sts = 1 inch

With cc, cast on as directed and work the border. Change to mc and continue yoke for 2 inches. *Break mc and join cc. Work 6 rows of reverse stockinette st (p side is right side). Break cc, join mc, and continue yoke for 2 inches more. Repeat from*. Continue in mc as directed.

Figure 31. It's the soft quality of this sweater that makes it look different, but it is actually the classic crew neck cardigan. Yarn: Darling Yarn by Unger.

TAM

The tam worn by the girl in Figure 31 is made with 2 oz mohair and #8 and #5 knitting needles.

With #5 needles cast on 90 sts, k 1, p 1 in rib for 1 inch. On next row, k across, inc 30 sts, evenly spaced. Change to #8 needle, continue in stockinette st on 120 sts for 2 inches more, ending with a p row. Shape top as follows:
Row 1: *K 18, k 2 tog, repeat from * across row.
Row 2: P across.
Row 3: *K 17, k 2 tog, repeat from * across row.
Row 4: P across.
Row 5: K 16, k 2 tog, repeat from * across row.
Row 6: P across.
Row 7: K 15, k 2 tog, repeat from * across row.
Row 8: P across.

Continue in this manner to dec every k row, always having 1 st less between decs, till 10 sts rem. Break yarn, leaving a long end. Pull this yarn through rem sts, sew seam with same yarn. Wet thoroughly with cool water, shape into tam shape, and let dry.

SHAWL-COLLARED WRAPAROUND

Knit a Classic Bulky Yarn or Knitting Worsted V Neck Cardigan, as directed in Chapter 3 and add a shawl collar. Figure 32 shows the sweater worn by a man; in Color Plate 11 it is worn by a woman. The tweed effect was achieved by using two colors of yarn.

Sizes:
Materials:
Needle:
Gauge:

Do you want to make the sweater in knitting worsted or bulky yarn? Is it for a man or a woman? Once you've decided, refer to the appropriate directions. Follow sizes, materials, needles, and gauge specifications. You will need 6 oz of knitting worsted or 10 oz of bulky yarn to make the collar.

Cast on 12 sts (if working with knitting worsted; cast on 7 for bulky yarn). Work in seed st till same length as front to beg of V shaping. Then inc 1 st on one side only. Repeat the inc on the same side every row, being sure to form new pat as sts are inc, till collar is 9 inches wide. Work even for 16 inches, then dec 1 st same side, every row, till you are back to 12 sts (7sts for bulky yarn). Work even to bottom, bind off.

Belt:
Cast on 9 sts (5 for bulky yarn). Work seed st for desired length.

Finishing:
Sew underarm seams and back of collar. Sew collar to front of sweater, sewing shaped edge to sweater edge and easing fullness of collar at back of neck.

Figure 32. Shawl collars are easy to make and wraparound styles such as this one are casual and easy to wear. The tweed effect, which can be seen in Color Plate 11 is done by holding two strands of different colors of yarn together. Yarn: Nantuck by Columbia-Minerva.

WOMAN'S CROCHET-TRIMMED CARDIGAN

Crocheted trimmings on sweaters can completely transform their look. The sweater on the left in Figure 33 is a good example. Basically, it is the Classic V Neck Cardigan taught in Chapter 3 with trim added at the neckline, cuffs, and bottom. The overall length and the sleeve lengths are shorter, too; and the tie at the waist thoroughly completes the look.

Women's Sizes: Which yarn to you want to use, sport
Materials: weight, knitting worsted, or bulky yarn?
Needles: Once you've decided, refer to the appro-
Gauge: priate directions in Chapter 3 and fol-
low sizes, materials, needles, and gauge
specifications.

Work sweater as directed. When doing sleeves, eliminate decs and make sleeves straight for 10 inches or 3 inches less than desired finished length, bind off. Body is also worked for 10 inches or 3 inches less than desired finished length.

Crocheted Trim:
Row 1: Starting at right underarm, work 1 row sc around entire outside edge, making 3 sc in each bottom corner. Join with a slst to start, ch 3.
Row 2: *1 dc in next st, ch 1, sk 1 st. Repeat from * around. Join with slst to start.
Row 3: Ch 3, 1 dc in each st around.
Row 4: Repeat Row 2.
Row 5: Repeat Row 3.
Row 6: Ch 3, *sk 1 st, 1 dc in next st, ch 3 (yo and pick up a loop around post of the dc just made) 3 times, yo and through 6 loops on hook, yo and through last 2 loops on hook. Repeat from * around.

Work same pat on sleeves.

Finishing:
Make a long chain using doubled yarn. Weave in and out of first row of crochet pat. Sew on buttons and use open row of crochet for buttonholes.

Figure 33. The sweater on the left is a knitted V neck cardigan with crocheted trim while the sweater on the right is a crew neck pullover. Both are delicate and feminine—just perfect for special occasions. Yarn: Frostlon Petite by Spinnerin.

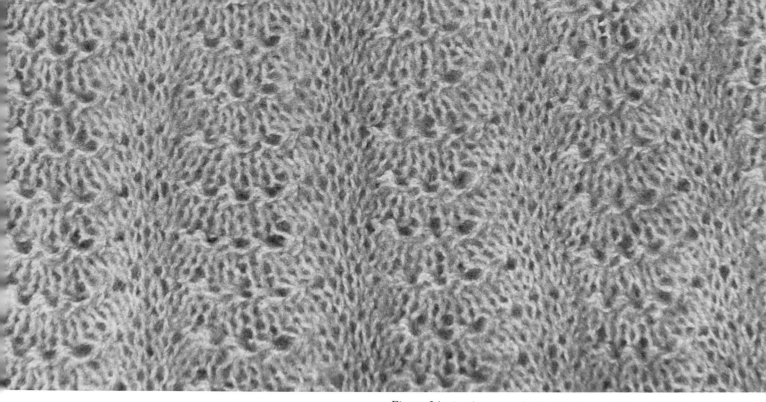

Figure 34. A closeup of the feather and fan stitching on the sweater on the right in Figure 33. Yarn: Frost-lon Petite by Spinnerin.

WOMAN'S FEATHER- AND FAN-STITCHED PULLOVER

The sweater on the right in Figure 33 is basically the Classic Crew Neck Pullover taught in Chapter 5, done with short sleeves and an interesting stitching pattern (see Figure 34).

Women's Sizes: Which yarn do you want to use, sport
Materials: weight, knitting worsted, or bulky yarn?
Needles: Refer to the appropriate directions in
Gauge: Chapter 5 and follow sizes, materials, needles, and gauge specifications.

Fan St Pat:
Row 1: K across.
Row 2: P across.
Row 3: * P 2 tog, p 2 tog (inc 1, k 1) 3 times (to inc pick up bar before the next st), inc 1, p 2 tog, repeat from * across row.
Row 4: P across.

Following directions, working fan-st pat. If pat does not work into your number of sts, keep extra sts in garter st at each side.

WOMAN'S ALPACA TUNIC

The sweater shown in Color Plate 5 is yet another variation of the Classic Crew Neck Pullover in Chapter 3, but the cowl neck, straight sleeves, turn-back cuffs, and ribbed body set it apart. The sweater was knitted in alpaca wool, which is the same weight as knitting worsted.

Sizes: Which yarn do you want to use, sport
Materials: weight, knitting worsted, or bulky yarn?
Needles: Once you've decided, refer to the appro-
Gauge: priate directions in Chapter 3 and follow sizes, materials, needles, and gauge specifications. Be sure you have a pair of circular #8 needles to do the cowl neck area.

With #8 needles, cast on 100 sts, join, work stockinette st for 8 inches. On next row, dec evenly spaced across row to the amount of sts in cast on for the size you want. K 1, p 1 in rib for 1 inch, without reversing sts. Continue as directed until raglan decs are made. For sleeves, do not make any decs. Work even till 5 inches less than desired finished length. Work in reverse stockinette st for 5 inches, bind off. For body, work in rib of 6 p, 2 k, till 5 inches less than desired finished length. Work reverse stockinette for 5 inches, bind off.

Finishing:
Sew sleeve seams.

Figure 35. Capes and ponchos are immensely popular these days. The cape on the left is a knitted version of the crew neck cardigan; the poncho on the right is crocheted and directions appear on page 136. Yarn: Windrush by Brunswick.

WOMAN'S RAISED-RIB CAPE

The cape on the left in Figure 35 is essentially the Classic Crew Neck Cardigan taught in Chapter 3. The basic difference is that stitches are not divided at the yoke to make front, back, and sleeve sections. The stripe pattern and fringing are easy to do. The reverse garter stitch stripe forms a raised pattern on yoke and bottom.

Women's Sizes: Which yarn do you want to use, knitting
Materials: worsted or bulky yarn? Once you've de-
Needles: cided, refer to the appropriate direc-
Gauge: tions in Chapter 3 and follow sizes, ma-
terials, needles, and gauge specifications.
You will need small amounts of 2 con-
trasting colors (cc), as well as the main
color (mc) of yarn.

For striping pat work 2 rows of reverse stockinette in each cc on yoke and bottom, alternating between cc and mc. Work as directed till raglan incs are completed. Do not divide. Continue working as before, making incs every 4th row, 3 times more, and then every 6th row, 3 times more. Work even till desired length, bind off loosely. Fringe.

WOMAN'S NUBBY TWEED JACKET

The jacket shown in Color Plate 1 was done in a nubby tweed yarn, but can be easily done following the basic directions in the Women's Classic Knitting Worsted Crew Neck Cardigan in Chapter 3. The sailor collar is not difficult at all. The turn-back cuffs are done simply by making sleeves straight (not decreasing) and longer.

Women's Sizes: Refer to the directions for the Women's
Materials: Classic Knitting Worsted Crew Neck
Needles: Cardigan in Chapter 3 and follow sizes,
Gauge: materials, needles, and gauge specifica-
tions.

Collar:
Add 14 sts to the cast on. With larger needles, k 1, p 1 in rib for 9 inches.

Yoke, Back, Front, and Sleeves:
Work as directed, keeping 7 sts each side in rib, being sure to allow for the 14 extra sts. When working sleeves, do not dec. Work sleeves straight for desired length. Do not change needles. K 1, p 1 in rib for 5 inches for deep turn-back cuff. When working body, work even for desired length, k 1, p 1 in rib for 1 inch, bind off.

Belt:
Cast on 7 sts, k 1, p 1 in rib for desired length.

Pockets (make 2):
Cast on 22 sts, work stockinette for 5 inches. K 1, p 1 in rib for 1 inch, bind off. Sew pockets in place.

Finishing:
Sew underarm seams. Ch 10 sts twice, sew in place for belt loops.

HAT

The hat shown in Color Plate 1 was made with 2 oz nubby tweed yarn and #8 needles.

Cast on 100 sts. K 1, p 1 in rib for 12 inches and shape top as follows:
Row 1: *K 3, k 2 tog, repeat from * across row.
Row 2: P across.
Row 3: *K 2, k 2 tog, repeat from * across row.
Row 4: P across.
Row 5: *K 1, k 2 tog, repeat from * across row.

Break yarn, leaving a long end. Draw this yarn through rem sts, weave seam together, and roll up cuff double.

WOMAN'S TWEED ENSEMBLE

If you're ready to commit yourself to a larger project, try the dress and coat ensemble shown in Color Plate 12. The coat is simply a variation of the Women's Classic Bulky Yarn Crew Neck Cardigan in Chapter 3 with turn-back cuffs and a sailor's collar, while the dress is based on the Classic Crew Neck Pullover. The lengths of the coat and dress will be up to you.

COAT

Women's Sizes: Refer to the Women's Classic Bulky
Materials: Yarn Crew Neck Cardigan directions in
Needles: Chapter 3 and follow sizes, materials,
Gauge: needles, and gauge specifications. You will need an additional 12 oz of yarn for the coat length.

Cast on as directed. Work pat for 5 inches as follows for collar:
Row 1: K across row.
Row 2: K 1, p 1 across row.

Complete as directed, still keeping pat till raglan incs are made. When working sleeves do not make any decs. Work even till desired length. Reverse pat and work for 3 inches more for turn-back cuff, bind off. Work as directed to any length you like.

DRESS

Women's Sizes: Refer to the Women's Classic Knitting
Materials: Worsted Crew Neck Pullover directions
Needles: in Chapter 3 and follow sizes, mate-
Gauge: rials, needles, and gauge specifications. You will need an additional 8 oz of yarn for the dress length.

Work as directed. Make neckband 2 inches instead of 1 inch. When raglan incs have been completed, work sleeves as follows: Work 1 inch stockinette st, change to smaller needles, k 1, p 1 in rib for 3 inches, bind off. Work body even for 5 inches, change to smaller needles, work k 1, p 1 rib till 9 inches from underarm. Place marker at underarm, continue working on large needles again, inc 1 st before and after underarm marker, every 3 inches, 5 times. Work even till desired length, k 1, p 1 in rib for 1 inch, bind off loosely.

Finishing:
Turn neckband to inside and tack down. Sew underarm seams. Make a chain using doubled yarn, weave in and out of rib at waistband for drawstring tie.

MAN'S BULKY, RUGGED PULLOVER

The sweater pictured in Figure 36 is really the Men's Classic Bulky Yarn Crew Neck Pullover taught in Chapter 3. It looks different because it was made with a tweed yarn. Follow the same directions.

Men's Sizes: Refer to the directions in Chapter 4 and
Materials: follow size, stitch, materials and gauge
Needles: specifications.
Gauge:

Cast on as directed and continue to follow instructions.

Figure 36. It's the yarn that makes this sweater look different. Variegated yarns such as this one add design and textural interest to any classic pattern. Yarn: Bim Bam by Stanley Woolen Company.

LACEY CHRISTENING OUTFIT—DRESS COAT, HAT, AND BLANKET

The christening outfit shown in Figures 37 and 38 consists of a dress, coat, hat, and blanket. The dress and coat are based on the Infants' Classic Crew Neck Cardigan and the Classic Crew Neck Pullover taught in Chapter 3. The lace pattern simply consists of four repeated rows.

DRESS

Infants' Sizes: Directions are for 3 months
Materials: 9 oz baby yarn; 5 yd ¼-inch satin ribbon; 5 yd lace
Needles: 24-inch cir #5 and #7; crochet hook #4
Gauge: 6 sts = 1 inch on #5 needles; 5 sts = 1 inch on #7 needles

Lace Pat (working cir):
Row 1: K around.
Row 2: K around.
Row 3: *P 2 tog, p 2 tog, (inc 1, k 1) 3 times (to inc, pick up bar before the next st), inc 1, p 2 tog, p 2 tog. Repeat from * across rnd.
Row 4: K around.

Yoke:
With #5 cir needles, cast on 92 sts, do not join. Work back and forth as follows: P 15 sts, place marker (back), p 16 sts, place marker (sleeve), p 30 sts, place marker (front), p 16 sts, place marker (sleeve), p rem 15 sts (back). *Next row, k across, inc 1 st before and after each marker (8 incs). Next row, p. Repeat from * till there are 60 sts on center front section of work. End with a k row.

Front, Back, and Sleeves:
Next row, p to first marker, leave these sts on needle. With same yarn, bind off sleeve section. Continue across front section, bind off next sleeve section. Continue to end of row. Next row, join and begin working cir and inc evenly spaced across row to 198 sts. Work lace pat till 12 inches from joining, change to #7 needles and continue till 20 inches, bind off on a k row.

Finishing:
With crochet hook, right side facing you, join yarn at bottom of back opening. Work 1 row sc all around opening and neck edge. Work 1 row sc up 1 side of opening to top of neck edge, ch 3, *sk 2 sts, (2 dc, ch 1, 2 dc) all in next st, sk 2 sts, (1 dc, ch 1, 1 dc) all in the next st. Repeat from * all around neck opening, then continue down other side with sc. Repeat last row once more, making buttonloops on one side as you work the 2nd row. Work the first 2 rows of neck finishing around each sleeve. Sew lace around waistband and around neck. Make little bows with long streamers out of ribbon and attach to front.

COAT

Infants' Sizes: Directions are for 3 months
Materials: 10 oz baby yarn
Needles: #5 and #7; crochet hook #4
Gauge: #5 and #7; 6 sts = 1 inch on #5 needles; 5 sts = 1 inch on #7 needles

Lace Pat (working back and forth):
Row 1: K across.
Row 2: P across.
Row 3: *P 2 tog, p 2 tog, (inc 1, k 1) 3 times (to inc pick up bar before the next st), inc 1, p 2 tog, p 2 tog. Repeat from * across.
Row 4: P across.

Yoke:
With the #5 needles, cast on 68 sts, do not join. Work back and forth as follows: P 12 sts, place marker (front), p 10 sts, place marker (sleeve), p 24 sts, place marker (back), p 10 sts, place marker (sleeve), p rem 12 sts, (front). *Next row, k across, inc 1 st before and after each marker (8 incs). Next row p. Repeat from * till there are 64 sts on center back section of work. End with a k row.

Front, Back, and Sleeves:
P to first marker, place these sts on a holder, p to 3rd marker, place sts between 2nd and 3rd marker on holder, p to 4th marker, place rem sts not worked on a holder. Mark this front and remove all other markers. You now have 2 sleeve sections left on needles. Working each sleeve with a separate ball of yarn, work stockinette st till sleeve is 6 inches, bind off. Joining yarn at underarm of front with marker, p this front. Now k across this front section, back section, and other front section. Working all 3 sections as 1 piece, work as follows: Next row, k 1, *yo, k 2 tog, k 1. Repeat from * across row. Next row, k all across, inc evenly across row to 202 sts. P 1 row. Continue with #5 needles and work 4 rows of lace pat, keeping 2 sts each side in garter st. Work for 12 inches, change to #7 needles and continue pat till 21 inches from beg. Bind off on a k row.

Finishing:

Starting at bottom right corner with #4 hook, work 5 rows sc all around front and neck openings, making 3 buttonholes on the 3rd row from the waist to the neck. Work sleeve edge same as for dress. Draw ribbon through eyelet holes at waist.

HAT

The hat worn by the baby is made with 1 oz of baby yarn and #5 needles.

With #5 needles, cast on 22 sts. Work stockinette st for 4 inches. At beg of next 2 rows, cast on 22 sts. Work 4 rows lace pat for coat for 4 inches, bind off.

Finishing:

Sew 2 rows of lace around front of hat. Sew side seams. Pick up 68 sts around neck, k 1, p 1 in rib for 1 inch, bind off. Sew ribbon ties.

BLANKET

The blanket is made with 12 oz of baby yarn and #7 needles. You will also need a #4 crochet hook.

With #7 needles, cast on 220 sts, do not join. Work 4 rows of coat lace pat for 40 inches. Bind off on a k row.

Finishing:

With hook, work 1 row sc around entire blanket, working 3 sc in each corner. On 2nd row, ch 3, work 1 dc in next st, *ch 2, sk 2 sts, 1 dc in next st. Repeat from * around, join with a slst to top of turning ch. Ch 3, *sk 2 sts, work 1 shell of (3 dc, ch 1, 3 dc) all in next st, sk 2 sts, work a V st of (1 dc, ch 1, 1 dc) all in next st. Repeat from * all around, making a shell in each corner to turn. Repeat the last row, 4 times, end off. Weave satin ribbon through the eyelet row all around blanket.

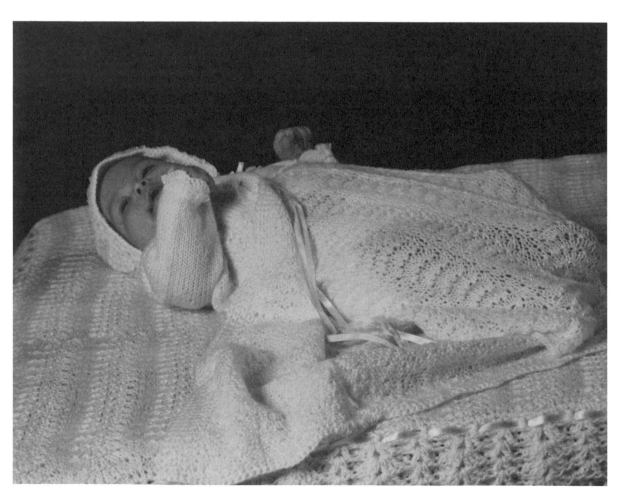

Figure 37. The hat and coat from the christening outfit shown in Figure 38. Yarn: Alouette by Joseph Galler Yarns.

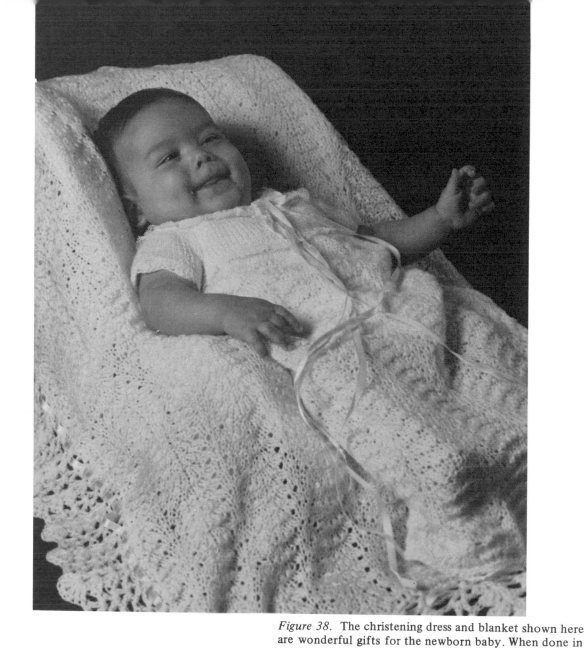

Figure 38. The christening dress and blanket shown here are wonderful gifts for the newborn baby. When done in one piece, the dress is simple to make. The hat and coat are shown in Figure 37. Yarn: Alouette by Joseph Galler Yarns.

WOMAN'S TOWN AND COUNTRY ENSEMBLE

Basically a variation of the Women's Classic Crew Neck Cardigan taught in Chapter 3, the coat, hat, and scarf set shown in Color Plate 4 makes a beautiful spring or fall ensemble. A closeup of the cable and garter stitch pattern can be seen in Figure 39.

COAT

Women's Sizes: Directions are for size 8. Changes for 10, 12, 14, 16, and 18 are in parentheses.
Materials: 48 (50, 52, 54, 56, 58) oz bulky yarn
Needles: 36-inch cir #10½
Gauge: 3½ sts = 1 inch

Cable Pat (worked on 16 sts):
Row 1: K across (right side).
Row 2: K 4, p 8, k 4.
Row 3: Repeat Row 1.
Row 4: Repeat Row 2.
Row 5: K 4, sl next 4 sts to dp needle, hold to back of work, k next 4 sts, k 4 from dp needle, k 4.
Row 6: Repeat Row 2.
Row 7: Repeat Row 1.
Row 8: Repeat Row 2.
Row 9: Repeat Row 1.
Row 10: Repeat Row 2.
Row 11: Repeat Row 1.
Row 12: Repeat Row 2.
  Repeat these 12 rows for cable pat.

Yoke:

Cast on 62 (62, 62, 68, 68, 68) sts. Do garter st for 8 rows. Work as follows: K 10, p 8 (8, 8, 9, 9, 9) sts, place marker (front), p 6 (6, 6, 7, 7, 7) sts, place marker (sleeve), p 14 (14, 14, 16, 16, 16) sts, place marker (back), p 6 (6, 6, 7, 7, 7) sts, place marker (sleeve), p 8 (8, 8, 9, 9, 9) sts, k 10 (front). *Next row, k all across, inc 1 st before and after each marker (8 incs). Next row, k 10, p to last 10 sts, k 10. Repeat from * till there are 56 (60, 62, 66, 70, 74) sts on back section. End on a right side row.

Front, Back, and Sleeves:

Divide as directed. Work sleeves as follows: Do garter st for 6 rows. Centering cable pat on sleeve, work sleeve even till 13 (13, 13, 14, 14, 14) inches from underarm. Reverse pat, continue in reverse for 5 inches more, work 8 rows garter st, bind off. Join yarn at underarm, work body in stockinette st, keeping 10 sts each end in garter st for front border. Work till 28 (28, 28, 29, 29, 29) inches or 3 inches less than desired length. Work garter st for 3 inches, bind off loosely.

Pockets (make 2):

Cast on 22 sts, centering cable pat. Work 20 rows cable pat, work 10 rows garter st, bind off.

Finishing:

Sew underarm seams. Be sure to reverse seam where pat reverses at cuff. Turn back cuff.

SCARF

The scarf is made with 10 oz of bulky yarn and #10½ needles.

Cast on 28 sts. Work in garter st for 64 inches, bind off. Fringe 2 strands in every other st along each end.

HAT

The hat is made with 4 oz bulky yarn and #10½ needles.

Cast on 56 sts. Work garter st for 18 rows. Next row, p 2, *k 4, p 8, k 4, p 2, repeat from * twice more. Next row k. Repeat last 2 rows, twisting cable on the rib of k-8, on the 5th row once, and every 12th row thereafter. Work till 2 twists have been completed. Dec 1 st in garter st rib every other row, 4 times. Next row k 2 tog all across. Gather top, sew seam.

Figure 39. A closeup of the cable stitch on the coat in Color Plate 4.

WOMAN'S ELEGANT BLOUSON

Believe it or not, the sweater shown in Color Plate 13 is based on the Classic Crew Neck Cardigan in Chapter 3. The interesting stripe on the cuffs and waistband is done by working a stockinette stitch row between the ribbed stripes.

Women's Sizes: Directions are for size 8. Changes for 10, 12, 14, 16, and 18 are in parentheses.
Materials: 12 (16, 16, 16, 20, 20) oz knitting worsted in main color (mc); 4 oz knitting worsted in contrasting color (cc)
Needles: #5 and #8
Gauge: 5 sts = 1 inch

Yoke:
With #8 needles, cast on 60 (60, 60, 64, 64, 64) sts and work as follows: P 10 (10, 10, 11, 11, 11) sts, k 1, place marker (front), k 1, p 6, k 1, place marker (sleeve), k 1, p 20 (20, 20, 22, 22, 22) sts, k 1, place marker (back), k 1, p 6 sts, k 1, place marker (sleeve), k 1, p 10 (10, 10, 11, 11, 11) sts (front). *Next row, k 9 (9, 9, 10, 10, 10), inc 1 in next st, p 2, inc 1 in next st, k 4, inc 1 in next st, p 2, inc 1 in next st, k 18 (18, 18, 20, 20, 20), inc 1 in next st, p 2, inc 1 in next st, k 4, inc 1 st in next st, p 2, inc 1 in next st, k 9 (9, 9, 10, 10, 10). Next row, p 11 (11, 11, 12, 12, 12) sts, k 2, p 8 sts, k 2, p 22 (22, 22, 24, 24, 24) sts, k 2, p 8, k 2, p 11 (11, 11, 12, 12, 12) sts. Repeat from * keeping pat as established, always making the inc before and after the 2 p sts. Work till there are 78 (82, 86, 90, 94, 98) sts on back section. End with a right side row.

Front, Back, and Sleeves:
P across to first marker, place sts just worked on needle, p to 3rd marker, place sts between 2nd and 3rd marker on holder, p to 4th marker, place rem sts not worked on holder. Mark this front and remove all other markers. You now have 2 sleeve sections left on needles. Working both at once and joining a 2nd ball of yarn for 2nd sleeve, work as follows: Work even till 12 (12, 12, 12, 13, 13) inches from underarm. On next row, dec 24 (24, 24, 26, 26, 26) sts on 1 row. Change to #5 needles and work cuff as follows: *With cc, k 1 row, then k 1, p 1 in rib for 5 rows. With mc, k 1 row, then k 1, p 1 in rib for 1 row. Repeat from * 4 times more, bind off in rib. Place fronts and back on needle and continue in reverse stockinette st for 5 inches more. Change to #5 needles and repeat striping pat of cuff.

Finishing:
Sew underarm seams. Work 2 rows sc along front and neck edges, making 3 sc in each corner. Sew in zipper and block lightly.

WOMAN'S HONEYCOMB ENSEMBLE

The dress shown in Color Plate 2 is a simple variation of the Classic Crew Neck Pullover taught in Chapter 3, while the coat, of course, is based on the cardigan. The coat features a textured honeycomb pattern.

DRESS

Women's Sizes: Directions are for size 8. Changes for 10, 12, 14, 16, and 18 are in parentheses.
Materials: 32 (32, 32, 36, 36, 36) oz knitting worsted
Needles: dp #5 and #8 and #10½, 24-inch cir #8
Gauge: 5 sts = 1 inch on #8 needles

Collar:
With dp #10 ½ needles, cast on 140 sts. Join, being careful not to twist. Work k 2, p 2 in rib for 6½ inches. Next rnd, *k 2 tog, p 2, repeat from * around. Next rnd, *k 1, p 2, repeat from * around. Next rnd, *k 1, p 2 tog, repeat from * around. Change to dp #8 needles and continue in k 1, p 1 rib till 8 inches from beg.

Yoke:
For sizes 8, 10, and 12 only, k 1 rnd, dec 4 sts evenly spaced around. Continue on dp #8 needles till you have inc enough sts to change to cir #8 and work as follows: K 24 (24, 24, 26, 26, 26) sts, place marker (front), k 9, place marker (sleeve), k 24 (24, 24, 26, 26, 26) sts, place marker (back), k 9 (sleeve). Next row, k all around, inc 1 st before and after each marker (8 incs). Next row k. Continue to k every row, inc 1 st before and after each marker, *every other row.* Work till there are 78 (82, 86, 90, 94, 98) sts on back section.

Front, Back, and Sleeves:
Place front, back, and 1 sleeve section on holders. Work rem sleeve as follows: *With dp #8, place marker at underarm and dec 1 st each side of marker every 1 inch, 12 (12, 12, 12, 13, 13) times. Work even till 14 (14, 14½, 14½, 15½, 15½) inches. Change to dp #5 needles, k 2, p 2 in rib for 4 inches. Bind off loosely. Repeat for 2nd sleeve. Join yarn at underarm. With cir #8 needles, pick up sts from holders, placing a marker at each underarm. Work in stockinette st, dec 1 st before and after the underarm markers, every 1 inch, 7 times. Work even for 1 (1, 2, 2, 2½, 2½) inch. Continue in stockinette st, inc 1 st each side of underarm markers. Repeat this inc, every 3 inches, 6 times more. Work even till desired length, make a turning ridge for hemline. (To make a turning ridge, p on a k row.) Work 1 inch more, bind off loosely.

Finishing:
Turn hem to inside stitch in place, steam gently. Do not steam ribbed sections. Sew small hole at underarm.

COAT

Women's Sizes: Directions are for size 8. Changes for 10, 12, 14, 16, and 18 are in parentheses.

Materials: 40 oz bulky yarn in main color (mc), 4 oz bulky yarn in 2 contrasting colors (col A and col B)

Needles: #11; crochet hook

Gauge: 2 sts = 1 inch (in pat)

St Pat

Row 1: K across (wrong side).

Row 2: *K 1, k in st in the row below, repeat from *, end with k 2.

Row 3: K 2, * k the slipped thread with st above, k 1, repeat from * across row.

Row 4: K 2, *k in next st in row below, k 1, repeat from * across row.

Row 5: *K 1, k the slipped thread tog with st above, repeat from *, end with k 2.

Front, Back, and Sleeves:

Starting at back, cast on 46 (48, 50, 52, 54, 56) sts with mc. *Work 5 pat rows. Repeat Rows 2 through 5, 6 times more. Repeat Row 2 once more. Join col A, p 1 row, k 1 row, join col B, p 1 row, k 1 row, p 1 row with mc *. Repeat between *s till 4 color groups are completed, ending with 2nd col B, stripe. With mc, cast on 24 (24, 26, 26, 28, 28) sts at beg of next 2 rows (sleeves). Continue pat, working till 17 rows beyond next color stripe (should be about 8½ inches from cast-on sts). Next row, work across 36 (37, 39, 40, 42, 43) sts, join new ball of yarn, bind off center 22 (22, 24, 24, 26, 26) sts (neck opening), work rem 36 (37, 39, 40, 42, 43) sts. Working both sides at once, and continuing in pat, cast on 5 (5, 6, 6, 7, 7) sts once at each neck edge and 6 sts once at each neck edge. You now have 47 (48, 51, 52, 55, 56) sts each side. Continue in pat, working each side with separate yarn. Reverse shaping and correspond to back, bind off.

Finishing:

Starting at first col A stripe, sew underarm and sleeve seams. With mc work 1 row sc around all edges.

HAT

The hat is made with 3 oz of bulky yarn in main color (mc) and a small amount in contrasting color (cc) on #11 needles and #10½ crochet hook.

Work st pat same as for coat. Cast on 20 sts. Work honeycomb and striping pat till there are 3 sets of color stripes and 4 groups of honeycomb st, bind off. Fold in half and sew short ends together to form tube. Thread needle with mc and, taking the very end of the st, work a running st along one side of tube, gather up, and fasten. Work 1 row sc around bottom edge.

WOMAN'S LACED TUNIC

Don't let the laces fool you. A study of the tunic in Figure 40 will show you that it is simply a variation of the Women's Classic Crew Neck Raglan Cardigan in Chapter 3. See Figure 41 for help when you get to the laces.

Women's Sizes: Directions are for small size. Changes for medium and large are in parentheses.

Materials: 20 oz knitting worsted in main color (mc); small amounts knitting worsted in 3 contrasting cols (col A, col B, and col C)

Needles: 24-inch cir #10; crochet hook #10

Gauge: 4 sts = 1 inch

Yoke, Front, and Back:

Rows 1–8: With #10 cir needles cast on 92 sts, do not join. K each row back and forth in garter st. Then work the main area in stockinette st and eyelet area in garter st as follows:

Row 9: K 6, p 12, place marker (front), p 16, place marker (sleeve), p 24, place marker (back), p 16, place marker (sleeve), p 12, k last 6 (front).

Row 10: K across, inc 1 st before and after each marker (8 incs).

Row 11: K 6, p across to last 6, k 6.

Row 12: K 2, yo, k 2 tog (1 eyelet made), k across row, inc 1 st before and after each marker, work to last 4 sts, yo, k 2 tog (1 eyelet made), k 2 (8 incs).

Row 13: Repeat Row 11.

Repeat Rows 10 through 13 till 8 eyelets are made. Now start working cir, (remember that when working cir stockinette st is done by k all rows and garter st is done by k 1 row, p 1 row) continuing to inc 1 st before and after each marker, every other row, discontinuing the eyelets, and making 1 st less in garter st and 1 st more in stockinette st each side of stockinette st area till there are no garter sts left (see Figure 42). Continue working in stockinette st and continue inc till there are 78 (84, 90) sts on back section. Place sleeves on holders and work body round and round in garter st for 8 rows. Continue in stockinette st till 14 (15, 16) inches or 2 inches less than desired length. Join col A, *k 3, sl 1, repeat from * around. K 1 rnd, break off col A. Join col B, * sl 1, k 3, repeat from * around. K 1 rnd, break off col B. Join col C, k 2 * sl 1, k 3, repeat from * around. K 1 rnd, break off col C. Join mc, * sl 1, k 3, repeat from * around. Work 7 more rnds of mc in stockinette st. Next rnd, k 1, * yo, k 2 tog, repeat from * around. Work 7 more rnds mc in stockinette st. Bind off loosely in pat.

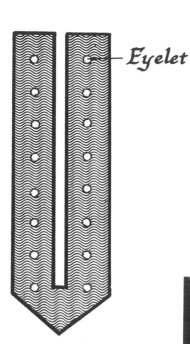

— *Eyelet*

Sleeves:

Pick up sleeve sts. Work back and forth in garter st for 8 rows and continue in stockinette st till 8 inches from underarm, inc 1 st each side of each sleeve. Repeat the inc every 2 inches twice more. Work even till 2 inches less than desired finished length. Repeat pat as on bottom of front and back except p every other row instead of k. Repeat last 15 rows of bottom of body, bind off.

Finishing:

Sew underarm seams. Fold hems to inside and st in place, forming picot edges. Make a ch using all 3 cols with #10 hook. Lace the ch through eyelets.

Figure 40. A sketch of the eyelets for lacing on the tunic shown in Figure 41.

Figure 41. The laces and tunic shape give this version of the classic pullover a unique look. Yarn: Germanntown Knitting Worsted by Brunswick.

MAN'S KANGAROO-POCKET PULLOVER

Aside from the cable pattern and that big kangaroo pocket, the sweater in Figure 42 is basically the Classic Crew Neck Pullover in Chapter 3. See Figure 43 for a closeup of the cable pattern.

Men's Sizes:
Materials:
Needles:
Gauge:

Decide whether you want to make the sweater in sport weight, knitting worsted, or bulky yarn and refer to the appropriate directions. Follow sizes, materials, needles, and gauge specifications. You will also need a regular cable needle to do the cable pattern.

Figure 42. Two entirely different sweaters that both feature cable patterns. The one on the right is taught on this page. That big kangaroo pocket is made separately and then sewn on. The short sleeve pullover on the left is taught on page 115.

Cable Pat for Center Front (worked on 34 sts):

Row 1: *K 6, p 1. Repeat from * 3 times, k 6.
Rows 2-3: Repeat Row 1.
Row 4: *K 6, p 1, sl next 3 sts to cable needle, hold to back, k next 3 sts, k 3 held back, p 1. Repeat from * once, p 1.
Rows 5-7: Repeat Row 1.
Row 8: *Sl next 3 sts to cable needle, hold to back, k next 3 sts, k 3 held to back, p 1, k 6, p 1. Repeat from * once, p 1.
   Repeat these 8 rows for cable pat for length of yoke.

Cable Pat for Sleeve (worked on 8 sts):

Rows 1-3: K across.
Row 4: Sl 4 sts to cable needle, hold to back, k next 4 sts, k 4 sts held to back.
Rows 5-8: K across.
   Repeat these 8 rows for length of yoke.

Cast on as directed. Work in k 1, p 1 rib 2 inches instead of 1 inch. Use p side as right side, and, keeping 1 st before and after each marker in reverse stockinette st, making incs before and after these 2 sts. Work cable pat on center front and sleeves. Work till raglan incs have been completed. When ready to divide, discontinue cable pat and complete sweater in reverse stockinette st.

Kangaroo Pocket:
Cast on 80 sts, work in reverse stockinette st for 10 inches. Bind off 20 sts at beg of next 2 rows, then dec 1 st each side, every other row, 6 times. Work even on rem sts till pocket reaches from beg of border to bottom of cable.

Finishing:
Turn neckband in half to outside and sew down. Sew pocket in place.

HAT

The hat shown in Figure 47 is made with 2 oz knitting worsted on #8 knitting needles.

Cast on 80 sts, work in k 1, p 1 rib for 8 inches. Shape top as follows:

Row 1: *K 8, k 2 tog, repeat from * across row.
Row 2: P across.
Row 3: *K 7, k 2 tog, repeat from * across row.
Row 4: P across.
   Continue to work in this manner, dec 8 sts every k row and always having 1 st less between decs, till 16 sts rem. Break yarn, leaving a long end. Pull this yarn through rem sts, gather up and sew seam with same yarn.

WOMAN'S CABLED OVERBLOUSE

   Possibilities for variation are endless. See the woman's sweater in Figure 42. The short sleeves and cable borders have completely transformed the Classic Crew Neck Pullover taught in Chapter 3.

Women's Sizes: Which yarn do you want to make it in,
Materials: sport weight, knitting worsted, or bulky
Needles: yarn? Once you've decided, refer to the
Gauge: appropriate directions in Chapter 3 and follow sizes, materials, needles, and gauge specifications. You will need #5 dp needles to do the cable pattern.

Cable Trim for Sleeve and Bottom Borders (worked on a multiple of 8 + 2 sts):
Row 1: *P 2, k 6. Repeat from * around.
Rows 2-3: Repeat Row 1.
Row 4: *P 2, sl 3 sts to dp needles, hold to back, k next 3 sts, k 3 being held. Repeat from * around.
Rows 5-6: Repeat Row 1.
   Repeat these 6 rows for cable trim.

Work as directed. Use the p side as the right side and keep 1 st before and after the marker in reverse stockinette st, making incs before and after these 2 sts. After dividing, work sleeves for only 1 inch, then work cable pat for 4 inches, bind off in pat. Work body even till 6 inches less than desired finished length. Work cable pat for 6 inches, bind off in pat.

Figure 43. A closeup of the cable pattern on the sweater shown in Figure 42. Yarn: Bernat Blarneyspun (imported from Ireland) courtesy of Emile Bernat & Sons Co.

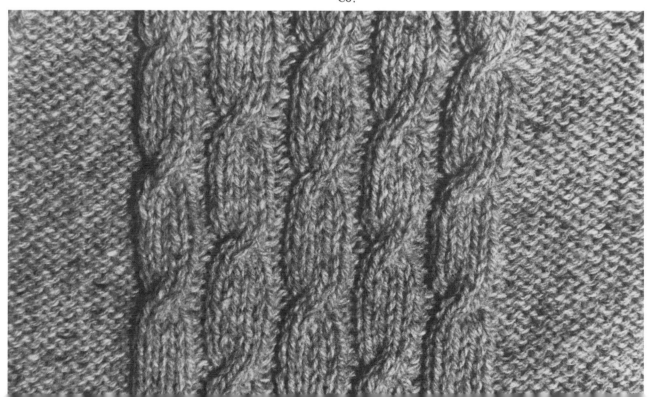

CHILD'S CHUNKY T TOP

It looks like a completely different sweater, but the child in Figure 44 is wearing yet another version of the Classic Crew Neck Pullover taught in Chapter 5. The cabled front, of course, sets it apart, as do the neckline and sleeves.

Children's Sizes:
Materials:
Needles:
Gauge:

Do you want to make the sweater in sport weight, knitting worsted, or bulky yarn? Refer to the appropriate directions in Chapter 5 and follow size, materials, needles, and gauge specifications. You will also need a cable needle to do the cable pattern.

Cable Pat Center Front (worked on 16 sts):
Row 1: P 2, k 12, p 2.
Row 2: K 2, p 12, k 2.
Row 3: Repeat Row 1.
Row 4: Repeat Row 2.
Row 5: P 2, sl next 6 sts to cable needle, hold to back, k next 6 sts, k 6 from cable needle, p 2.
Row 6: Repeat Row 2.
Row 7: Repeat Row 1.
Row 8: Repeat Row 2.
Row 9: Repeat Row 1.
Row 10: Repeat Row 2.
Row 11: Repeat Row 1.
Row 12: Repeat Row 2.
   Repeat these 12 rows for cable pat.

Follow directions and center cable on sts. When sleeves are cast on, keep 5 sts each end in garter st. Work till 1 inch before neck opening. Work garter st in center for 1 inch. After dividing for neck, keep 5 sts of neck edges and sleeve edges in garter st. Continue as directed.

Figure 44. This child's cabled tunic on the left is taught on this page and the nubby tunic on the right is taught on page 127. Both tunics are comfortable and easy to wear. Yarn: left—Nantuck by Columbia-Minerva, right—Apollo by Plymouth Yarn Company.

INFANT'S AUTUMN DAY CARDIGAN

The baby in Figure 45 is wearing a mock-cable version of the Classic Crew Neck Cardigan taught in Chapter 3. Directions for the hat are included.

Infants' Sizes: Directions are for 6 months. Changes for 1, 2, and 3 are in parentheses.
Materials: 8 oz knitting worsted
Needles: #5 and #8; crochet hook #6 or G
Gauge: 5 sts = 1 inch

Mock Cable Pat for Front (worked on 6 sts):
Row 1: P 2, k 1, yo, k 1, p 2 (right side).
Row 2: K 2, p 3, k 2.
Row 3: P 2, sl 1, k 2, psso both k sts, p 2.
Row 4: K 2, p 2, k 2.

Yoke:
With #5 needles, cast on 56 sts, k 1, p 2 in rib for 1 inch. Change to #8 and work pat as follows:
Row 1: K 7, p 2, k 1, yo, k 1, p 2, k 2, p 2, k 1, yo, k 1, p 2, k 14, p 2, k 1, yo, k 1, p 2, k 2, p 2, k 1, yo, k 1, p 2, k 7.
Row 2: P 7, k 2, p 3, k 2, p 2, k 2, p 3, k 2, p 14, k 2, p 3, k 2, p 2, k 2, p 3, k 2, p 7.
Row 3: K 5, inc 1 st in next st, k 1 *p 2, sl 1, k 2, psso both k sts, p 2*, inc 1 st in each of next 2 sts. Repeat between *s once, k 1, inc 1 st in next st, k 10, inc 1 st in next st, k 1. Repeat between *s once, inc 1 st in each of next 2 sts. Repeat between *s once, k 1, inc 1 st in next st, k last 5 sts.
Row 4: P 8, k 2, p 2, k 2, p 4, k 2, p 2, k 2, p 16, k 2, p 2, k 2, p 4, k 2, p 2, k 2, p 8.
Continue in pat as established, following the front cable pat rows on the 6 sts and making incs in the 2nd st before and after each cable, every k row. Work till there are 48 (50, 52, 54) sts on back section.

Front, Back, and Sleeves:
Place fronts and back on holders. Dec 1 st each side of each sleeve, every 3 inches, twice. Work even till 6 (6¼, 7, 7½) inches. Change to #5 needles and work k 1, p 1 rib for 1 (2, 2, 2) inches, bind off in rib. Work body all in 1 piece, working 1 cable pat at each front edge, 1 cable pat 8 sts over from first pat. Continue in this manner till 5 (5½, 6, 6) inches from underarm. Change to #5 needles, k 1, p 1 in rib for 1 (2, 2, 2) inch.

Finishing:
Sew underarm seams. Work 2 rows sc on front edge. On 3rd row sk 2 sts, ch 2 for every buttonhole desired. On 4th row work 2 sc in every ch-2 sp. Work 1 more row sc (5 rows in all). Be sure to make buttonholes on right side for girls, left side for boys. After last row, do not break yarn and do not turn. Work 1 row sc backwards over sts just worked, end off.

Figure 45. Another cabled version of the classic crew neck cardigan. This one features mock cables and a hat with earflaps. Yarn: Windrush by Brunswick.

The hat shown in Figure 45 is made with 2 oz knitting worsted and #5 and #8 needles. You also need a #6 or G crochet hook.

With #5 needles, cast on 84 sts. K 1, p 1 in rib for 2 inches. Change to #8 needles and work pat as follows:
Row 1: K 4 *p 2, k 1, yo, k 1, p 2, k 8. Repeat from * 5 times, ending last repeat with k 4.
Row 2: P 4 *k 2, p 3, k 2, p 8. Repeat from * 5 times, ending last repeat with p 4.
Row 3: K 4 *p 2, sl 1, k 2, psso both k sts, p 2, k 2, repeat from * 5 times, ending last with repeat k 4.
Row 4: P 4, * k 2, p 2, k 2, p 8. Repeat from * 5 times, ending last repeat with p 4.

Repeat the last 4 rows, 4 times more.

Continue in pat as established, dec 1 st each end of the rib of k 8, every right side row, 8 times. K 2 tog all across next row. Break yarn, leaving a long end. Pull through rem sts, gather up, and sew seam, weaving rib.

Earflaps:
Fold rib border in half to right side. Starting 1½ inches in from back seam, pick up 20 sts along folded edge. Work stockinette st for 3 rows, then dec 1 st each side, every k row, till 2 sts rem, bind off. Work other earflap to correspond.

Finishing:
Starting at back seam, work 1 row sc along back and one side of earflap to point. Ch 45 for tie, work sc along tie, and continue around hat, making another tie at other earflap. When you are back to start, join with a slst, do not turn. Work 1 row sc backward around entire outer edge, omitting ties.

Figure 46. Two color tones were delicately used on this classic pullover. The buttons on the diagonal raglan increase line are particularly interesting. Yarn: Darling Yarn by Unger.

WOMAN'S TWO-TONED PULLOVER

Figure 46 shows a subtle variation of the Classic Crew Neck Pullover in Chapter 3. A contrasting color yarn (cc) is used on the ribbed sections and the raglan openings. Buttonloops and buttons are added at the end.

Women's Sizes:	Which yarn do you want to use, sport
Materials:	weight, knitting worsted, or bulky yarn?
Needles:	Once you've decided, refer to the ap-
Gauge:	propriate directions in Chapter 3 and follow sizes, materials, needles, and gauge specifications. You will need a main color (mc) of yarn and a contrasting color (cc), as well as 10 small buttons.

With cc, cast on as directed, do not join. Work k 1, p 1, in rib for 1 inch. Work back and forth in mc, keeping 2 sts each side of your markers in cc and making incs before and after the 2 cc sts. Continue as directed till 5½ inches from beg. Join and begin working in rnds, keeping the cc stripes till raglan is completed. Finish as directed, working the cuffs and waistband for 4 inches in cc.

Finishing:
Sew underarm seams. Work 1 row sc around raglan opening, making 10 evenly-spaced buttonloops as you work.

Figure 47. Beading, picots, drawstring; they all contribute to this pretty little dress for a baby girl. Add embroidery as shown here in matching colors. Instructions are on page 120. Yarn: Fore and Aft Sport Yarn by Brunswick.

INFANT'S FIRST PARTY DRESS

The baby in Figure 47 is wearing an adaptation from the Classic Crew Neck Pullover in Chapter 3. Beading, which is explained on page 15, accents the dress; the sleeve effect and the bodice tie are easy to accomplish. Finish the dress with embroidery, if you wish.

Infants' Sizes: Directions are for 6 months. Changes for 1, 2, and 3 are in parentheses.

Materials: 2 (2, 3, 4) oz sport weight yarn in main color (mc). 1 oz sport weight yarn in 2 contrasting cols (col A and col B)

Needles: 24-inch cir #5

Gauge: 6 sts = 1 inch

Neck:
Cast on 74 sts, do not join. Working back and forth, work 4 rows stockinette st. On next row, k 1, *yo, k 2 tog. Repeat from * across row. Work 4 more rows stockinette st. Work yoke as follows, do not join.

Yoke:
Row 1: K 12, yo, k 1, yo, k 11, yo, k 1, yo, k 24, yo, k 1, yo, k 11, yo, k 1, yo, k 12.
Row 2: P 1 row.
Row 3: K 13, yo, k 1, yo, k 13, yo, k 1, yo, k 26, yo, k 1, yo, k 13, yo, k 1, yo, k 13.
Row 4: P 1 row.

Continue in this manner, always having 1 more st on each back section, 2 sts more on each sleeve and front section, between yo. Work till there are 60 (64, 66, 68) sts on front section.

Front, Back, and Sleeves:
Place back and front sections on holders. On sleeves, work 1 row of beading as follows: K 1 *yo, k 2 tog. Repeat from * across row. Work 4 rows stockinette st, bind off. Pick up back and front sections and start working circular. Join col A, work 2 rows stockinette st, 1 beading row, 2 rows stockinette st, join col B, k 1 row, on next row inc 20 sts, evenly spaced, around. Continue working round and round till 4 inches less than desired finished length. Work 1 more beading row, work 2 rows stockinette st. Join col A, work even for 5 rows, break off. Join col B, work 2 rows stockinette st, 1 beading row, 4 rows stockinette st, bind off loosely.

Finishing:
Turn the 4 rows of stockinette st at neck, sleeve, and bottom edges to the inside and stitch down, forming picot edge. Work 1 row sc around back opening, making 3 buttonloops as you work. Make a chain long enough to fit in around chest and draw through the beading row at bodice. Block lightly.

WOMAN'S WISHBONE CABLE CARDIGAN

There are some spring days when cabled cardigans are just the perfect garment. The young woman on the right in Color Plate 8 is wearing a wishbone cabled cardigan that is simply a variation of the Classic Crew Neck Cardigan in Chapter 3. Wishbone cables are like any other; just follow the direcitons. See Figure 48 for a closeup of wishbone cable.

Women's Sizes: Directions are for small size. Changes for medium and large are in parentheses.

Materials: 20 (24, 28) oz knitting worsted

Needles: #8; regular cable needle

Gauge: 5 sts = 1 inch

Cable Pat (worked on 16 sts):
Row 1: *P 2, k 12, p 2, k 5, repeat from * twice more, end with p 2, k 12, p 2.
Row 2: *K 2, p 12, k 2, p 5, repeat from * twice more, end with k 2, p 12, k 2.
Rows 3-4: Repeat Row 1.
Row 5: *P 2, sl next 3 sts to cable needle, hold to front of work, k next 3 sts, k 3 sts from cable needle, sl next 3 sts, hold to back of work, k next 3 sts, k 3 sts from cable needle, p 2, k 5. Repeat from * twice more, end with p 2, cable twist, p 2.
Row 6: Repeat Row 2.
Row 7: Repeat Row 1.
Row 8: Repeat Row 2.
Row 9: Repeat Row 1.
Row 10: Repeat Row 2.
Row 11: Repeat Row 1.
Row 12: Repeat Row 2.
Repeat these 12 rows for cable pat.

Collar:
Cast on 79 sts and work 24 rows of cable pat. Next row, make a turning ridge (k across row from wrong side). Continue in stockinette st for 24 rows (collar facing), end with a k row.

Yoke:
K 2, p 12, place marker (front), k 2, p 5, k 2, place marker (sleeve), p 12, k 2, p 5, k 2, p 12, place marker (back), k 2, p 5, k 2, place marker (sleeve), p 12, k 2 (front). Continue in cable pat, inc 1 st before and after each marker (8 incs in all), every k row. You will have to form the p sts on the side of the cable as sts are inc. There will be a wishbone cable on each front, 2 on the back, and a 5-st rib on the sleeves. Continue working the cables and making the inc until there are 87 (91, 95) sts on back section. End with a right side row.

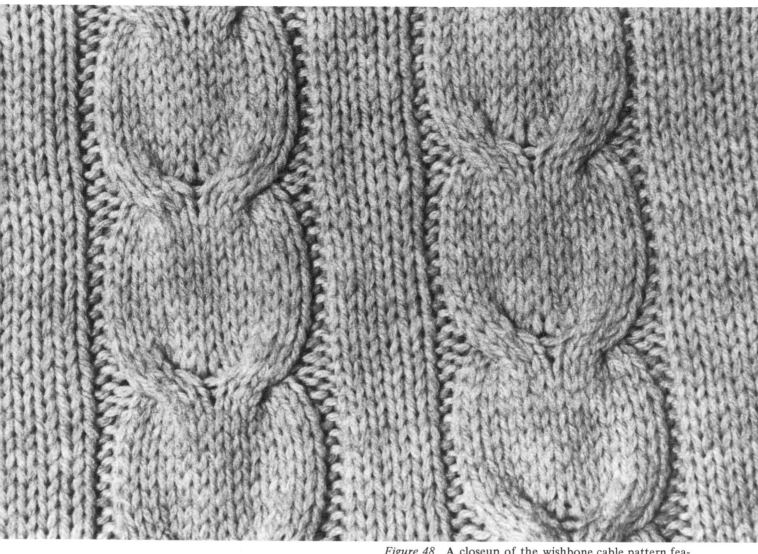

Figure 48. A closeup of the wishbone cable pattern featured in the sweater shown in Color Plate 8.

Front, Back, and Sleeves:
Place front and back sections on holders. Keeping 5-st rib in center, dec 1 st each side of each sleeve, every 1 inch, 11 (12, 12) times. Work even till 12 (13, 13) inches or 3½ inches less than desired length. Work cable pat, keeping 2 (4, 4) sts each side in stockinette st for 24 rows. Make a turning ridge (to make a turning ridge, k a p row), work stockinette st for 24 rows (cuff facing), bind off loosely. Place fronts and back section on needles, placing a marker at each underarm. Join yarn and work all 3 sections as one. Continue cable pat as established, inc 1 st before and after each marker every k row twice. Do not remove markers. Work even for 8 inches from underarm or desired length to waistline. Inc 1 st each side of each marker. Repeat this inc every 1 inch (if longer sweater is desired, make incs further apart), 4 times more. There are now 197 (201, 205) sts on needle. Work cable pat as on collar as follows: For small sweater only, there will be a 4-st rib between cables, instead of a 5-st rib, except on center back cable already established.

For medium size only, there will be a 4-st rib between every other cable and a 5-st rib between other cables, starting with a 5-st rib. For large size only, there will be a 5-st rib between each cable as on collar. Work 24 rows of cable pat, make a turning ridge, work stockinette st for 24 rows, bind off loosely (hem facing).

Finishing:
Sew underarm seams. Tack facings to inside of collar, cuffs, and bottom. Starting at bottom right front, work 1 row up front, ch 1, turn. Work 2nd row. On 3rd row make 6 evenly spaced buttonholes. Work 2 more rows. Work other front to correspond. *For Buttonholes:* On 3rd row work 2 chs, sk 2 sts. On 4th row make 2 sc in ch-2 sp. Be sure to make buttonholes on the right front for girls, left front for boys.

Do not block sweater by steaming. To block, wet thoroughly with cold water and lay flat to dry, patting into shape with fingertips.

WOMAN'S ALPACA STRIPED TUNIC

Color Plate 7 shows a woman wearing a tunic knitted from the side over. An interesting fact about the sweater is that it looks just as attractive right side out as it does right side in. See Figures 49 and 50. Alpaca wool is the same weight as knitting worsted.

Women's Sizes: Directions are for small size. Changes for medium and large are in parentheses.

Materials: 6 oz knitting worsted in 4 contrasting cols—col A, col B, col C, and col D

Needles: #10; crochet hook #9 or I

Gauge: 4 sts = 1 inch

Starting at sleeve edge, cast on 64 sts with col A. K 10 rows, join col B, k 10 rows, join col C, k 10 rows, join col D, k 10 rows, join col A, k 10 rows. With col B, cast 50 sts on free needle. With same yarn, k across 64 sts on other needle. Cast on 50 sts other side (164 sts on needle), work 1 more row with col B. Continue stripes in col pat as established, alternating 2 rows of each col. (Do not break yarn after each color change. Carry loosely across bottom.) Work in this manner for 6 (6½, 7) inches. Work across 80 sts, join new yarn, bind off center 4 sts, work rem 80. Continue 2-row stripe as established, working each side on separate yarn. Work for 6 inches more. Next row, work across 80 sts, cast on 4 sts. Continue as 1 piece again, work 6 (6½, 7) inches more. At beg of next 2 rows, bind off 50 sts. You are now left with 64 sts for other sleeve. Work to correspond, reversing striping pattern.

Finishing:
Sew underarm seams. Work 1 row sc around neck. Work 1 row sc around bottom and sleeves. Make a twisted cord for belt.

Figure 49. A closeup of the front side of the alpaca striped tunic shown in Color Plate 7.

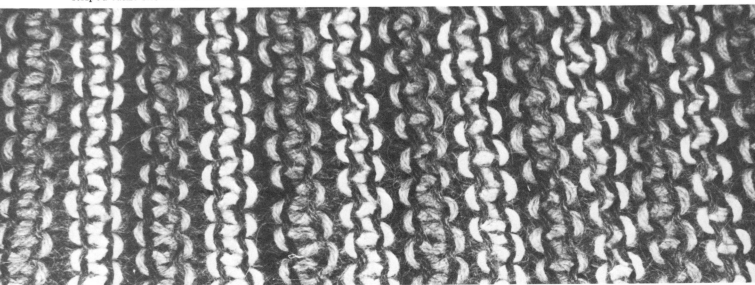

Figure 50. The back side of the tunic shown in Color Plate 7.

CHILD'S GOING-TO-GRANDMA'S SWEATER SET

The child in Color Plate 9 is wearing a cabled sweater set based on the Classic Knitting Worsted Crew Neck Cardigan and Pullover taught in Chapter 3.

CREW NECK CARDIGAN

Children's Sizes: Directions are for size 2. Changes for 4 and 6 are in parentheses.
Materials: 6 (6, 7) oz knitting worsted
Needles: #5 and #8
Gauge: 5 sts = 1 inch

Yoke:
With #5 needles, cast on 54 (58, 62) sts. Work 1 row of *k 2, p 2 rib. Repeat from * across row. Work cable pat twice.

Cable Pat (worked on a multiple of 4 + 2 sts):
Row 1: * P 2, k 1, yo, k 1, repeat from * across row.
Row 2: * K 2, p 3, repeat from * across row.
Row 3: P 2, sl 1, k 2, psso both k sts, repeat from * across row.
Row 4: * K 2, p 2, repeat from * across row.

Change to #8 needles, k 1 row, keeping cable pat. Keeping pat, p next 8 (9, 10) sts, place marker (front), p next 4 (4, 5) sts, place marker (sleeve), p next 18 (20, 20) sts, place marker (back), p next 4 (4, 5) sts, place marker (sleeve), p next 8 (9, 10) sts (front). Work cable pat on last 6 sts. (Cable pat is continued on first and last 6 sts throughout garment for front border.) *Next row, work pat on 6 sts, k across, inc 1 st before and after each marker, work cable pat on last 6 sts (8 inc). Next row, work cable pat on 6 sts, p to last 6 sts, work cable pat on last 6 sts. Repeat from * till there are 52 (56, 60) sts on back section. End with a right side row.

Front, Back, and Sleeves:
Place front and back sections on holders. Work sleeves (each with a separate ball of yarn) as follows: Dec 1 st each side of each sleeve, every 1 inch, 5 (6, 7) times. Work even till 2 inches less than desired finished length. Change to #5 needles, work cable pat for 16 rows, bind off loosely in k 2, p 2 rib. Place all 3 body sections on #8 needles, work stockinette st, still keeping 6 sts each side in cable pat. Work for 5½ (6½, 7¼) inches or 2 inches less than desired finished length. Change to #5 needles, work cable pat for 16 rows, bind off loosely in k 2, p 2 rib.

Finishing:
Sew underarm seams. Work 1 row sc on each front edge. Sew 6 buttons on one front side and use cable openings for buttonholes on the other side.

CREW NECK PULLOVER

Sizes: Directions are for size 2. Changes for 4 and 6 are in parentheses.
Materials: 4 (5, 6) oz knitting worsted
Needles: dp #5 and #8, 24-inch cir #8
Gauge: 5 sts = 1 inch

Cable Pat (worked on a multiple of 4 + 2 sts):
Row 1: *P 2, k 1, yo, k 1, repeat from * around.
Row 2: *P 2, k 3, repeat from * around.
Row 3: *P 2, sl 1, k 2, psso both k sts, repeat from * around.
Row 4: *P 2, k 2, repeat from * around.

Yoke:
With dp #5, cast on 56 (60, 64) sts. Join, being careful not to twist. Work p 2, k 2 for 1 rnd. Work the 4 pat rnds twice. Change to dp #8 (use these needles till there are enough sts to change to the cir #8) and work as follows: K 22 (22, 24) sts, place marker (back), k 6 (8, 8) sts, place marker (sleeve), k 2 (2, 3) sts, work cable pat on next 18 sts, k 2 (2, 3) sts, place marker (front), k 6 (8, 8) sts, place marker (sleeve). Continue working in stockinette st, keeping 18 sts center front in pat as established, inc 1 st before and after each marker (8 incs) every other row, till you have 50 (54, 58) sts on front and back sections of sweater.

Front, Back, and Sleeves:
Place back and front sections on holders. Using dp #5, work 8 (8, 12) rows of cable pat, bind off loosely in k 2, p 2 rib. Place back and front sections on cir #8, k all as 1 piece in stockinette st for 5 (5½, 6) inches. Change to dp #5, work cable pat for 24 (28, 28) rows, bind off loosely in k 2, p 2 rib.

Finishing:
Sew small hole at underarm.

TAM

The tam shown in Color Plate 9 is made with 2 oz of knitting worsted with #5 and #8 needles. Directions are for size 2. Changes for 4 and 6 are in parentheses.

With #5 needles, cast on 74 (82, 90) sts. K 2, p 2 in rib for 1 row. Work cable pat as on cardigan for 8 rows. On next row, make evenly spaced incs to 120 (130, 140) sts. Change to #8 needles and work in stockinette st for 2½ inches, end on a p row. Next row, *k 8, k 2 tog. Repeat from * across row. Next row, p. Continue to dec every k row, always having 1 st less between dec each time. Work in this manner till there are 2 sts left between decs. K 2 tog across row. Break yarn, leaving a long end, pull through rem sts, gather up. Sew seam.

CASUAL TEXTURED PULLOVER

The child in Color Plate 6 is wearing a very simple variation of the Classic Crew Neck Pullover in Chapter 3. The interesting texture is achieved by knitting one row and ribbing the next.

Sizes:
Materials:
Needles:
Gauge:

Do you want to make the sweater for an infant, child, woman, or man? Which yarn do you want to use, sport weight, knitting worsted, or bulky yarn? Refer to the appropriate directions in Chapter 3 and follow sizes, materials, needles, and gauge specifications. You will also need a #6 or G crochet hook.

Work as directed, using the following pat instead of stockinette st:
Row 1: K around (wrong side).
Row 2: *K 1, p 1, repeat from * around.

Make all incs on the k rnds. The incs work into the pat and there is no need to adjust after each inc rnd. Continue following directions till sleeves. After dividing, work sleeves as follows: Continue in pat without decs, till desired sleeve length. Then reverse pat for turn-back cuff, working 3 inches more (for children, 4 inches more for adults), bind off in pat. Join yarn at underarm, work body in pat till desired length. Work 1 inch stockinette st for hemline, bind off loosely.

Finishing:
Sew underarm seams and finish as directed. Turn hem to outside and stitch in place. Make a chain using doubled yarn and crochet hook. Draw tie through bottom, pulling tie through sts at center front.

HAT

The hat worn by the child in Color Plate 6 was made with 2 oz knitting worsted and #8 needles.

Cast on 90 sts and work pat as follows:
Row 1: K across.
Row 2: *K 1, p 1, repeat from 8 across.
Repeat Rows 1 and 2 for pat.
Work in pat for 3 inches, now reverse pat and continue for 4½ inches more. Shape top as follows:
Row 1: *K 8, k 2 tog, repeat from * across row.
Row 2: P across.
Row 3: *K 7, k 2 tog, repeat from * across row
Row 4: P across.
Continue in this manner, dec 9 sts every k row, always having 1 st less between decs, till there are 9 sts left. Break yarn, leaving a long end. Pull this yarn through rem sts, gather up and sew seam, being sure to reverse seam at cuff.

CASUAL TEXTURED CARDIGAN

The green sweater in Color Plate 6 is based on the Classic Crew Neck Cardigan in Chapter 3. The only difference is that a knit-row, knit-one-purl-one-row pattern is followed, instead of the stockinette stitch.

Sizes:
Materials:
Needles:
Gauge:

Do you want to make the sweater for an infant, child, woman, or man? Which yarn do you want to use, sport weight, knitting worsted, or bulky yarn? Once you've decided, refer to the appropriate directions in Chapter 3 and follow sizes, materials, needles, and gauge specifications.

Work as directed, using the following pat instead of stockinette stitch:
Row 1: K across (wrong side).
Row 2: *K 1, p 1, repeat from * across.

Make all incs on the k rows. The incs work into the pat and there is no need to adjust after each inc row. Continue following directions till sleeves. After dividing, work sleeves as follows: Continue in pat, without dec, till desired sleeve length. Then reverse pat for turn-back cuff, working 3 inches more (for children, 4 inches more for adults), bind off in pat. Join yarn at underarm, work body in pat till desired length. Work 1 inch of stockinette st for hemline, bind off loosely.

Finishing:
Sew underarm seams. Turn hem to inside and stitch in place, leaving ends open for tie. Make a chain using a doubled yarn and crochet hook. Draw tie through bottom, pulling the tie through sts at center front. Finish as directed.

HAT

The hat worn by the young woman in Color Plate 6 is made with 4 oz knitting and #8 knitting needles.

Cast on 100 sts and work pat as follows:
Row 1: K across.
Row 2: *K 1, p 1, repeat from * across row.
Repeat Rows 1 and 2 for pat.
Work for 4 inches, now reverse pat. Continue in reverse pat for 6 inches more, shape top as follows:
Row 1: *K 8, k 2 tog, repeat from * across row.
Row 2: P across.
Row 3: *K 7, k 2 tog, repeat from * across row.
Row 4: P across.
Continue in this manner, dec 10 sts every k row and always having 1 less st between decs, till there are 10 sts left. Break yarn, leaving a long end. Pull this yarn through rem sts, gather up, and sew seam, being sure to reverse seam at cuff.

WOMAN'S DIAMOND-MOTIF TUNIC

The woman on the left and in the inset of Color Plate 8 is wearing a bulky tunic made with one strand of mohair and one strand of sport weight yarn held together. The sweater can be made with any yarn, however, and it is just a simple variation of the Women's Classic Crew Neck Pullover in Chapter 5. Figure 51 is a stitching guide for the diamond motif.

Women's Sizes: Directions are for all sizes.
Materials: 12 oz mohair; 10 oz sport weight yarn
Needles: #10; crochet hook
Gauge: 3½ sts = 1 inch

Starting at sleeve, cast on 40 sts. Work garter st for 20 ridges (every 2 rows makes 1 garter st ridge) and then work stockinette st till 17 inches or desired length to underarm. At beg of next 2 rows, cast on 52 sts. Keeping the added 52 sts each side in garter st and all rem sts in stockinette st, work for 4 inches. Keeping 14 sts each side in garter st and all rem sts in stockinette st, work for 1 inch more. Keeping pat as established, work across 68 sts, join new ball of yarn, bind off center 8 sts. Work rem 68, working both sides each with separate yarn, still keeping 14 sts garter st each end. Work for 2 inches more. Follow chart (see Figure 51), starting first diamond 16 sts from garter st border. Work diamonds in garter st and center sts in stockinette st. Work till chart is completed. Work stockinette st for 2 inches more, still keeping the 14 sts in garter st. On next row, cast on 8 sts at neck edge. Join as one piece again, work 1 inch more stockinette st. Keeping 52 sts each side in garter st, work to correspond to other side.

Finishing:
Work 3 rows sc around neck edge. Sew underarm seams.

HAT

The hat shown in Color Plate 8 is made with 2 ozs mohair, 1 oz sport yarn.

With #10 knitting needles, cast on 64 sts. K every row in garter st for 7 inches. Continue in garter st, dec to shape top as follows:
Row 1: *K 6, k 2 tog, repeat from * across row.
Row 2: *K 5, k 2 tog, repeat from * across row.
Row 3: *K 4, k 2 tog, repeat from * across row.
Row 4: *K 3, k 2 tog, repeat from * across row.
Row 5: *K 2, k 2 tog, repeat from * across row.
Row 6: *K 2 tog, repeat from * across row.
Break yarn, leaving a long end. Pull this yarn through rem sts, gather up and sew seam.

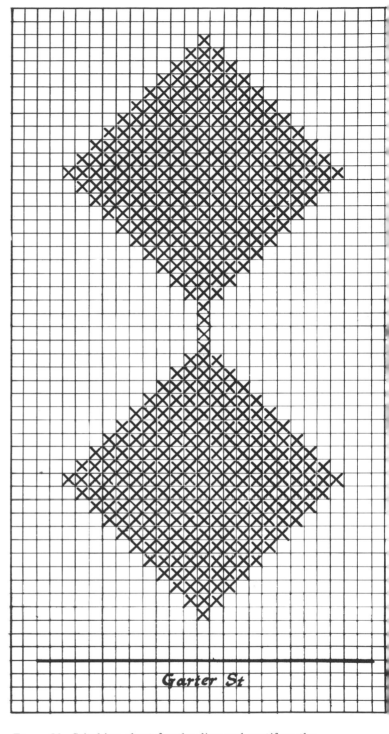

Figure 51. Stitching chart for the diamond motif on the tunic shown in Color Plate 8.

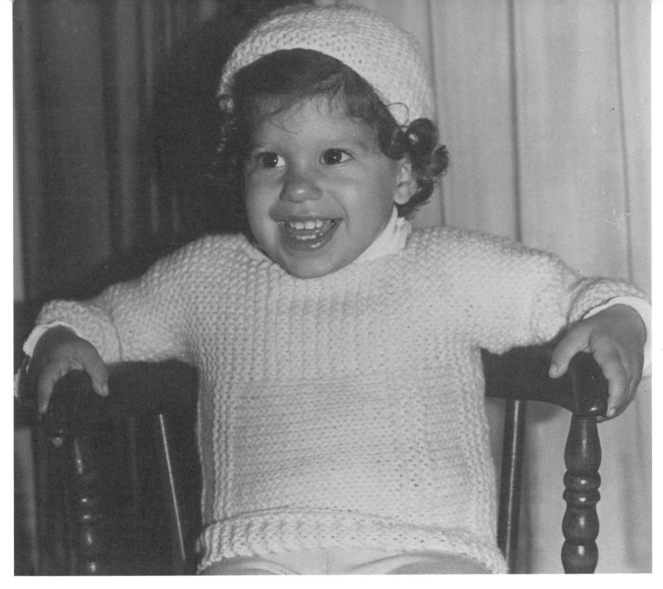

Figure 52. This textured pullover was knitted from the side over. Yarn: Nantuck by Columbia-Minerva.

INFANT'S PLAYTIME PULLOVER

Take a close look at the sweater in Figure 52. Do the stitches look different? Turn the book on its side and you'll see that this sweater was worked from the side over. Read over the Infants' Classic Knitting Worsted Crew Neck Pullover in Chapter 5 for help.

Infants' Sizes: Directions are for 6 months.
Materials: 4 oz knitting worsted
Needles: #10
Gauge: 4 sts = 1 inch

Starting at sleeve edge, cast on 32 sts, work garter st for 6½ inches. At beg of next 2 rows, cast on 25 sts, work garter st for 8 rows more. Next row, k 5, p 20, k 32, p 20, k 5. Next row, k all across. Repeat last 2 rows twice more. K every row for 6 rows. Next row, k 39 sts, join new yarn, bind off next 4 sts, k rem 39. Work both sides, each with a separate ball of yarn, keeping yoke sts in garter st, center sts in stockinette st, and bottom edges in garter st. Work for 4 inches more. On next row, k all sts, casting on 4 and joining as one piece again. Work to correspond to other side.

Finishing:
Sew underarm seams.

HAT

The hat shown in Figure 52 is made with 1 oz knitting worsted on #10 needles.

Cast on 64 sts, k every row in garter st for 5½ inches. Next row, k 2 tog all across next 2 rows. Break yarn leaving a long end, pull this yarn through rem sts, gather up, and sew seam. Make small poms-poms for top.

CHILD'S BULKY TWEED SWEATER SET

The little girl in Color Plate 10 is wearing both a bulky tweed cardigan and pullover. They are variations of the Children's Bulky Crew Neck Cardigan and Pullover in Chapter 3, but are each made with double strands of knitting worsted to give the tweed effect.

CARDIGAN

Sizes: Refer to the directions in Chapter 3 and
Materials: follow sizes, materials, needles, and gauge
Needles: specifications. Use knitting worsted instead
Gauge: of bulky yarn but use 2 different colors of yarn. You will also need a zipper.

Using 2 strands of knitting worsted held together and starting with the larger needles, work in k 1, p 1 rib for 3 inches. Change to smaller needles and continue in rib for 1 inch more. Complete as directed.

Finishing:
Work 1 row sc along each front edge. Sew in zipper.

PULLOVER

Sizes: Refer to the directions in Chapter 3 and fol-
Materials: low size, materials, needles, and gauge spec-
Needles: ifications. Use 2 different colors of knitting
Gauge: worsted held together instead of the bulky yarn. See notes on turtlenecks in Chapter 2.

Using 2 strands of knitting worsted held together and starting with the larger needles, work in k 1, p 1 rib for 3 inches. Change to smaller needles and continue in rib for 1 inch more. Complete as directed.

WOMAN'S NUBBY, BULKY TUNIC

The sweater on the right in Figure 44 is a classic T tunic with short sleeves and V neck. The interest lies in the bulky, nubbed yarn that was used. All the classics take on new interest when the lovely new yarns of today are used.

Women's Sizes: Which yarn do you want to use, sport
Materials: weight, knitting worsted, or bulky yarn?
Needles: Refer to the appropriate directions in
Gauge: Chapter 5. Follow size, materials, needles, and gauge specifications.

Follow directions, but cast on 4 sts for sleeve. When binding off for sleeve, bind off 4. Finish as for long sleeve.

8. Crocheted Raglans and T Tops

Figure 53. This crocheted tunic is easy and quick. Add decorative stitching at the borders to set it off a bit. Yarn: Germanntown Knitting Worsted by Brunswick.

Crocheted raglans and T tops, as you've seen from Chapters 4 and 6 are easy to make, and there are many ways to expand upon the classics taught in those chapters.

The very intricate crocheted patterns do not lend themselves well to this method of crocheting. The fact that you must increase 8 stitches every row works only in simple stitches—single crochet, double crochet, etc. In spite of the drawback, some very interesting effects can be achieved and quite easily. One of the easiest variations is to make the top of a raglan section in simple, single, double, or triple crochet and then work a more intricate stitch from the armhole down. T tops lend themselves well to many patterns.

All the great texture stitches, filet crochet, stripes, and open work, work well with this style. Add pockets, turn back cuffs, pull a drawstring through a waistline but, most of all, have a good time creating.

WOMAN'S LONG-FRINGED TUNIC

The tunic in Figure 53 is another variation of the Women's Classic Crew Neck Pullover taught in Chapter 6. The short sleeves make it appropriate for the layered look. Slits at the sides are made by leaving side seams open for 14 inches or desired length. A closeup of the stitching can be seen in Figure 54.

Women's Sizes: Do you want to crochet the tunic in
Materials: sport weight, knitting worsted, or
Hook: bulky yarn? Refer to the appropriate
Gauge: directions in Chapter 6 and follow sizes, materials, hook, and gauge specifications.

Follow directions, working dc cross sts instead of regular dc. (To make cross sts *sk 1 st, 1 dc in next st, 1 dc in the skipped st.) Repeat from * across row, ending 1 dc in top of turning ch. Cast on 3 sts each side for sleeves and complete as directed.

Finishing:
Sew side seams, leaving 14 inches open for side slit. Work 1 row sc around side, sleeve, and neck edges in cc. Fringe the bottom.

Figure 54. A closeup of the stitching pattern done on the tunic in Figure 53—a cross stitch double crochet—can be seen here.

GIRL'S SHORT-SLEEVED POPOVER

The girl on the right in Figure 55 is wearing another version of the Women's Classic Crew Neck Pullover. By using a bulky yarn and adding stripes in contrasting colors, it takes on a bold look. The sweater is great with jeans and turtlenecks.

Children's Sizes: Do you want to make the sweater
Materials: in sport weight, knitting worsted,
Hook: or bulky yarn? Refer to the appro-
Gauge: priate directions in Chapter 6. Follow sizes, materials, hooks, and gauge specifications. You will need a main color (mc) and contrasting color (cc) yarn.

Start as directed. Work in striping pat. Continue in mc till sleeve section. Ch 6 for sleeves each side and continue as directed. Work 1 row sc in mc, 1 row sc in cc, 1 row sc in mc, 2 rows dc in cc, adding same striping pat at bottom edge, other side.

Finishing:
Sew underarm seams. Work 1 row sc with cc, 1 row sc with mc around neck.

Figure 55. The girl on the right is wearing a simple pullover with stripes and short sleeves. The girl on the left is wearing another pullover with a different stitching pattern and a striped yoke and sleeve. Yarn: left—Nantuck by Columbia-Minerva, right—Belding Lily Craft Yarn.

GIRL'S TWO-TONED T TOP

The little girl on the left in Figure 55 is wearing another version of the Classic Crew Neck Pullover taught in Chapter 6. The sleeves are mid-length, the yoke is done in a contrasting color, and the sweater was worked in a stitching pattern of 1 double crochet, chain 1, skip 1 (see Figure 56).

Children's Sizes: Which yarn do you want to use, sport
Materials: weight, knitting worsted, or bulky
Hook: yarn? Refer to the appropriate direc-
Gauge: tions in Chapter 6 and follow sizes,
materials, hooks, and gauge specifications. You will need a main color
(mc) and a contrasting color (cc) of
yarn.

Work as directed in a st pat of 1 dc, ch 1, sk 1. Work till you have added the sts for both sleeves on back piece. Work 1 row sc all sts, break yarn. Join cc, work 5 rows with cc, join mc, and complete neckline. Work cc color stripe on front section same as back section and complete as directed.

Finishing:

Sew underarm seams, leaving 3 inches open each side for slit. Work 1 row sc around bottom and slit, work 1 row sc around neckline. Block by steaming lightly.

Figure 57. This jacket can be seen as a coat in Color Plate 3. Either way, it is easily crocheted from the top down. The collar is easy to do. See instructions on page 130. Yarn: Knob Tweed by Unger.

Figure 56. A closeup of the stitching pattern used on the sweater on the left in Figure 55.

WOMAN'S AFTERNOON JACKET/COAT

It may look fancy, but the jacket shown in Figure 57 is based on the Classic Crew Neck Cardigan in Chapter 4. The short sleeves, sailors collar and leather frogs create a special effect. If you wish, make the jacket longer and turn it into the coat shown in Color Plate 3.

Women's Sizes: Do you want to make the jacket/coat
Materials: in sport weight, knitting worsted, or
Hook: bulky yarn? Refer to the appropriate
Gauge: directions in Chapter 4 and follow sizes, materials, hook, and gauge specifications. You will need an extra 10 oz of bulky yarn, 8 oz of knitting worsted, or 6 oz of sport weight for the coat length.

Working 1 row dc, 1 row sc, make collar 5 inches before starting rows. Work sleeves straight with no decs. Work body about 18 inches for jacket, 28 inches or desired length for coat. Starting at bottom right, work 1 row sc all around front and collar. Break yarn. Work 1 row backward sc around collar edges only. Use leather frogs for closing.

Pockets:
Ch 18, work pat for 7 inches, end off.

Finishing:
Sew underarm seams. Sew pockets in place.

CHILD'S FRONT-POCKET PULLOVER

The sweater worn by the second child from the right in Figure 58 is a favorite among children. Other than the front pocket (see Figure 59), shorter sleeves, and trim, it's simply a variation of the Classic Crew Neck Pullover in Chapter 4.

Children's Sizes: Do you want to make the sweater
Materials: in sport weight, knitting worsted, or
Hook: bulky yarn? Refer to the appropriate
Gauge: directions in Chapter 6 and follow sizes, materials, hooks, and gauge specifications. You will need a main color of yarn (mc) and a small amount of contrasting colors (col A and col B).

Work as directed, trimming neck and sleeves with 1 row of col A and 1 row of col B and then 1 row of mc around sleeves.

Pocket:
Ch 14. Work sideways, making 1 row sc in col A, 1 row sc in col B, 8 rows sc in mc, 1 row sc in col B, and 1 row sc in col A.

Finishing:
Sew underarm seams. Work 1 row sc in mc around pocket and sew in place.

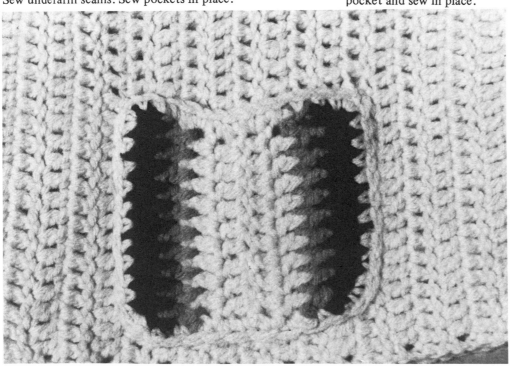

Figure 58. A closeup of the pocket shown on one of the sweaters in Figure 59.

CHILD'S DEEP V TUNIC

The second child on the left in Figure 59 is wearing a deep V neck tunic. It's very easy to crochet this version of the Classic V Neck Pullover taught in Chapter 4 (see Chapter 2 for specific V neck pullover instructions). It's simply a matter of increasing every other row, instead of every row for the V neck area.

Children's Sizes:
Materials:
Hook:
Gauge:

Decide whether you want to make the tunic in sport weight, knitting worsted, or bulky yarn. Refer to the appropriate directions in Chapter 4 and follow sizes, materials, hooks, and gauge specifications. You will need a main color (mc) and a small amount of yarn in a contrasting color (cc).

With mc, ch required number of sts, do not break yarn. Join cc, work 1 row sc. With mc, work 1 row sc, with cc work 1 row dc. Continue to follow pat with mc until back is completed and you are ready to divide for neckline. After dividing, work 4 rows even, then start to inc for V neck, every 4th row. Take off for sleeves as directed. Continue neckline till 3 inches below sleeve. Complete front, working same stripe pat as on back. Work 1 row sc around neckline with cc, work 1 row sc around neckline with mc, end off.

Finishing:
Sew underarm seams. Block by steaming lightly.

Figure 59. Four crocheted children's sweaters. The one on the far end is seen again in Figures 64 and 65. Yarn: two on left—Belding Lily Craft Yarn, two on the right—Germanntown Knitting Worsted by Brunswick.

CHILD'S HOODED, MULTISTRIPED CARDIGAN

The first child in Figure 58 wears a colorful, interesting version of the Classic Crew Neck Cardigan taught in Chapter 4. The sweater on the end is shown again in Figures 67 and 68.

Children's Sizes:
Materials:
Hooks:
Gauge:

Decide whether you want to make the sweater in sport weight, knitting worsted, or bulky yarn. Refer to the appropriate directions in Chapter 4 and follow sizes, materials, hooks, and gauge specifications. You will need a main color (mc), as well as small amounts of two contrasting colors (col A and col B) of yarn.

Ch required number of sts with mc. Follow directions, making hood 9 inches before starting incs. When starting yoke, alternate rows of mc and each cc. Work body in mc till 2 inches less than desired length, then repeat striping pat. Also repeat stripe on sleeves.

Finishing:
Sew underarm seams. Sew top of hook. Starting at bottom right, work 5 rows sc. Work first row in sc with mc up front, around hood, and down other side. Work 2nd row with col A, work 3rd row with mc, making buttonholes on this row. Work 4th row in col B, 5th row in mc.

WOMAN'S INITIALLY YOURS T TOP

The tunic in Figure 60 is an interesting one. Slits at the sides, short sleeves, the initialled motif, and the filet crochet stitching pattern and puff stitches make this variation of the Classic Crew Neck Pullover taught in Chapter 6 look much more complicated than it is.

Women's Sizes:
Materials:
Hook:
Gauge:

Which yarn do you want to make it in, sport weight, knitting worsted, or bulky yarn? Refer to the appropriate directions in Chapter 6 and follow size, materials, hook, and gauge specifications.

Follow directions, working filet crochet pat instead of sc as follows: Ch 3 to start row, *sk 1 st, 1 dc in next st, ch 1. Repeat from * across row, ending 1 dc in top of turning ch. Repeat this row for pat. Work 10 rows of pat. Work halfway across next row, make 1 puff st in next sp (to make a puff st, yo and pick up a long loop 3 times, yo through all but last loop on hook, yo through last 2). Following charts for diamond pat (see Figure 61) and your own initial (see Figure 62 and page 14), work puff sts in the filet spaces. When the diamond pat is completed, ch the sleeve sts. When 7 rows of pat are completed on sleeve, work a puff st every 4th sp on next row. Next row, work 1 puff st in sp before and after puff st from row below. Next row, work 1 puff st every 4th sp. Complete as directed.

Finishing:
Sew underarm and sleeve seams, leaving 10 inches from bottom open for side slits. Work 2 rows sc around sleeves, slits, and bottom edges. Work 1 row sc and 1 row backward sc around neck.

Figure 61. A closeup of the initial used in Figure 60.

Figure 60. The filet crochet stitching pattern shown in this tunic is fun and easy to do. See Figure 61 for a closeup of the initial and follow charts in Figure 62 for your own initial. Yarn: Columbia-Minerva Sport Yarn.

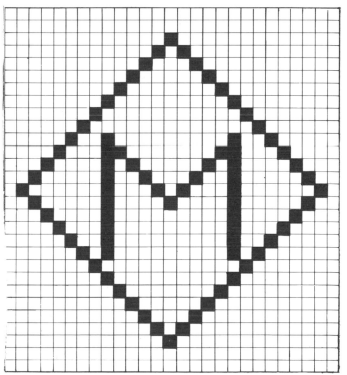

Figure 62. Stitching chart for the letter M. For other letters of the alphabet see page 14. These will enable you to personalize the sweater shown in Figure 60.

WOMAN'S V-SHAPED PONCHO

Just as the knitted poncho on the left in Figure 35 is a variation of the Classic Crew Neck Cardigan taught in Chapter 3, the crocheted poncho on the right is a variation of the Classic Crew Neck Pullover taught in Chapter 4.

Women's Sizes: Which yarn do you want to use, knitting
Materials: worsted or bulky yarn? Once you've
Hook: decided, refer to the appropriate direc-
Gauge: tions in Chapter 4 and follow sizes, materials, needles, and gauge specifications. You will need a main color (mc), as well as a contrasting color (cc), of yarn.

Work cc stripes wherever desired, always joining new color at back. Work as directed, not dividing yoke. Work till desired length, making incs at the 4 points right to bottom. Bind off loosely. Fringe.

Neckband:
Work 1 row sc around neck, ch 5 (counts as 1 dc, ch 2), sk 1 st, * 1 dc, ch 1, sk 1, repeat from * around ending with a slst to 3rd ch of starting ch–5. Work 2 sc in each sp, end off. Make a long ch using doubled yarn. Weave in and out of neckband for tie.

Figure 63. The woven yoke is what catches the eye in this sweater; it's quite simple to do. Yarn: Germanntown Knitting Worsted by Brunswick.

GIRL'S WOVEN-YOKE PULLOVER

The woven yoke and cap sleeves set it apart, but the sweater in Figure 63 is actually a simple variation of the Classic Crew Neck Pullover taught in Chapter 4. If you wish, adapt the directions here to make a Crew Neck Cardigan.

Children's Sizes: Which yarn do you want to make it in,
Materials: sport weight, knitting worsted, or
Hook: bulky yarn? Refer to the appropriate
Gauge: directions in Chapter 4 and follow sizes, materials, hook, and gauge specifications. You will need 3 colors of yarn—one main color (mc), and 2 contrasting colors (col A and col B).

Follow directions, working 2 rows in mc. Join col A. Work 7 rows col A, 5 rows mc, 7 rows col B. Work rem yoke in mc. Finish sweater in mc, following body only. Sleeves are left as cap sleeves.

Finishing:
Work 3 rows sc around neck edge. Thread a needle with a doubled strand of col B and weave in and out of dc on the 3rd and 5th rows of col A stripe. Repeat with mc on col B stripe.

GIRL'S BULKY CHILL CHASERS

By working in single crochet, rather than double crochet, an interesting version of the Classic Bulky Yarn Crew Neck Pullover taught in Chapter 4 can be achieved. Figure 64 shows the sweater as a pullover. Yet, if you wish, follow these directions and the Classic Bulky Knit Crew Neck Cardigan directions in Chapter 4 to make the cardigan shown in Figure 65.

Children's Sizes: Which yarn do you want to use, knitting worsted or bulky yarn? Refer to the appropriate directions in Chapter 4 and follow sizes, materials, hook, and gauge specifications. You will need a main color (mc) and a contrasting color (cc) of yarn.
Materials:
Hook:
Gauge:

Follow the directions, working in sc instead of dc. Work sleeves without decs for 1 inch, then work 1 row of cc, 1 row of mc, 1 row of cc, end off. Work bottom and finish with same striping pat as sleeve.

Finishing:
Work 1 row sc around all edges with cc.

Figure 64. A single crochet version of the classic bulky yarn pullover. Yarn: Belding Lily Craft Yarn.

Figure 65. The cardigan version of the sweater shown in Figure 64. Yarn: Belding Lily Craft Yarn.

WOMAN'S DEEP-CUFF WRAP

Often a particular stitching pattern can completely transform the look or style of a sweater. The woman's sweater shown in Figure 67 is, of course, the Classic Crocheted V Neck Worsted Cardigan taught in Chapter 6. It's the stitching (see Figure 66) and striping pattern that make it look so different.

Women's Sizes: Refer to the appropriate directions
Materials: in Chapter 6 and follow sizes, ma-
Hook: terials, hook, and gauge specifica-
Gauge: tions. You will need 12 oz of a main color (mc.) as well as 2 contrasting colors (cc) 2 oz of one color (col A) and 4 oz of another (col B).

Striping Pat:

Rows 1–4: Work with mc.
Rows 5–8: Work with col B.
Rows 9–10: Work with mc.
Rows 11–12: Work with col A.
Rows 13–14: Work with mc.
Rows 15–18: Work with col B.
Rows 19–40: Work with mc. (For some sizes it may be necessary to work more than 22 rows of mc.)

Stitching Pat:

Row 1: *Ch 4, sk 3 sts, 1 sc in next st, repeat from * across.
Row 2: Ch 4, * 4 dc in the ch-4 loop, repeat from * across, end 1 dc in top of turning ch.
Row 3: Ch 1, 1 sc between the first 2 dc, *ch 4, 4 dc, 1 sc in next sp, repeat from * across row.

Repeat Rows 2 and 3 for pat, always joining new col on Row 3.

Follow directions, working stitching and striping pats. Ch sleeve sts and repeat first 22 rows of striping pat. Reverse entire striping pat for front, shaping V and forming new pat as sts are inc.

Belt:

With mc make a 46-inch chain. Work rows 1 and 2 of st pat, end off.

Finishing:

Sew underarm seams. Work 5 rows sc around front and neck edges with mc.

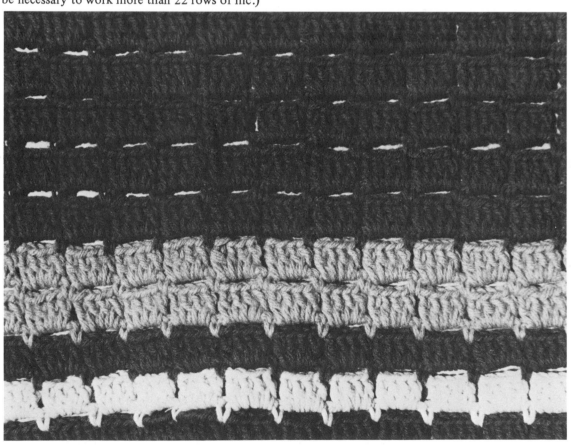

Figure 66. A closeup of the stitching pattern of the woman's sweater shown in Figure 67.

Figure 67. The stitching and striping pattern of the sweater on the left is particularly interesting. A closeup can be seen in Figure 66. The man's sweater is done in another interesting stitch pattern. Instructions for that sweater are on page 138. Yarn: Nantuck by Columbia-Minerva.

MAN'S SHAWL-COLLARED CARDIGAN

The shawl collar in Figure 67 is easy to crochet; the patterned stitching is interesting, yet very basic. Otherwise, this sweater is basically the Men's V Neck Cardigan taught in Chapter 4.

Men's Sizes:
Materials:
Hook:
Gauge:

Do you want to make the sweater in sport weight, knitting worsted, or bulky yarn? Refer to the appropriate directions in Chapter 4 and follow sizes, materials, hook, and gauge specifications.

Stitching Pat:
Row 1: *1 sc, 1 dc, repeat from * across, end with 1 sc.
Row 2: Ch 2, turn (counts as first dc), sk first st, *1 sc in next st (top of dc from row below), 1 dc in next st.

Follow directions, working pat. Continue pat of 1 sc, 1 dc (the sc comes on top of the dc, the dc on top of the sc) being sure to keep pat as you inc. Work till raglan incs are completed. Work sleeves as directed. Ch 5 at each front edge. Complete body, working 5 sts on each added ch.

Collar:
Ch 6, work in pat, inc 1 st on one side only, every row, till collar is 6 inches wide. Work even for 18 inches, then dec 1 st same side, every row, till you are back to 5 sts, end off.

Pockets:
Ch 21, work pat for 7 inches, end off.

Finishing:
Sew underarm seams. Sew collar in place. Work 1 row sc, 1 row backward sc around bottom, front, collar, sleeve, and pocket edges. Sew pockets in place.

WOMAN'S ORIENTAL TUNIC

The tunic shown in Figure 68, with its long vertical stripes, is very easy to wear and easy to make, comfortably topping any outfit. It's just another version of the Classic Crew Neck Pullover taught in Chapter 4.

Women's Sizes:
Materials:
Hook:
Gauge:

Refer to the appropriate directions in Chapter 4 and follow sizes, materials, hook, and gauge specifications. You will need 22 oz of main color (mc) and 2 oz of a contrasting color (cc).

Stitching Pat:
Row 1: *1 sc, 1 dc, repeat from * across row, ending with 1 sc.
Row 2: Ch 3 (counts as dc), sk the first st, *1 dc, 1 sc, repeat from * across row.

Starting at sleeve with cc, ch 80. Work pat with cc for 10 rows, join mc and work for 2 rows, join cc and work for 2 rows, join mc and work for 30 rows more. Ch 90, work pat back on ch, across established sts. Ch 90 on other side. Continue on all sts for 28 rows more. Work across 120 sts, ch, and turn. Continue on this side only for 14 rows more, end off. Sk 20 sts for neck opening. Work front center to correspond to back, ending at neck edge. Ch 20, join to other side of neck. Work to correspond to other side.

Figure 68. Another interesting, but easy, stitching pattern is seen in this Oriental-looking tunic. Yarn: Columbia-Minerva Sport Yarn.

Index